Seed to Seed

Seed Saving Techniques for the Vegetable Gardener

by Suzanne Ashworth

Photography by David Cavagnaro

Edited by Kent Whealy
Editorial Assistance by Arllys Adelmann
Designed and Typeset by Steve Demuth

ISBN 0-9613977-7-2 (Softcover)

Library of Congress Catalogue Card Number 90-62386

Printed in the United States of America

Seed Saver Publications
Rural Route 3, Box 239
Decorah, Iowa 52101

CONTENTS

SECTION III - OTHER FAMILIES WITH VEGETABLE MEMBERS

INTRODUCTION

An estimated 60 million Americans grow a portion of their own food in a vegetable garden. Their planting needs are supplied by 215 mail order seed companies, countless local outlets for seeds and plants, and the ever-present grocery store seed racks. Indeed, American vegetable gardens seem to magically appear each spring as if conjured up directly from the glossy color photographs in the seed catalogs. At first glance, seeds appear to be little more than a convenient way of transferring vegetables from corporation to backyard vegetable patch, from image into juicy reality.

There has always been a substantial minority of gardeners, however, who bypass the garden seed industry completely by saving their own seeds from year to year. Some of these seed savers, remnants of a recently-lost peasant agriculture which purchased nothing that could be produced at home, are still planting the same vegetable varieties that their great-grandparents once grew. Other new converts to seed saving may be trying to save something special discovered along the way, or obtain unique plant material not available commercially. Still others have simply been touched by the powerful satisfaction that comes from a garden which is genuinely self-perpetuating.

For some years now, I have been one of these seed saving gardeners. Like many of my fellow seed savers, I have often been frustrated by not having access to detailed information on saving seeds from garden vegetables. Do turnips cross with Chinese cabbage, watercress with garden cress, red Malabar spinach with white? During the spring and summer months, hardly a week went by without a question arising about how to save seed from various vegetables.

As these questions became more numerous, I felt sure that somewhere within the walls of this country's libraries was just the book that gardeners in my situation needed. But, with every new interlibrary search, it became more evident that a comprehensive guide to saving vegetable seeds on a small scale was not to be found. Instead, bits and pieces of relevant information were hidden in obscure publications on such diverse topics as food sources for honeybees, hybridization of vegetable crops, and commercial seed production techniques.

What was needed, I realized, was a book that would pull these various sources together and facilitate small-scale seed saving of all common and obscure vegetables grown in the United States. Eventually, with encouragement from the Seed Savers Exchange and others, I decided to write *Seed to Seed*.

In creating this reference book, I have tried to be comprehensive enough to satisfy the needs of most seed savers, both beginners and those with more advanced skills. For example, techniques have been included for every vegetable appearing in the annual Yearbooks of the Seed Savers Exchange to assist members in growing pure, high quality seeds. Most vegetatively propagated herbs and most grain or forage crops have been excluded, but all forms of corn are discussed along with amaranths and sunflowers, which often appear in the vegetable garden.

In order to offer proven techniques for saving seeds, I have grown seed crops in my own garden of every vegetable discussed in this book. There have been some problems, of course. Some subtropicals refused to ripen completely, so seed extracting techniques had to be tested using purchased ripe fruits. Rutabagas, celery and parsnips had a hard time in the 110° summer heat, cassabanana fruits grew only three inches before succumbing to frost, and pepino and tamarillo rarely set fruits without encouragement from the plant hormone gibberelic acid. After three years of persistent effort, I have grown out seed from every species that could conceivably be coaxed into maturity in central California.

During my research, I found that the literature that does exist on the pollination of vegetable crops is often quite contradictory. This confusion is due mainly to site-specific environmental factors, especially the vast differences in the sizes of crops and insect populations. In all cases, the information on pollination, seed viability and isolation distances in *Seed to Seed* has been based on the most recent research available.

The only isolation distances ever published for some crops are the recommendations made by commercial seed producers. Such publications deal with large acreages that produce massive amounts of pollen which attract huge insect populations. These commercial isolation distances have been used throughout this text without any attempt at modification. While these distances will ensure absolute seed purity, some may argue that such distances are excessive for small plantings in home gardens and for the related insect populations which can vary widely from location to location and even with the weather from year to year. Extensive research far beyond the scope of this project would be needed, however, to make recommendations which would ensure seed purity for specific garden sites.

Since the Seed Savers Exchange was founded in 1975, techniques for growing and saving seeds in home gardens have been tried and tested by numerous members. *Seed to Seed* only includes proven seed saving techniques that have been revised and refined over the course of several gardening seasons. For example, Glenn Drowns' techniques for the hand-pollination of cucurbits have proven to be as successful as any methods currently being used in the United States. In general, though, extensive research would also be necessary to prove which home methods are successful across a wide range of locations. Again, such research was beyond the scope and time frame of this project, so most home techniques have not been included in *Seed to Seed* unless confirmed by the published literature.

Information on various techniques for saving vegetable seeds is a dynamic and evolving area on which far too little has been written. Certainly, a project of this magnitude cannot hope to answer every question that may arise concerning home seed saving. Still, I sincerely hope that *Seed to Seed* will be widely useful and provide a foundation upon which future research and publications can be based.

Seed to Seed would not have been possible without the help of several talented and dedicated persons. Kent Whealy, director of the Seed Savers Exchange, has offered frequent encouragement and support in getting the book into print. Kent's editing skills and some of his previously published material have added greatly to the readability and content of this book. David Cavagnaro has taken hundreds of photographs during the last two summers which he has donated to clearly illustrate the text. I wish to also thank Arllys Adelmann, who typed all of the extensive revisions to the text, and Steve Demuth, technical consultant for the production of *Seed to Seed*.

Finally, it seems most appropriate that the research, text and photographs that comprise *Seed to Seed* should be donated to help support the work of the Seed Savers Exchange. And it is to the members of the Seed Savers Exchange that this book is dedicated.

Suzanne Ashworth
Sacramento, CA
August 1990

I

SAVING VEGETABLE SEEDS

SAVING VEGETABLE SEEDS

The seeds that gardeners hold in their hands at planting time are living links in an unbroken chain reaching back into antiquity. Today's gardeners cannot possibly comprehend the amount of history contained in their seeds, both what has come before and what may potentially come after their brief involvement. Our Stone Age ancestors began identifying and domesticating food plants thousands of years ago, with the simple act of selecting seeds for replanting. Whenever gardeners begin to save their own seeds, they also become part of this ancient tradition.

SAVING OUR GARDEN HERITAGE

Because the United States is a nation of immigrants, today's gardeners are blessed with access to an immense cornucopia of vegetable varieties. Gardeners from every corner of the world invariably brought along cherished vegetable seeds when their families immigrated. Afraid that their treasures might be confiscated, these seeds were often smuggled into this country hidden in the linings of suitcases, under the bands of hats and sown into the hems of dresses. Seeds provided a living reminder of their past and ensured continued enjoyment of foods from the old country. This unique heritage of seeds, steadily accumulating for nearly four centuries, was first brought over by passengers on the Mayflower and is still arriving today with the boat people from Laos.

HEIRLOOM VARIETIES: AN ENDANGERED TRADITION

Our grandparents and their ancestors were seed savers by necessity. Their best plants were carefully selected to produce the next year's seeds, which were traded over the back garden fence with neighbors and faithfully passed down to each new generation of gardeners. Few of these *family heirloom varieties* have ever been available commercially, until just recently. Many have been grown on the same farm by different generations of a family for 150 years or more. This often resulted in the seeds slowly developing resistances to local diseases and insects, and also gradually becoming well adapted to climates and soil conditions in family gardens throughout the United States.

Countless heirloom varieties are still being maintained by gardeners and farmers in isolated rural areas. But today's society has become extremely mobile with young families moving every few years, often to urban homes where gardening may not be possible. The steady erosion of rural populations was rapidly accelerated by the farm crisis, leaving ever fewer farmers and gardeners to save the family history growing in their own backyards.

Untold numbers of old-time varieties are lost each year, because elderly gardeners can no longer find family members willing to grow and maintain these living heirlooms. When elderly seed savers pass away, unless their

Facing Page: Preservation gardens at Heritage Farm, headquarters of the Seed Savers Exchange, where 1,200 endangered varieties are multiplied each summer.

seeds are replanted by other gardeners, their outstanding strains become extinct. Invaluable genetic characteristics are lost forever to future generations of gardeners and plant breeders.

There are a few bright rays of hope in what is otherwise a bleak situation. During this last decade, several grassroots genetic preservation projects have started to reverse these losses by collecting and distributing heirloom varieties. Four of these groups are described in the section entitled "Seed Saving Organizations" at the end of the book.

RAPID LOSSES AMONG COMMERCIAL NON-HYBRID VARIETIES

Today's commercial vegetable varieties have also evolved from the same ancient tradition of seed saving as the heirloom varieties, but often were further refined by public breeding programs. Until recently, most of the Agricultural Experiment Stations at land-grant universities had active vegetable breeding programs that developed varieties specifically suited for growers in their state. Such programs have largely been abandoned and those that remain are in rapid decline, with a few notable exceptions. Enrollments at agricultural colleges have also steadily decreased, especially during the past two decades, with ever fewer students choosing careers in traditional plant breeding. The dynamic breeding programs which characterized the first half of this century will probably never happen again.

Tremendous consolidation is currently occurring within the garden seed industry. Multinational corporations, including many agrichemical conglomerates, are buying out family-owned seed companies and replacing their regionally-adapted collections with more profitable hybrids and patented varieties. The new corporate owners usually switch to generalized varieties that will grow reasonably well in areas across the country, thus assuring the greatest sales in the company's new nationwide market.

During the period from 1984-1987, 54 of the 230 mail-order seed companies in the United States and Canada went out of business. The majority were smaller companies that had been rich sources of unique varieties. The loss of those 54 companies resulted in 943 non-hybrid varieties (19%) becoming unavailable. The collections being dropped, which sometimes represent the life's work of several generations of seedsmen, are often well adapted to specific regional climates and resistant to local diseases and pests. Far from being obsolete or inferior, these may well be the best home garden varieties ever developed. It is entirely possible that half of the non-hybrid varieties still available from seed companies could be lost during the next decade.

Gardeners who are interested in helping rescue these endangered commercial varieties should send for the information brochure of the Seed Savers Exchange (see "Seed Saving Organizations" at the end of this book). Their organization has compiled an inventory of all non-hybrid vegetable varieties available by mail order in the United States and Canada entitled *Garden Seed Inventory: Second Edition.* Concerned gardeners can use the book to purchase and permanently maintain varieties that are about to be dropped, and then share those seeds with other gardeners.

HYBRID VARIETIES GAIN DOMINANCE

The one factor most responsible for destroying garden diversity has been the massive shift to hybrid varieties. Seed companies favor these proprietary varieties for several reasons. Hybrid seeds, while somewhat more expensive to produce, usually sell for several times more than "standard" (non-hybrid) seeds. Also, seeds saved from hybrids are worthless for replanting, so farmers and gardeners must return to the companies for new seeds every year. And the parentage of hybrid varieties can be kept secret, so competing companies can never reproduce them.

Standard varieties will come "true-to-type" (produce plants like their parents) if not allowed to cross with similar varieties growing nearby. In contrast, hybrids are the result of deliberately crossing two different parent varieties, usually inbreds. Hybrids should be avoided for seed saving purposes, because they are incapable of producing plants like the previous generation. Seeds saved from hybrids will either be sterile or will begin reverting to one of the parent varieties during succeeding generations.

Hybrid corns are markedly more vigorous and productive than their open-pollinated counterparts, due to a phenomenon known as "hybrid vigor" (the synergistic effect that results when two extremely diverse varieties are crossed). There is much less difference, however, between hybrid and standard varieties of self-pollinated crops. Plants that self-pollinate are naturally inbred and contain relatively little diversity compared to cross-pollinated crops, therefore the hybridization of such self-pollinated crops results in less hybrid vigor.

Most of today's breeding programs produce hybrid varieties for commercial growers, often designed to facilitate mechanical harvesting and long distance shipping. Commercial hybrids exhibit highly uniform characteristics, often ripening almost simultaneously. Hybrid uniformity is essential for commercial growers who must mechanically harvest huge fields with one pass, but is often poorly suited for home gardeners who wish to spread canning chores and fresh produce over the longest possible harvest season. Some commercial varieties rely on tough skins and solid flesh to withstand mechanical picking and cross-country shipping. Gardeners, on the other hand, are primarily concerned with tenderness and outstanding flavor.

The old varieties are threatened today, not because of any deficiencies, but because they are not suitable for factory farmers and the food processing industry. As long as food crops are being bred for machines and large commercial growers, the needs of the home gardener will be of marginal importance. The old varieties will survive and flourish only if they continue to be grown by backyard gardeners and sold in local farmers markets.

PASSING HEIRLOOMS ON TO OTHERS

Seed savers put a great deal of effort into locating and preserving heirloom varieties. Just learning how to grow various seeds isn't enough, unless ways are also found to pass those seeds on to other interested growers. Most gardeners are deservedly proud of their gardens and produce, both of which can easily spark interest in others. Entering visually unique heirloom varieties in county and state fairs takes little time and often causes quite a stir.

Some vegetables may not fit into the limited categories allowed by most fairs, but can sometimes be entered in miscellaneous categories.

Garden clubs, arboretum societies and environmental groups are always looking for speakers and opportunities for field trips. Most seed savers enjoy giving short guided tours of their gardens, answering questions about special gardening techniques, and talking about heirlooms varieties. Stage fright is never a problem during such garden tours, because the heirloom plants provide plenty of cues for discussion. Giving out small samples of seeds or a taste of an unusual variety will always bring rave reviews. Also, a local newspaper interview with pictures of visually unique heirlooms can often help reach an even larger audience and contact like-minded gardeners.

If an unusual variety produces a bumper crop, try taking a sample to a favorite restaurant. The reputations of chefs, who must continually offer new items on their menus, depend on their ability to concoct unique and unusual dishes. Most chefs are enthusiastic about extraordinary or beautiful produce, often bemoaning the fact that produce suppliers don't offer more unusual vegetables. Produce companies counter that their growers can't risk growing an unusual crop without an established market.

Give the chef enough of a particular vegetable to allow for several culinary experiments. If the experiments are successful, try to establish how much produce would be used during a growing season. Then either grow the requested produce yourself, or help locate another gardener or farmer who would be willing to work with the restaurant. Some gardeners exchange produce for dinner at the restaurant, rather than become involved with cash receipts and record keeping. Heirloom varieties that find their way into commercial production, no matter how limited, are much less likely to die out.

Whenever far more seeds are produced than can be used, consider selling the surplus to a regional seed company. Many companies can use relatively small amounts of seeds of unusual varieties. The time and labor required to produce the seeds may only result in a cash reimbursement of less than a dollar per hour. Some companies offer seeds in trade, however, which may be advantageous. If becoming a grower for a small seed company is appealing, contact several companies and compare their requirements and prices. Always insist on a contract, no matter how small the amount of seeds, or the company will be under no obligation to buy what you have grown.

Finally, and perhaps most important of all, always try to involve children in both gardening and seed saving. Efforts to preserve heirloom vegetable varieties will not be passed on to future generations without the participation of children, grandchildren, scout troups and 4-H Clubs. Share the joy of gardening with a child, along with a gift of seeds. That gift could easily last a lifetime, and may create the next link in this unbroken chain of seed savers.

GARDENERS AS STEWARDS

Seed to Seed is an invaluable handbook for both beginning and experienced seed savers who are interested in maintaining unique varieties and conserving our vegetable heritage. Seed saving offers gardeners the opportunity to grow a bit of history in their own backyard. Be forewarned that seed saving often starts out as a hobby, but can quickly become a passion. Many seed savers become totally enthralled with heirloom varieties and with the sparks of life that the seeds contain.

It seems ironic that today's gardeners have access to such a vast array of the best home garden varieties ever developed, yet so many are in immediate danger of being lost forever. For thousands of years, seed savers have been the stewards and guardians of this invaluable and irreplaceable genetic heritage. The number and quality of vegetable varieties currently available are unequaled throughout history, the end result of a tradition of selection and improvement stretching back more than 10,000 years. Vegetable gardeners must do everything in their power to maintain what remains, because extinction is forever. *Seed to Seed* will hopefully play a valuable and timely role in helping to conserve our vanishing vegetable heritage.

_____ Botanical Classifications _____

Each vegetable discussed in this book is grouped according to its botanical FAMILY, *Genus* and *species*. The common name of each vegetable is also included next to its Latin name. Latin names are often unfamiliar, but without them we are unable to identify plants that are not indigenous to our area, or are new to our culture.

For seed savers, botanical nomenclature and classification are even more important. Different varieties of plants within the same species will cross with one another, but crosses are rare between plants that belong to different species. Therefore, knowing the species names of common vegetables is essential for proper preservation of specific plant varieties.

Plant classification was one of the most important scientific endeavors of our forefathers. As information and trade increased between villages, cities and countries, it became essential to know if what two separate groups of people called a lace-flower berry was in fact the same plant. More complicated still was the fact that the lace-flower berry was considered poisonous by one group, while another group ate the berries without ill effects. Scholars, attempting to solve these problems, were unable to communicate with one another without detailed pictures of each plant.

In 1727, Charles Linnaeus began classifying plants using a system of binomial nomenclature, a two-word designation for each plant that belonged to the same family. Plant families are large groups of plants that share similar botanical characteristics. Typically, plant families are based on similarities in flower and fruit structure.

Plant families are divided into natural groupings called genera (the plural of genus). Genera are groups of more closely related plants which share even closer similarities in morphology. Plants within a genus are also divided even further into species. The genus is the first of the two Latin words that make up a plant's botanical designation, and the species is the second word in its Latin name. For example, a zucchini squash (*Cucurbita pepo*) is classified as belonging to the genus

Cucurbita and the species *pepo*.

Within the genus *Cucurbita* there are several distinctive species of squash, each of which has unique leaf, flower and fruit characteristics. The plants within each of those species possess such similar characteristics that, in fact, all of the members of a species can be thought of as the maximum interbreeding unit. Each species of squash, for example, contains a number of "cultivars" (cultivated varieties) which will all cross with one another, but will not cross with any varieties that belong to other species of squash.

This taxonomic progression can be seen more easily in the following illustration:

> **Family - CUCURBITACEAE**
>   Genus - *Cucurbita*
>   Species - *pepo*
>   Variety - Black Beauty zucchini
>   Variety - Yellow Crookneck squash
>   Variety - Connecticut Field pumpkin
>   Variety - Patty Pan scallop
>   Variety - Spaghetti squash

All of the taxonomic classifications in this book are based on *Hortus Third* (Macmillan Publishing, New York, 1976). *Hortus Third* includes botanical names for 281 families, 3,301 genera and 20,397 species. Each entry also includes detailed plant descriptions as well as the names of the botanists who have previously contributed to the identification of that plant. *Hortus Third* is limited to plants grown in North America, including those from Hawaii and Puerto Rico, and reflects the most current horticultural and taxonomic research.

Because of the rapid evolution of such knowledge, entries in *Hortus Third* often conflict with *Hortus Second* and with other books based on the classifications in *Hortus Second*. For example, many readers may possibly possess taxonomic texts or seed catalogs which classify onions as Liliaceae. As a result of recent research, however, onions are now considered to be members of the Amaryllidaceae family. When *Hortus Fourth* is published, it will undoubtedly conflict with some of the classifications in *Hortus Third*. Botanical classification is a dynamic and rapidly evolving field and it is important to keep abreast of changes as the state of our knowledge increases.

Pollination and Flower Structure

Before becoming a seed saver, it is necessary to know a few things about the reproductive abilities of plants. Plants, like all other living organisms, have a sex life. Unlike animals, however, most plants carry both male and female reproductive organs, often within the same flower. The male portion of the flower is called the *stamen* and consists of one or more hairlike *filaments*, each of which has a pollen-producing sac at its tip called an *anther*. The anthers gradually ripen and split open, exposing the pollen grains.

The female portion of the flower is called the *pistil* and consists of a stigma, a style, and an ovary which contains one or more ovules (egg cells). The *stigma*, that portion of the pistil which is receptive to pollen, can vary in shape from just the tip of the *style* of a tomato to a single strand of corn silk which is receptive along its entire length. When a fertile grain of pollen touches a receptive *stigma*, the pollen

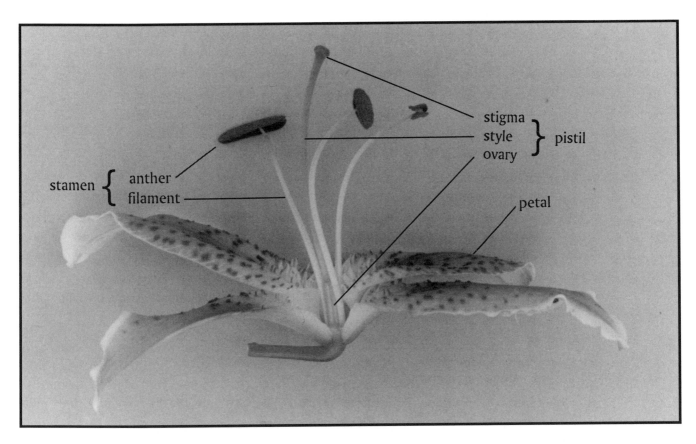

Cross section of a *Lilium rubrum* blossom showing the parts of a perfect flower.

grain begins to form a pollen tube which grows down through the *style* until it reaches and fertilizes the ovules within the *ovary*. The ovary eventually develops into the fruit or seedpod, while the fertilized ovules become the seeds for the next generation.

In order to maintain pure seed of a variety, pollen from that variety must reach the stigma of the plant, while contaminating pollen from all other varieties within that species must be excluded. If pollen from a different variety within that species comes in contact with the plant's stigma, resulting in fertilization, the fruit's seeds will be crossed and not true-to-type.

Squash and other cucurbits which produce separate male and female flowers on the same plant are referred to as *monoecious* species (which literally means "one house"). Some other species that produce separate male and female plants are *dioecious* ("two houses"). For example, spinach is a dioecious species with male plants that produce only pollen and female plants that produce only seed.

Imagine that a Yellow Crookneck squash and a Dark Green zucchini (which both belong to *Cucurbita pepo*) are growing in the same garden. A honeybee gathering pollen lands on a male flower and collects Dark Green zucchini pollen. Not quite overburdened, the bee then flies to an open female flower on the Yellow Crookneck squash. While the bee is foraging on the flower, some of the Dark Green zucchini pollen is deposited on the stigma of the Yellow Crookneck squash.

The crossed fruit which results will develop and look exactly like all of the other Yellow Crookneck squash on that plant, but any seeds inside that were fertilized by zucchini pollen will carry the genetic code of both parents. If those crossed seeds (known as the F$_1$ hybrid) were saved and replanted, they would produce plants that were uniquely different from the parent plants. A green crookneck zucchini with bumpy skin would be just one possibility. Each of the plants grown from the crossed seeds could possibly produce a new and different fruit, but all of the fruits on each individual plant would look exactly alike.

Such crosses can be stabilized after a few years (generally 6-12 generations) of continued selection, which is the process used by plant breeders to develop new standard varieties. Such experimentation is beyond the scope of this book and has little to do with preserving the vegetable varieties we already have. In order to preserve our vegetable heritage, cross-pollination must be prevented so that pure varieties can be maintained.

SELF-POLLINATED PLANTS

Self-pollinated plants have functional male and female flower parts within the same flower. Such blossoms are referred to as *perfect flowers* (see illustration on page 19). Fertilization in perfect flowers usually takes place within each individual flower and usually does not depend on insects or the wind. For example, self-fertilization occurs in some garden beans before the flowers even open. Some self-

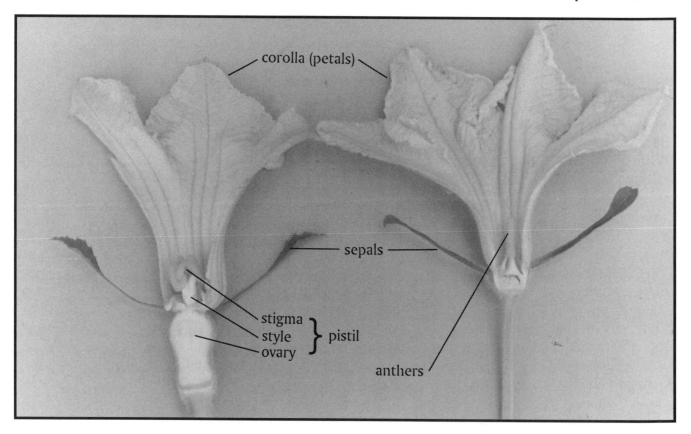

Cross sections of squash blossoms with female at left and male at right.

pollinated plants, such as peppers for example, can also be easily cross-pollinated by insects and must be grown in isolation or in screened cages to prevent such crossing.

There are several genera with perfect flowers that cannot fertilize themselves, and such flowers are said to be *self-incompatible*. The pollen produced by these flowers will not grow in the flower style on the same plant, but it will grow in the style on a different plant. Such plants generally depend on insects to move the pollen from one plant to another.

INSECT-POLLINATED PLANTS

Many vegetables produce separate male and female flowers on the same plant. Such plants are said to have *imperfect flowers*, since each blossom only displays the organs of one sex. A good example is the Cucurbitaceae family, which includes squash, cucumbers, muskmelons and watermelons. Female squash blossoms are easily identified by the ovary located at the flower's base, which is actually the tiny, immature fruit just beginning to form. When the female flower opens (ripens), its multi-segmented stigma is receptive.

Male squash blossoms, also quite easy to recognize, are just a flower at the end of a long, straight stem. The anthers, the pollen-producing structures inside the male flower, are also readily apparent and begin shedding pollen when the flower opens. Squash plants rely on insects to move the pollen from the anthers of the male flowers to the stigmas of the female flowers. Insect-pollinated plants must either be grown in isolation away from any other varieties of their species or be hand-pollinated to maintain seed purity.

Honeybees

Honeybees are the most efficient pollinators of commercial vegetable crops. Frequently bees are in short supply and must be brought in by the truckload, not only to work the crops but also to produce honey. Without bee pollination, many of our food crops would have greatly reduced yields.

Honeybees are covered with dense, branched hairs. As the bees brush up against the anthers of the flowers while collecting pollen and nectar, grains of pollen become entangled in their hairs. When its body is covered with pollen, the bee combs the pollen into pellets which are collected in the pollen baskets on its back legs.

Normally the number of bees foraging for pollen and nectar decreases as the distance from the hive increases. Most foraging is done within one-fourth mile of the hive. If food is scarce, however, bees will travel considerably further. Squash bees, a type of wild bee which has co-evolved with the genus *Cucurbita*, have been known to travel as far as seven miles.

The locations of nearby pollen and nectar sources are made known to the worker bees by a dance-like behavior that conveys direction, distance and other information. Having received these instructions, the worker bees leave the hive and exhibit a behavior called "flower constancy" (the tendency to forage on flowers of the same color and type, instead of foraging on mixed colors and types). For example, a worker bee might be informed of a good source of pollen on bright yellow flowers in a garden just south of the hive. Upon arrival the bee will diligently visit all of the open squash and pumpkin blossoms in the garden, not caring a bit that it has just crossed a Yellow Crookneck squash with a Connecticut Field pumpkin. Thus, bees are not only beneficial pollinators, but are also extremely efficient cross-pollinators.

Bumblebees, Sweat Bees and Wild Solitary Bees

Bumblebees, sweat bees and wild solitary bees are also covered with pollen-collecting branched hairs, but are far more random in their search for nectar and pollen than honeybees. (An exception are two species of wild "squash bees" which exhibit a strong preference for cucurbits and forage extensively on squash.) Bumblebees, which are too large to get inside most vegetable flowers, will often hang upside down from the flowers, shaking pollen onto their bodies. Bumblebees, sweat bees and wild solitary bees are minor pollinators on certain crops when compared to honeybees, but are quite capable of causing a significant amount of cross-pollination on the crops that they do frequent.

Moths and Butterflies

Moths and butterflies are covered with scales rather than hairs, which makes them inefficient pollinators because pollen grains are unable to stick to their scales. Moths and butterflies consume only nectar and do not collect food for nesting or rearing young. Their proboscis, which is usually quite long and delicate, is also unlikely to transfer pollen. The bodies of moths and butterflies seldom come into contact with flower pollen during feeding. Although a few moth species are highly specialized pollinators, moths seldom transfer vegetable pollen.

Wasps

Wasps are covered with coarse spines which are not adapted to the transfer of pollen. Although wasps feed on the nectar of many flowers, only in a few rare exceptions do they transfer pollen.

Flies

Flies will visit flowers having open, exposed "nectaries" (the part of a flower that secretes nectar), such as various members of the Umbelliferae and the Brassicaceae families. Flies have hairy legs that are capable of transferring pollen and can easily cross-pollinate varieties. The caging and bagging techniques used to exclude bees will also exclude flies.

WIND-POLLINATED PLANTS

Many grains, grasses and trees are dependent upon the wind for pollen dispersal. Although many grasses are self-pollinated, cross-pollination often occurs as a result of the wind. Pollen picked up by the wind can travel for miles on the air currents before coming to rest.

Corn is one of the most notable plants that relies on the wind for pollination. Corn pollen is produced in the tassel at the top of each stalk, which contains the plant's male flowers. When the wind shakes the plant, pollen falls from the tassels onto the silks that protrude from the ears, which are the plant's female flowers.

Spinach is another example of a plant that is primarily wind-pollinated. Spinach pollen is very fine and can be carried long distances by the wind, easily drifting a mile or more.

Maintaining Varietal Purity

The vegetable varieties gardeners enjoy today are the result of thousands of years of selection and adaptation in diverse worldwide ecological niches. Vegetable seeds have accompanied travelers and immigrants to every corner of the world, being traded from region to region and from continent to continent in order to satisfy mankind's desires for new and different produce. Serious gardeners have never been content to grow and eat only one type of pepper or one type of corn. Instead, gardeners are constantly experimenting with different varieties including many which are nearly impossible to grow in their climates. A tremendous heritage is available to today's garden experimenters, but protecting these countless varieties from loss and maintaining their purity is a constant challenge.

ISOLATION DISTANCES

Pure seeds can be saved from cross-pollinated vegetable crops, without resorting to caging or hand-pollination, by isolating a single variety of a species. Such varieties must be isolated by a distance that is large enough to prevent contamination from insect pollination or wind-blown pollen. That distance varies from species to species and is commonly referred to as the plant's "isolation distance."

To produce pure seed, seed savers must properly isolate their own crops and also check the gardens nearby as well. For example, if Nizza zucchini is being grown in isolation and saved for seed while a neighbor a block away is growing Yellow Scallop squash, bees will most likely cross the two varieties. For most gardeners in similar situa-

tions, especially those living in communities where vegetable gardening is prevalent, isolation only works for species that are not being commonly grown. The more widely grown cross-pollinated vegetable crops will usually require hand-pollination, bagging or caging to ensure seed purity.

Isolation distances are given for almost all of the vegetable species in this book. The distances cited are primarily those used by commercial seed producers. For many home seed savers these isolation distances will seem excessive. Isolation distances are highly site specific and depend on many factors such as plant population size, pollinator population density, presence of alternate insect forage sources, geographical barriers, vegetation barriers, and other habitat-related factors.

These commercial recommendations should be viewed as maximum starting points for individualized experiments to determine isolation distances that would be more appropriate for specific garden sites. Although buildings, trees and tall crops such as sunflowers, amaranth and corn all act as barriers for insects and help decrease the distances required for maintaining purity, this is certainly not to suggest that isolation distances should be ignored. When in doubt, always err on the side of caution. Of course, any experiments should only involve varieties that are widely available.

Pollination experiments are often hard to interpret, because many variables can be involved whose effects on cross-pollination as a function of isolation distance are only partially understood. Some variables that would tend to increase the need for isolation: a greater number of plants, a greater number of varieties, extremely diverse varietal characteristics, and the presence of a large number of highly efficient pollinators. Variables that would tend to decrease isolation distances: the presence of barrier crops, the presence of alternate pollen sources, staggered flowering times (seed collected from first blooms of the first blooming variety), and the collection of seed from the center of block plantings.

TIME ISOLATION

Annual varieties that cannot be isolated by distance can sometimes be isolated by time. To save seeds from more than one variety, plant the first crop as early as possible. When the first crop is beginning to flower, sow the second variety. Time isolation will only succeed if the first crop sets its seeds before the second crop reaches the flowering stage.

Some examples of annual crops which can be easily isolated in time include corn, sunflowers, lettuce and annual Umbellifereae. Corn is a relatively easy crop for time isolation, provided that accurate information on maturity dates is known. For example, an early season Orchard Baby sweet corn could be planted at the beginning of the season. Two weeks later a late season Country Gentleman sweet corn could be planted. If the weather cooperates and both corn varieties grow normally, the Orchard Baby will have finished tassling and its silks will have dried up before the Country Gentleman begins to tassel and shed pollen. Both varieties could then be saved for seed even though they were grown in adjacent plots.

Time isolation usually works best using two varieties that have very different maturity dates. Two varieties having equal or similar maturity dates can still be time isolated, however, when the season is long enough for them to be sown at least four weeks apart. In southern locations for example, it is possible to sow three varieties of solitary-headed sunflowers, if the plantings are spaced a month apart and the maturity dates are well known. When time isolating three varieties, however, always be careful to allow sufficient time for seeds of the last variety to mature and dry properly.

Weather variability in the spring and fall may cause problems in various time isolation sequences. The earliest variety often does not grow quite as quickly very early in the season because of cooler temperatures, while the second variety may grow more quickly than expected due to warmer weather. That could cause the flowering periods of the two varieties to overlap so that neither variety could be saved for seed. If, due either to miscalculation or weather variations, some flowers of both varieties are present simultaneously, the seed crops can still be kept from crossing by manually removing the flowers and flower buds of the earlier variety from that point on. In some cases, such as okra for example, this might involve simply pruning off the top of the plant.

MECHANICAL ISOLATION

Mechanical isolation involves constructing a physical barrier which prevents unwanted pollination. The mechanical isolation techniques discussed in the following sections are as varied as the plants being protected. Sometimes the technique is as simple as tying a cloth bag around a fertile okra blossom until it self-pollinates. Some self-pollinated plants can also be easily cross-pollinated by insects. Populations of peppers, for example, are often grown inside a screened cage to prevent any insect crossing with nearby varieties. Other more elaborate variations, which will be explained shortly, can involve alternate day caging techniques or introducing insects into a cage to pollinate the plants inside.

BAGGING TECHNIQUES

Bagging involves covering the flowering portion of a plant, in order to isolate those flowers from insect pollinators or wind-blown pollen. Except for corn, bagging is usually used to prevent cross-pollination of self-pollinating plants. For example, a cluster of currant tomato blossoms could be bagged with spun polyester cloth to prevent any possible insect crossing. Bagging individual flowers or clusters of blossoms is especially useful in cases where only a small amount of seeds is needed and caging methods are not possible.

Spun polyester cloth, often known by the trade name Reemay, is a popular bagging material as are other lightweight fabrics. Pieces of Reemay can be tied around individual flower heads or groups of flowers to prevent any insects from entering. Reemay can also be sewed, heat-sealed or rolled and stapled to make bags for flowers. Always be certain, however, that the base of the bag is tightly secured around the stem. In some cases it may be necessary to wrap a cotton ball or cotton batting tightly around the flower stem before securing the bag with a twist tie, in order to prevent insects from crawling into the bag.

Later when the bag is removed, the pods or fruits inside can be marked with pieces of bright yarn so that only their seeds will be saved. These bagging techniques don't work for some wind-pollinated plants such as spinach, whose extremely fine-grained pollen is small enough to pass through Reemay and muslin. Such species are identified throughout the text of this book.

Paper bags are often used, but can become a problem where summer rains are prevalent. Treated paper bags are available from Lawson Bag Co. (see "Supplies for Seed Savers" at the end of this section). Never use clear plastic bags or glassine envelopes, which can cause the flower to cook in the hot sun or become slimy from lack of ventilation. Suitable bagging techniques are discussed for each of the applicable vegetables in Section II and Section III.

CAGING TECHNIQUES

Some crops that are naturally self-pollinating can also be readily contaminated by insect cross-pollination. A good example would be peppers which, given the right conditions, can be crossed by sweat bees at rates exceeding 80%. When a population of peppers is grown under a cage covered with window screen, however, the fruits will all be pure. Because the species is naturally self-pollinating, the fruits will develop normally on the pepper plants growing inside of the cage. Eggplants can also be kept pure using exactly the same caging technique.

Pollination cages are usually covered with spun polyester cloth or window screen over a frame made of wood, wire, or lightweight plastic pipe or metal tubing. Both coverings allow air, water and light to pass through to the

Screened cages prevent insects from crossing various self-pollinated crops.

plants while excluding insects. Larger wood frames covered with nylon mesh or wire window screening can be custom designed to fit eight or more plants into a single cage. A short row of low-growing plants can be caged using half-circles of stiff wire pushed into the ground at intervals and then covered with Reemay whose outer edges are buried in the dirt. Spun polyester cloth can also be wrapped around whole plants and secured with clothespins, or used to cover three-ring tomato cages. Vegetables that re-spond well to these various caging techniques are identified throughout *Seed to Seed*.

ALTERNATE DAY CAGING

Alternate day caging is a method of isolating two or more varieties that are flowering simultaneously. This method allows insects to pollinate each variety for one day, then excludes insects during the next day. The trade-off is that seed production is somewhat restricted due to the lack of daily polli-nation. The plants sometimes compensate for this by producing flowers over a longer period of time.

In order to use alternate day caging, a minimum of two cages must be constructed. Every morning one cage is removed and is then replaced that evening; the following day the other cage is removed and replaced. Alternate day caging is ideal if, for example, seeds are being saved from both a cabbage and a kale. Six or more cabbage plants would be covered under one cage, with six or more kale plants under the second cage. These two vegetables both require insects for pollination, but will easily cross with one another. Remember to make absolutely certain that no other varieties of *Brassica oleraceae* are flowering in neighboring gardens, or insects could certainly cross the uncovered kale or cabbage.

For maximum seed set, alternate day cage removal and replacement would continue until all of the plants stop flowering. The process can be stopped, however, when a sufficient number of seedpods have formed. Then, to ensure seed purity, leave the cages on both plant groups until all flowering has stopped and the seeds have begun to dry.

Alternate day caging can be expanded to handle up to four varieties. If, for example, four varieties of cabbage are being saved, four cages would be constructed with one cage being removed each day on a four-day rotation. As the number of cages increases, the amount of seed set by each variety will definitely decrease. A two-cage rotation seems to only minimally reduce seed production. A four-cage rotation, however, results in a much greater decrease in the amount of seed that is set.

CAGING WITH INTRODUCED POLLINATORS

Caging with introduced pollinators requires the use of trapped flies or newly emerged bees. The cage needs to be large enough to cover the plants, yet allow the insects some flying space. In commercial applications such cages are often the size of small greenhouses. In a home garden situation this method is rather costly, difficult to put into effect, and is usually outside the means or interests of most gardeners. The technique is certainly an option, however, for advanced seed savers.

Honeybees can be easily trapped by setting out a plate of honey. Typically, 20 or more bees can be expected within half an hour. The bees are usually so intent on feeding that the plate can be moved without any covering for a short distance and placed inside the cage. Often the bees will then spend the entire day trying to escape from the cage, doing little or no pollinating. Also, there is always the possibility that trapped bees may be carrying pollen from other crop plants. Using trapped bees as introduced pollinators is usually quite ineffective.

Some government facilities use specially-constructed alternate day hives which are built into one wall of large cages. The bees are allowed to forage outside every second day and are turned into the cage on alternate days. Pollination is often relatively poor, because the bees usually spend their day in the cage trying to escape. Queenless hives, called nucs, filled with ready-to-hatch bees are sometimes placed inside the cages with greater success. The bees hatch and, having no prior flying experience, are content to fly about as if the cage were their world.

Some plants are naturally pollinated by flies, which can be attracted using rotten meat and trapped. The flies are then introduced into the cage, without the meat of course, but their pollination efficiency is often low and seed set may be only marginally effective. Trapping flies with rotten meat usually ensures that every cat and dog in the neighborhood will be present. To avoid possible damage to plants or cages by animals, make sure that such trapping occurs well away from the garden.

Although caging with introduced pollinators is not commonly used outside of the Agricultural Experiment Stations, additional information on using such techniques can be obtained from the agriculture or entomology departments of most colleges and universities.

HAND-POLLINATION TECHNIQUES

Next to isolation, either by space or time, hand-pollination is probably the most commonly used method of producing pure seeds in the home garden. Hand-pollination techniques are mainly used for vegetables that require insects for pollination, but are also used for some wind-pollinated crops, especially corn. The various techniques all involve transferring uncontaminated pollen from a male flower onto the receptive stigma of a female flower which has also been protected from contamination. After the pollination has been made by hand, the female blossom must then be protected from any further contamination by foreign pollen. Specific hand-pollination techniques for each of the applicable vegetable species are discussed in Section II and Section III.

SELECTION AND POPULATION SIZE

Vegetable plants and their seeds are in a constantly evolving state of flux, always slowly changing due to either environmental factors (drought, short seasons, disease, pests, etc.) or genetic factors (mutations, genetic shifts, etc.). Seed savers must learn how to select the right plants to save for seed, so that these changes will be for the better.

Seed savers must also learn to closely and attentively observe vegetable plants throughout the entire season, keeping seed selection constantly in mind. Look at the whole plant, not just the fruit. Plant characteristics to consider during selection could include earliness, disease resistance, insect resistance, drought resistance, stockiness, vigor, color, lateness to bolt, hardiness, uniformity or lack of it, and trueness-to-type. Fruit characteristics that can be selected for include color, shape, size, thickness of flesh, productivity, storage ability, flavor and many others.

Vigor is the seed's ability to germinate rapidly with good disease resistance. Only plants that display good vigor should be selected to save for seed. For example, if one plant within a population is always covered with aphids, has smaller leaves and stunted growth, or produces fewer fruits, seeds from that plant should definitely not be saved. Also, if all of the best cabbages are harvested for eating each year and only the poorly formed heads are saved for seed production, subsequent crops will eventually include poorly formed heads, more with each generation.

Seed savers can also select for plant characteristics of value in their specific climate, such as bolt resistance in cool season crops. For example, out of a row of 20 lettuce plants, 14 may bolt to seed very early in the season while the remaining six plants bolt two weeks later. Since late bolting is a very desirable characteristic in lettuce, only the six late bolters might be allowed to flower. The seed saved from these plants may demonstrate a greater incidence of late bolting than the original crop. If this selection for late bolting continues over a sufficient period of time, a late bolting strain of the original variety will gradually be developed.

Population size is an extremely important factor during seed production and must always be considered during selection procedures. To avoid decreasing the genetic diversity within a crop, seed should be obtained from the greatest possible number of plants that meet the selection criteria. Maintaining the genetic diversity within a population is the key to continued evolution and the ability of the plants to adapt to varying environmental conditions. Never select only the largest or best-looking fruit for seed, which could create a severe and irreversible bottleneck during that generation. Instead, always strive to save an equal amount of seed from as many plants as possible that are the most true-to-type within the population.

An exception to focusing strictly on trueness-to-type is required when working with a population of plants that contains a relatively high degree of natural variability. Such populations usually require growing a larger number of plants, with some seed being saved from each plant in order to maintain the diversity being exhibited. In general, naturally diverse populations and truly unique varieties will require larger growouts than, for example, modern commercial varieties

which are usually quite stable and often relatively similar.

Two other notable exceptions to any general suggestions concerning population sizes involve self-pollinated plants and corns. Most self-pollinated plants, especially ones that are not insect cross-pollinated, are naturally inbred and contain relatively little diversity within any given population. An excellent example would be garden beans which generally self-pollinate before the flowers open, and have often been saved from one or only a few plants for countless generations. At the other end of the spectrum are corns, which are highly sensitive to inadequate population sizes. Significant and irreversible damage can occur in a single generation if a large enough population is not grown or if a mixture of seeds from a sufficient number of plants isn't prepared properly. These precautions are described in detail when corns are discussed in Section III.

ROGUING FOR TRUENESS-TO-TYPE

Commercial seed companies require their contract growers to rogue crops in order to remove any off-type plants. Onion seed crops, for example, may be rogued four or more times before the plants actually go to seed. During the first season of growth, crews of workers walk through the fields and remove any plants with off-type foliage, bulbs or color. Any plants that bolt to seed during the first year are also removed, because such onions have very poor keeping abilities. During storage, any onions with thick necks, bottle necks, split bulbs, double bulbs or damaged bulbs are removed. Finally, during the second season of growth when the bulbs begin to flower, the blossoms are checked for color and shape, and any off-types are removed.

Small-scale seed savers should also rogue their plants, being sure to plant large enough populations so that roguing is meaningful and doesn't lead to inbreeding. Garden plants undergo almost daily inspection during watering, weeding and picking. Off-type plants are easy to spot within a population, and their removal helps eliminate the effects of any slight crossing that may have occurred during a previous generation or any accidental mixing of home-saved seeds.

For many gardeners, who often are concerned with food production and seed saving simultaneously, roguing is a hard thing to do. Letting an off-type plant remain in the garden is fine, if the plant is harvested for food before it flowers. For example, an off-type lettuce is usually just as tasty as its more uniform neighbors. It is a mistake, however, to let any off-type plants stay in the garden long enough to flower and cross-pollinate with neighboring plants being saved for seed. In general, off-type plants can remain in the garden as long as they are in a non-reproductive, vegetative stage, but should be removed before the onset of flowering. Most biennials can therefore be grown for produce during their first season without creating any problems.

With certain vegetables, off-type plants can be extremely difficult to recognize until the fruits form. Imagine, for example, that several plants of Guatemalan Blue Banana squash are being grown for seed. Several flowers on each of the plants have been hand-pollinated. The plants initially all look the same, but the banana-shaped fruits on one of the plants are bright pink. To make matters worse, blossoms from the pink-fruited plant were used for the hand-pollinations on some of the blue-fruited plants.

Whether or not this problem can be remedied during the current season depends entirely on the length of the local growing season and if sufficient time remains before frost. First, tear out the pink-fruited plant to avoid any chance of it causing further damage. Then remove all of the small squashes on the blue-fruited plants, including those that were hand-pollinated. The plants will start to flower vigorously shortly thereafter, and the new flower can again be hand-pollinated.

During this second round of hand-pollinations, only male and female blossoms from the same plant should be used. This technique is called *selfing*, meaning that the plant has been pollinated by itself, and should be used whenever seed purity is in question. This situation graphically illustrates the importance of good record keeping, which would have shown whether pollen was taken from the same vine or from a different vine.

Let's follow our imaginary problem through a different set of circumstances. Suppose there wasn't enough time remaining before frost to repollinate, so none of the fruits were removed. Also imagine that the blue-fruited plants represent all of the remaining seed and no more is available. There is still a slight chance of salvaging the variety. First, save the seeds from several hand-pollinated blue-fruited squash that appear to be true-to-type. Select fruits from plants that were farthest away from the uprooted pink-fruited plant and therefore possibly less likely to have received its contaminating pollen. Keep the seed harvested from each fruit separate from the seeds of the other fruits. Next season grow one seed from each of the fruits to check for purity. If a plant produces true-to-type fruits, that probably means other seeds from that fruit are also pure, and could be checked with further growouts. Seeds from fruits that produce off-type plants should be discarded.

Seed Cleaning Methods

Seed cleaning methods can be divided basically into wet processing or dry processing. The wet processing method is used for any seeds that are embedded in the damp flesh of fruits or berries, such as tomatoes, cucumbers, muskmelons or ground cherries. Seeds that are dry processed include those that are harvested from pods or husks that have usually dried in place on the plant, such as corn, radish, beans or lettuce.

WET PROCESSING, FERMENTATION AND DRYING

Wet processing is a three-step method that involves *removal* of the seeds from the fruit, *washing* to clean the seeds, and finally *drying*. Large fruits are cut open and the seeds are scraped out. Small fruits are usually crushed or mashed. Depending on the species, the seed, pulp and juice from the fruits may need to go through a fermentation process. Fermentation occurs in the garden as a natural process to some degree, as unharvested fruits fall to the ground, ferment and rot. During the fermentation process, microorganisms such as bacteria and yeast destroy many of the seed-borne diseases that can affect the next generation of plants. Water should usually not be added to the fermenting mixture, because dilution may slow the fermentation process and can cause premature sprouting of the seeds near the end of the process. Specific fermentation techniques are described for all applicable species in Section II and Section III.

The seeds must then be washed to either remove them from surrounding pulp or to separate them from the fermenting mixture. For most fruits this process is basically the same. The seeds and pulp are usually placed in a large bowl or bucket. Add at least twice as much water as the volume of seeds and pulp, and stir the mixture vigorously. Viable seeds tend to be more dense and sink to the bottom, but poor quality seeds tend to float. The debris and hollow seeds can be gently poured off. Add more water and repeat the process until only clean seeds remain. The seeds are then poured into a strainer and washed under running water. Always be sure, however, that small seeds cannot pass through the strainer holes.

The final processing step involves drying the seeds. The bottom of the strainer can be wiped on a towel to remove as much moisture as possible. The seeds are then dumped out onto a glass or ceramic dish, cookie sheet, window screen or sheet of plywood. Do not attempt to dry the seeds on paper, cloth or non-rigid plastic, because it can be extremely difficult to remove the seeds from such surfaces.

It is important to dry the seeds fairly quickly, because warm, wet seeds have a tendency to either germinate or mold. Spread the seeds as thinly as possible on the drying surface and stir the seeds several times during the day. Always remember that damage begins to occur whenever the temperature of the seeds rises above 96° F. For that reason, never dry seeds in an oven. Even at the lowest settings, the temperatures in a stove's oven can vary enough to damage the seeds. It may be possible, however, to place a tray of seeds on the racks inside an oven with just the pilot light on and the door cracked open. Another relatively warm place in most kitchens is on top of the refrigerator.

Never dry seeds in the direct sun if there is any chance that the temperature of the seeds will exceed 96° F. Also, always remember that the air temperature is often not the same as the temperature of the seeds. Even at air temperatures around 85° F., dark-colored seeds can sometimes become hot enough to sustain damage. Direct sun can sometimes heat plates and cookie sheets enough to cause seed damage. In humid climates it often helps to place seeds in front of a low-speed fan to hasten the drying process. Ceiling fans are ideal, because the seeds are less likely to blow while drying. Another option is to dry the seeds on window screen which allows for excellent air circulation, stirring as often as once an hour at first.

DRY PROCESSING AND WINNOWING

Plants that produce seeds in pods or husks are usually harvested dry. Bean or pea pods, radish pods and carrot umbels are allowed to dry in the garden whenever possible, depending on the weather. In most cases the dry pods are harvested individually. It is also possible to remove the entire plant, although this makes cleaning much harder. Gardeners in cold climates are sometimes forced to pull entire plants the evening before a hard frost. The plants are then hung for a week or so in a garage or shed that doesn't freeze. As the plants gradually dry down, the seeds continue to mature and gain some additional strength. The pods can be picked as they dry.

Threshing is the process that breaks the seeds free from their coverings. The dry seed heads or pods are rubbed, beaten or flailed until the seeds fall free. Commercial machines are capable of harvesting, threshing and, to some degree, winnowing the seed crop as it is harvested. For small-scale seed saving there are many options. One popular method is to place the dry pods in a feed sack or pillow case, which is then jogged on or flailed. Mashing the pods between two pieces of board works well with smaller seeds. Always be careful, however, because threshing or mashing the seedpods too vigorously can cause split seeds in legumes and can cause hairline cracks in corn. Gradually you will learn to use just the right amount of pressure.

Winnowing is the process used to separate the debris and chaff from the seeds. Most gardeners have seen pictures of Indian women tossing seeds into the air out of baskets, allowing the wind to do the separating. In reality, wind speed is usually quite variable and a considerable amount of seed can be lost easily during a heavy gust of wind. Also, when the wind changes direction, it is easy to end up covered with dust and chaff. Good substitutes for the wind include old hair dryers with the heating element removed, the blower from a discarded vacuum cleaner, small high-speed computer fans, household fans, and variable speed squirrel cage blowers.

No matter what winnowing method is used, the area should be covered with a sheet of cloth or plastic. This way seeds that are accidentally blown away with the chaff can be recovered. Always be careful, however, to completely shake out the sheet before starting a new variety.

When the seeds and chaff are nearly the same weight, it can be extremely difficult to successfully winnow the seeds. A good example is the feather-like chaff that surrounds lettuce seeds. This can, however, sometimes be separated by repeatedly rubbing the material through a screen of the correct size. In similar cases, another process called reverse screening can also be used. First, a screen is used which is just large enough for the seeds to pass through, but which excludes larger pieces of chaff and plant debris. After this initial screening, all that remains are the seeds and any chaff that was smaller than the seeds. The process is then repeated using a screen that is smaller than the seeds, which removes the remaining chaff.

A method of gravity separation using a bowl can be useful when very small amounts of seeds are being cleaned. The bowl method requires either sturdy lungs or a small fan. Place the seeds and chaff in a bowl and swirl the material around. The chaff and debris will begin to collect on the surface while the seeds remain underneath. Gently tip the bowl and blow the chaff out. This process is repeated until only clean seeds remain.

Another home version of gravity separation works best with rounded seeds and is usually a two-person job. This method requires a smooth board such as a bread board, a fan of some

sort, and either a shallow, flat cake pan or a cookie sheet with low sides. A very light air current is positioned next to the bottom edge of the slightly tilted board. A handful of seeds and chaff is placed near the top of the board. The angle of the board is gradually increased until the round seeds begin to roll down the board and into the cake pan. The chaff does not roll and will be blown up and over the top edge of the board.

HOT WATER TREATMENT

Hot water treatment was commonly used by seed companies to disinfect seeds before chemical seed treatments became popular. This safe and effective technique is seldom used today, but should be quite valuable for seed savers and organic seed producers. Hot water treatment is a method of controlling the seed-borne phase of diseases such as black rot, black leg and black leaf spot in the cabbage family. The treatment can also be used against bacterial canker and target spot in tomato, downy mildew in spinach, black rot and black leg in turnip, and Septoria spot in celery.

The technique requires the use of an accurate thermometer, electric frypan, large saucepan and kitchen sieve. Try a practice run without the seeds. Heat some water in the saucepan to 50° C. (122° F.). Pour a little of this water into the warm electric frypan, leaving the saucepan about 2/3 full, and then set the saucepan into the water in the frypan. Regulate the temperature of the water in the saucepan by either turning up the heat on the frypan or taking the saucepan out of the frypan. When the desired temperature can be steadily maintained, pour in the seeds, stir until all are wetted and not floating, then stir gently throughout the whole process.

Use the following treatment times and temperatures for various crops: treat broccoli, Brussels sprouts, kale and Chinese cabbage seeds for 20 minutes at 50° C. (122° F.); eggplant, spinach and turnip seeds for 25 minutes at 50° C.; celery and pepper seeds for 30 minutes at 50° C.; cauliflower for 25 minutes at 52° C. (126° F.); cabbage seed for 30 minutes at 52° C.; and tomato seed for 25 minutes at 55° C. (131° F.). Then sieve the seeds, spread on a hard surface away from direct sunlight, dry and store.

SEED CLEANING EQUIPMENT

Seed companies and universities often rely on small scale threshing and winnowing equipment to clean small amounts of experimental seeds. The Hance Corporation manufactures both large and small scale seed cleaning equipment. The Mini-Vac, their small electric tester and cleaner, is widely used in offices and laboratories for small applications. The unit incorporates a three-screen cleaning process with an adjustable air stream for removal of dust and fine material. The screens are 12" x 12" with one top scalping screen for large trash removal, and two bottom screens for grading the seeds, as well as removing splits, weed seeds and other foreign material. The Mini-Vac comes with a set of 15 screens to clean most standard seeds and grains, and costs about $750. Additional screens are available for nearly all types of seeds. In fact, these screens cost only about $15 each and can be used for hand processing many types of seeds. For additional information contact the Hance Corporation, 235 E. Broadway, Westerville, Ohio

43081 (614/882-7400).

Clipper seed cleaners are manufactured in a variety of sizes and have been used on farms and in laboratories for decades. The Clipper Office Tester and Cleaner, which retails for about $850, is a small, compact, desk-top machine similar to the Mini-Vac. The unit is popular with vegetable and flower growers and is often used in seed stores for specialized cleaning, grading and sizing. Clipper is manufactured by the Blount Industrial Products Corp., 805 S. Decker Dr., Bluffton, IN 46714 (219/824-3400).

The relatively new I-Tech Seed Thresher is a valuable tool for small-scale seed saving. Originally developed as a low-tech, human-powered machine for Third World countries, the I-Tech thresher cracks sunflower shells without smashing the kernels, and can thresh dry beans, peas, peanuts, sesame seeds, basils, endives, soybeans, all the brassicas and more. The hand-operated seed thresher comes with four different screens and costs around $250. The I-Tech Seed Thresher is available from Abundant Life Seed Foundation (see "Supplies for Seed Savers" at the end of this section) or from I-Tech's originator: Al Dong, 1610 L Street, Davis, CA 95616.

Many types of seeds can be processed using an assortment of hand-held seed cleaning screens. These can be made by assembling frames made of wood lath (1 1/2" x 3/4") into 12" squares, and then attaching the screening material to the bottom of each frame. Some hardware stores carry galvanized wire mesh (hardware cloth) in the following sizes: 1/2", 3/8", 1/4", 1/8" and window screen. If different-sized meshes are not available locally, Abundant Life Seed Foundation carries six different sizes of seed-cleaning screens from 1/4" to 1/30". The screens can be purchased either mounted or unmounted (see "Supplies for Seed Savers" at the end of this section).

Seed Storage Techniques

The collection and storage of vegetable seeds necessitates a variety of containers. Seedpods can be easily collected in woven baskets or even bushelbaskets, but always make sure that the basket's weave is tight enough to prevent the seeds from falling through. Many traditional Indian baskets are woven with seed collection specifically in mind. Baskets allow the air to circulate around the seeds, which encourages further drying.

Paper bags, feed sacks and cardboard boxes are also commonly used to collect seeds and seedpods. Such containers are especially useful when relatively large portions of the plants are being collected. It is best not to reuse bags or boxes, however, because seeds from the first collection often get stuck in their seams and can become mixed with a second seed harvest.

Fruits, berries and other seeds that are embedded in moist flesh are usually collected in plastic buckets, plastic deli tubs from the grocery store, and various kinds of bowls. One-gallon jugs are also quite useful and can often be obtained from restaurants and bakeries. Five-gallon plastic buckets are available from some fast-food restaurants or drywall contractors. Such containers are especially useful for collection and processing, because the seeds can then be fermented or washed right in the same container. Cooking bowls that are used for fermention should always be thoroughly cleaned and sterilized with a bleach solution before being used again for food preparation.

AIRTIGHT STORAGE CONTAINERS

Vegetable seeds are at their peak when they reach maximum dry weight on the mother plant. Vigor is the seed's ability to germinate rapidly with good disease resistance. Home-saved seeds will retain maximum vigor when thoroughly dried and stored in a moisture-proof container. The most vigorous seeds at harvest time will keep the longest in storage. The two greatest enemies of stored seeds are high temperature and high moisture. Seeds that are stored at fluctuating temperature and moisture levels lose their ability to germinate very quickly. As a rule of thumb, the sum of the temperature (degrees F.) and relative humidity should not exceed 100. In actuality, humidity is probably more important than temperature, because it allows for the growth of microorganisms which degrade seed quality. Always realize that seed vigor can be lost during storage well before the seed dies completely.

Containers used for seed storage should always be airtight. Glass and metal are the only common materials that are completely moisture-proof. Glass jars with good rubber seals under their lids, such as baby food jars or canning jars with new lids, provide a nearly airtight seal when screwed on really tight. Gallon glass jars that do not have a common-sized canning lid can be modified into excellent storage containers by cutting gaskets for their lids out of used automobile inner tubes.

Lightweight plastic bags are not moisture-proof and make poor storage containers. However, seeds can be put into Self Seal T-Bags™, Seal-A-Meal™ bags, Zip Lock™ bags, small draw-string muslin bags, or paper envelopes, before being stored inside of a large, airtight jar. Each bag of seeds should be securely sealed and carefully labeled. The jar should then be stored in a cool, dry, dark place where the temperature fluctuates as little as possible. Locations at floor level are better than those near the ceiling, which can be significantly warmer. The constant cool temperature of an underground root cellar is excellent, for those lucky enough to have access to such a structure. Finding the right storage location may take a bit of experimentation, but will ensure the long-term vigor and viability of home-saved seeds.

LONG-TERM FROZEN STORAGE

Most seed savers grow out their seeds on a fairly regular basis. Imagine that three varieties of leeks are being maintained, for example, with one variety being grown each year on a rotating basis. Leek seeds will maintain 50% germination for three years, if properly dried and well stored. The proposed three-year rotation would result in each variety reaching 50% germination before being regrown, but 50% is really too low. Seed vigor declines well before germination is actually lost, so always try for at least 70% germination. The three-year rotation cycle and a germination level above 70% can both be attained, if long-term frozen storage techniques are used.

Seeds of all species can be stored

for many years with almost no loss of germination and only minimal loss of vigor, when dried to about 8% seed moisture, sealed into an airtight container and frozen. Seeds stored using these techniques will maintain their viability for up to ten times longer than normal germination rates. Freezing does not hurt seeds that have been dried to moisture levels of 8% or less. If the seeds are not thoroughly dry, however, the excess moisture expands when frozen and will rupture cell walls. A quick and easy test is that seeds will break instead of bending when folded, if their moisture level is 8% or less.

Color-indicating silica gel is an excellent "desiccant" (moisture absorbing material) for drying seeds. By comparison, powdered milk is less than 10% as effective as a drying agent. Silica gel, which looks like little plastic beads, is often treated with cobalt chloride which indicates how much moisture has been absorbed. The beads are deep blue when completely dry, but gradually change to light pink as moisture is absorbed. Silica gel can be reactivated indefinitely by drying for eight hours in a 200° F. oven. Batches weighing over a pound should be stirred occasionally to speed up the drying process. Always dry silica gel slowly, because temperatures that are too high can scorch and ruin it, turning the beads black.

Silica gel can also be easily dried in a microwave which works on the moisture in the material. It only takes about 25 minutes to dry an 8" x 12" glass dish that is filled with silica gel to a depth of 1.5-2". Progress can be checked by watching through the glass door of the microwave as the silica gel changes from pink to deep blue. Whichever drying method is used, the silica gel is then stored in an airtight container to keep the material dry until it is needed.

The drying process requires a glass jar with an airtight lid, at least half a pound of dry silica gel, and the seeds. Each sample of seeds should be placed in a paper packet and carefully labeled. Determine the total weight of the seeds and packets, and then measure out an equal weight of dark blue silica gel. Place both the packets and silica gel into the jar and screw the lid on tightly. The silica gel will immediately start absorbing moisture from the seeds.

Both large and small seeds reach optimum moisture levels for storage after seven or eight days in the container. Peas, beans and corns usually contain 6-8% moisture at the end of that period, which is dry enough to greatly increase their storage life while avoiding dormancy problems that can occur when legumes are dried to under 5% moisture. Small, soft seeds such as peppers and tomatoes will reach a lower 4-5% moisture level during that period, because their mass is so small. Small seeds aren't damaged if moisture levels remain above 3%.

After seven or eight days, open the jar and separate the packets of seeds from the silica gel. The seed packets are then stored in another moisture-proof container without any silica gel in order to maintain the low moisture content of the seeds. The second container could be another glass jar or any similar moisture-proof container. Thoroughly dry seeds reabsorb moisture quickly, so always try to minimize the time that the seed packets are exposed to the moisture in the air while being shifted to the second container.

Another type of container proving to be really versatile is a flat bag that has laminated walls made from layers of paper, plastic, foil and another layer of plastic. Individual paper packets of dry seeds can be heat-sealed inside of these pouches with a Microseal II™ that is available for about $20 from Southern Exposure Seed Exchange listed in "Supplies for Seed Savers" at the end of this section.

Paper/poly/foil/poly pouches can even be sealed shut with an ordinary clothes iron set on "wool" and applied to the open end of the bag for three seconds. When the pouches are filled with water and sealed, a person can stand on them without the seals leaking. If that person jumps on them until the pouch breaks, the sealed edges are still perfect. The sealed edge can be cut off with a pair of scissors, seeds can be taken out and the pouch can be resealed. The outside of the pouch can be written on, since that layer is paper, but for safety's sake always put a label inside with the seeds as well. Several small packets can be sealed into each laminated pouch. The pouches can be stored directly in the freezer, take up very little space, and are inexpensive.

The very best place to store an airtight container of thoroughly dried seeds is in a freezer. The next best place is in a refrigerator, followed by any cool area where the temperature fluctuates as little as possible. When retrieving seeds from frozen storage, always allow the sealed jar to reach room temperature before opening. Let the jar set out overnight, whenever there is sufficient time. If the jar is opened before the seeds reach room temperature, moisture will condense on the cold seeds and rehydrate them. Also try to limit the number of times seeds are retrieved from the jar, because temperature fluctuations gradually reduce the viability of the seeds.

When removing seeds from storage that have been dried to low moisture levels, expose the seeds to the air for a few days before planting, if time allows. This will let the seeds slowly pick up some moisture, instead of going immediately from low moisture storage to a very moist planting environment.

Color indicating silica gel and paper-poly-foil-poly packets are available from Southern Exposure Seed Exchange listed in "Supplies for Seed Savers" at the end of this section.

OVERWINTERING BIENNIAL PLANTS

Probably the most difficult task faced by seed savers involves overwintering biennials, especially in northern climates where roots or plants must be dug, stored and then replanted the next spring. In extremely mild climates overwintering may be as simple as making a fall planting, caring for plants that are left in the soil during the winter, and then harvesting seed during the next summer. In areas where the ground freezes only to a slight extent, special mulching techniques are used to cover plants or roots that are left in the garden over the winter. In northern areas where the ground freezes deeply, gardeners who successfully save vegetables in a root cellar for eating during the winter months will probably also be able to save some of the vegetables a bit longer for use in seed saving. The same techniques are used with only a few minor exceptions.

Saving biennial plants and roots requires some sort of storage area, clean storage containers, clean paper for wrapping and shredding, clean dry leaves or sphagnum moss, peat moss or sand, water containers for providing moisture and increasing the humidity, a thermometer and humidity gauge. Root cellaring is commonly used to hold vegetables several months after harvest in a cold, moist atmosphere. Care must be taken to prevent the vegetables from freezing or drying out during storage. Generally root cellaring is most successful when temperatures are held between 32 and 40° F., a temperature range that slows down the microorganisms which cause spoilage and also retards plant growth.

So many variations of root cellaring are used in various climates, that whole books have been written on the subject. Specific guidelines for commonly grown biennial vegetables are given in the applicable sections of *Seed to Seed*. These techniques include preparation for storage, optimum temperature and humidity levels, and expected storage life.

Basement storerooms designed to overwinter vegetables are often no more than a closed-off corner of the basement. Usually the north or east corner is chosen, because temperatures are most likely to be stable in areas least affected by the sun. Storage areas should not contain any heating ducts, oil pipes or water pipes. All of the designs incorporate insulated walls and ceilings, tightly closing doorways, air ducts and passive ventilation systems.

Occasionally garages or sheds are utilized for cold storage. These areas are subject to a great deal of temperature fluctuation, however, and usually are not recommended for winter storage of vegetables. Also, garages used to park cars or other machinery often have emissions that interfere with temperature and air quality. Never use attics for seed storage because such areas are especially prone to temperature fluctuation on sunny winter days.

Many different types of outdoor storage pits are popular in various areas of the country. Cone pits are often constructed by layering straw and vegetables, and then covering the entire mound with a layer of soil 6" or deeper. A special cone is inserted in the top of the mound to allow for ventilation. Often only one type of vegetable is stored in each pit and, once the pit is opened, the entire contents are usually removed. A partially buried barrel laid on an insulating bed of straw and covered with straw and earth is also a popular type of outdoor storage pit. Another variation is the Walter Needham pit which is designed to meet storage needs in extremely cold climates such as Vermont.

Complete descriptions of these special pits and other storage techniques are described in *Putting Food By* by Ruth Hertzberg, *Root Cellaring* by Nancy and Mike Bubel, and USDA Bulletin No. 119: *Storing Vegetables and Fruits in Basements, Cellars, Outbuildings, and Pits.*

GERMINATION TESTING

Usually the time and expense involved with long-term frozen storage are only warranted for seeds that have high germination rates. An exception would be in cases where frozen storage is used to maintain seeds with low germination rates until they can be grown out. In either case, germination testing is easily done at home and closely mimics commercial testing.

Most vegetable seeds will germinate when exposed to moisture and warmth. Moist conditions are easily provided by using blotter pads or heavy paper towels. Cut the material into 12" x 12" squares and spray with warm water. Lay the moistened squares on a piece of plastic for easy handling and place 10, 25, 50 or 100 seeds, evenly spaced, on the surface. If there is an ample supply, use a minimum of 25 seeds. If an accurate count is needed, use 100 seeds due to sampling error. Cover with another moistened square, roll the layers up and place inside a lightweight plastic bag, such as a bread sack. Always remember that the seeds need air in order to grow. Punch a number of holes in the plastic sack, enough to let in some air without drying out the contents. Don't make the blotters too soggy, especially for melon seeds, which rot easily.

Finding a spot in the home that provides constant warmth at a specific temperature is sometimes difficult. The tops of refrigerators will sometimes suffice, as will areas near appliances with pilot lights. Natural gas inhibits many of the Solanaceae species, however, so do not try to germinate such seeds near gas stoves or water heaters. A 25 or 40 watt light bulb in a plywood box can provide an excellent source of heat at minimal expense, but should be closely checked with a thermometer. The temperature can be regulated by connecting the light bulb to a dimmer switch. The box may also need to be equipped with a heat-activated rheostat in order to maintain a constant temperature.

The importance of proper germination temperatures cannot be overstated. A constant minimum temperature of 75° F. is appropriate for most garden seeds. Some species, however, won't germinate if temperatures are slightly too high or too low. For example, eggplants and peppers germinate best at 80° F., but lettuce won't germinate if temperatures exceed that level. Malabar spinach, on the other hand, requires a constant temperature of at least 85° F.

If the proper level of warmth is constantly provided, most vegetable seeds will start to germinate in seven days. Check the seed daily and remoisten the seeds with warm water when necessary. After seven days, make the first count of germination and then remove the sprouted seeds. Make a second count a week later and add the first and second counts before figuring the germination percentage. Germination may not be complete for 21-28 days for some vegetables. The germination requirements for each species being tested should be checked before aborting a germination test. The most accessible source for such information is *Knott's Handbook for Vegetable Growers* (Third Edition) by Oscar A. Lorenz and Donald N. Maynard, Wiley and Sons, 1988.

RECORD KEEPING

Gardeners who grow their own vegetable seeds need to keep accurate records of seed sources and plant characteristics. An easy way to keep such records is to develop a card file. Any local office supply store should be able to provide a small metal recipe box, some 3" x 5" cards and dividers. Write all of the different plant types being kept on the dividers, and then fill out a card for each variety of seeds being maintained.

Each card should include the following information: type of plant, variety name (synonyms if any), name and address of source, date obtained, germination if known, date the seeds were stored, year the seeds were last grown,

accession number, and any pertinent history or cultural notes. If more seed needs to be obtained for some unforeseen reason, the source information could be invaluable. For computer storage, the information that is most important for retrieval includes: plant type, variety name, accession number, year last grown and date stored. Accession numbers are particularly important when different varieties with the same name have been obtained from different sources.

Data taken on the plants throughout the gardening season can also be written onto the cards. Such information might include: days to maturity (number of days from sowing to dry seed, or from transplant to ripe fruit); plant height and habit; fruit size, color and shape; productivity; disease resistances or susceptibilities; flavor; and storage qualities.

Detailed records called descriptor lists often become important as seed savers begin maintaining ever larger collections of rare and heirloom varieties. Descriptors are used by researchers worldwide to give as much data as possible about a plant. With practice it is relatively easy to visualize a plant and its fruit by looking only at the data on a descriptor list.

Descriptor lists are often specially formulated for each vegetable species, however there are usually a number of similarities. Each set of descriptors will show: botanical and common names, accession number or seed source, location where the data was taken, name of the evaluator, number of days to maturity from seeding or transplanting, maturity in relation to the maturity of a standard variety, plant characteristics at the time of first flower, description of the flower's color and size and shape, description of the leaf's size and color and shape, dimensions and color of a mature fruit, disease problems, insect problems, and possibly even a taste comparison to a standard variety.

Taking descriptor data requires a substantial investment in time and energy, and therefore such data is usually kept only by serious seed hobbyists on rare and little-known varieties. Descriptor lists are as varied as the individual growers and their data requirements. It would be wonderful if standard descriptors were developed and if all growers maintained complete descriptor lists, however that would require more time than most seed savers can afford.

A photograph taken on a grid of 1" squares showing fruits, flowers and a cluster of leaves can partially replace lengthy descriptor lists. Such photos are usually taken from a tripod with the camera aimed downward and the grid resting on the ground. A fairly inexpensive grid can be made from four photographers "gray cards" taped together and marked off in 1" squares with a waterproof marker. This middle-gray background gives the perfect meter reading in the light available at the time. The best light for grid photos occurs on bright but overcast days. Never take such photos in full sun, which always results in dark shadows and bright highlights.

SUPPLIES FOR SEED SAVERS

Often it is difficult for seed savers to find the supplies that they need, especially in small quantities and at reasonable prices. The following companies offer various supplies that should be of interest to gardeners who are saving vegetable seeds.

Southern Exposure Seed Exchange (PO Box 158, North Garden, VA 22959) offers the best line of supplies for seed savers in the United States. Their catalog includes heat-sealable paper-poly-foil-poly pouches, color-indicating silica gel, and an inexpensive Microseal II™ heat sealer. Other items available include small and large ziplock plastic bags, ear shoot bags, professional quality thermo-impulse heat sealer for all types of material, two sizes of airtight Seed Saver Vials™, non-leak coin envelopes, row marking stakes, plant labels, pollination tape and flags, hand-held corn and popcorn shellers, and Reemay in 25' and 250' rolls. Their catalog is $3 (free to previous customers) or a copy of just their price list is $1.

Johnny's Selected Seeds (305 Foss Hill Rd., Albion, ME 04910, phone 207/437-9294) used to carry the white spun polyester cloth called Reemay, but recently switched to a similar material called Kimberly Farms floating row cover. Unlike Reemay which pulls apart fairly easily, the new material is "point bonded" (melted together at thousands of tiny points) which makes it much more durable, sometimes lasting several years instead of just one. The material is extremely lightweight, lets the light and rain in, holds heat in, but keeps insects out. In addition to its uses for caging and bagging, seeds or pods or even whole plants can be placed on pieces of used material, tied into bundles and hung under cover to dry. The applications seem endless. Kimberly Farms floating row cover comes in 64" wide rolls in lengths of 50', 250' and 2,550'. Wider sizes for acreage plantings are also available: 29' x 100', 29' x 600' and 50' x 300'. Johnny's catalog is free.

Abundant Life Seed Foundation (PO Box 772, Port Townsend, WA 98368) is a nonprofit corporation dedicated to acquiring, propagating and preserving plants and seeds of native and naturalized flora of the North Pacific Rim. Their seed catalog offers self-sealing seed envelopes, cloth bags for storing seeds, the I-Tech Seed Thresher, and stainless steel screens for seed cleaning. The screens, which are available in six different meshes (1/4" to 1/30") and come either mounted or unmounted, can even be used to wash berry and other fruit seeds from their pulp without rusting. A $5 annual membership will bring you their seed catalog, book list and periodic newsletters.

Lawson Bag Company (PO Box 8577, Northfield, IL 60093, phone 708/446-8812) makes all sizes of pollinating bags for corn, sorghum, wheat, grasses, millet and sunflowers. Their tassel and shoot bags, which are used for the hand-pollination of corns, are made of sturdy paper, tough adhesive and are designed to withstand the elements. Although Lawson is primarily a supplier to large companies and government programs, the company offers smaller quantities (lots of 1,000) of their #402 tassel bags and #217 shoot bags to amateur growers. These are the sizes of bags that are most commonly used by seed savers. The tassel bag expands to about 5" x 5" x 14 1/2" and the shoot bag to 2" x 1" x 7". Call or send for their price list.

Chicopee Co. (PO Box 2537, Gainesville, GA 30503) manufactures a caging material called Natural Lumite Screen (product #51821-00) which is used extensively by the Plant Introduction Station in Ames, Iowa. Natural Lumite Screen is a woven synthetic screen that will last up to five years.

Peaceful Valley Farm Supply (PO Box 2209, Grass Valley, CA 95945, phone 916/272-4769) is a western source for Kimberly Farms floating row cover. Their catalog is $2, refundable when placing first order.

II

MAJOR VEGETABLE FAMILIES

THE AMARYLLIDACEAE FAMILY

James Beard, premier American chef, once said that without alliums there would be food, but no cuisine. Alliums are such an important crop that many cultures have used allium flowers in deity worship ceremonies. Onions, leeks and garlics have all been grown since prehistoric times and have spread worldwide. There are more than 400 species of alliums. Many species that are grown only as flowers in the United States are eaten in other parts of the world.

FAMILY TAXONOMY

Nearly all gardeners can identify members of the genus *Allium*. A strong onion or garlic odor is their most common characteristic. The odor is caused by sulfur compounds in the leaves and bulbs of the plants. The hollow round leaves that are so characteristic of onions are also found in many other allium species. Flat leaves that bend at a 45° angle in the middle are characteristic of leeks and garlics.

Topsetting onions and rocambole produce small bulbs called bulbils at the top of their flower stalk. Most garlics, shallots, multiplier onions and potato onions are "multicentric" (dividing vegetatively under the ground to form many bulbs). It is very unusual for any of these types of onions to produce seed, but some occasionally do when subject to extreme variations in the weather. Possibly such plants are responding to a little understood survival mechanism.

Common chives grow in low clumps and do not form bulbs. Garlic chives look like miniature clumping leeks and have a garlic-like flavor. Common chives and garlic chives both form seed.

POLLINATION CHARACTERISTICS AND TECHNIQUES

Allium flowers are perfect, but are unable to self-pollinate. The anthers open first and shed pollen before the

Amaryllidaceae in the Garden		
Genus	Species	Common Name
Allium	*ampeloprasum*	leek
	cepa	common (seed-producing) onion, shallot, multiplier onion, potato onion, top setting onion
	fistulosum	Japanese bunching onion
	sativum	garlic, rocambole
	schoenoprasum	common chives
	tuberosum	garlic chives (Chinese chives)

style and stigma are receptive. The anthers continue to shed pollen for three days, and the style and stigma are receptive for six days. The individual flowers open over a period of 30 days with the largest number open during the second week. Thus, on each seed head, some anthers are shedding pollen and some of the stigmas are receptive at any one time.

Allium flowers are visited by many types of insects. Flies and bees are the primary pollinators; wind is not a pollination vector. Different varieties within the same species are commer-

Facing Page: Common members of the Amaryllidaceae Family.

cially isolated by 1-3 miles depending on the geography.

Most home seed savers isolate varieties rather than deal with caging or daily hand-pollination. Another relatively easy method is alternate day caging, which can be used when working with more than one variety (see "Alternate Day Caging" in Section I).

Hand-pollination needs to be done every day for at least two weeks and preferably for 30 days, if good seed is to be produced. The immature flower heads are bagged before any of the individual flowers open. At least 10 flower heads of each variety should be bagged. Reemay bags or weather resistant corn tassel bags may be used. The bags should be secured with removable strings or plastic twist ties.

Each morning between 9:00 and noon, remove the bags from as many flower heads as can be kept free of insects. Use a camel hair brush to transfer pollen between the open flowers, moving from head to head and back again. Cover each flower head twice in rotation, which will help to ensure that some flowers are pollinated with pollen from another plant. Rebag the flowers and repeat the process daily. The bags can be removed when all of the seeds have set. Be sure to tag the hand-pollinated flower heads for identification during harvest.

Caging with introduced pollinators, another method of pollination, is also described in detail in Section I.

GENERAL PRODUCTION AND PROCESSING TECHNIQUES

It is very important to examine all alliums that are to be saved and replanted for seed production. Plants with off-type foliage should be removed early in the growing season. Also remove any plants that bolt or start to flower during the first season. Save only the best, most true-to-variety bulbs (or bulbils from the nonseeding alliums).

Garden rotation is very important when growing any nonseeding allium species. Invariably a few bulbils are unknowingly left in the soil after harvest. If a different variety is planted in the same location the following year, differences in the two varieties may not be obvious and the varieties could become mixed.

Two different methods are used for growing biennial alliums. Most common is the seed-to-bulb-to-seed method. Seeds are planted in the spring and mature bulbs are harvested, sorted or rogued in the fall. Only healthy true-to-type bulbs are stored over the winter for replanting the following spring. Shortly after being replanted, each bulb will begin to produce a seed stalk.

In mild winter areas it is also possible to grow alliums using the seed-to-seed method. Seeds are planted in the late summer or early fall, the plants grow throughout the winter, and bolt to seed in the spring. The seed-to-seed method does not allow for the bulbs to be sorted prior to flowering. Off-type bulbs are difficult to see and are usually not removed. It is best to use the seed-to-bulb-to-seed method if there is any question about the purity of seed that is being renewed.

It is easiest to let the seed heads mature on the stalks. In arid climates the stalks and seed heads dry quickly when irrigation is withheld. Harvest should begin as soon as the heads are dry. Many seeds will shatter and be lost if the plants are left too long. In humid regions of the country, seed heads often are cut off and dried on tarps or pieces of plastic in an area that can be protected from the rains. Seed heads can also be dried in a food dehydrator, but only if the temperature can be accurately controlled. Drying temperatures higher than 95° F. will damage the seeds.

Allium seeds will easily fall out of the seedpods when the heads are dry. The remainder can be removed by jogging on top of the heads or using a small seed thresher. Winnowing is then used to separate any remaining seedpods and other debris.

_____ *Allium ampeloprasum* - Leek _____

Leeks are a favorite vegetable in northern European countries. Their soft bulbs and leaves tolerate freezing temperatures and are more resistant to diseases than onions. Wild relatives of leeks can be found as far north as Germany.

Elephant garlic, sometimes known as greathead garlic, is also a true leek. The large bulbs are used like a mild garlic. Most elephant garlics produce a single large bulb, but do not flower. The few that do flower produce several cloves around a large central flower stalk. Flowers of these varieties are usually sterile.

Left: Two elephant garlic bulbs with a cluster of basel bulbils removed from around their roots.
Right: Smaller rocambole bulb (*Allium sativum*) and two flower stalks.

BOTANICAL CLASSIFICATION

Leeks are members of the genus *Allium* and the species *ampeloprasum*. Different varieties of *A. ampeloprasum* have been selected for long white bulbs, resistance to bolting, bluish green leaf color and cold tolerance. Leeks are most commonly grown in France and England where numerous heirlooms are documented.

POLLINATION, CROSSING AND ISOLATION

Leeks, like other seed producing alliums, have perfect flowers. Leeks do not cross with onions or with any other allium species. Leeks will, however, cross with kurrat, a wild leek that grows in Egypt and along the Mediterranean.

SEED PRODUCTION, HARVEST AND PROCESSING

Leeks are true biennials, but will produce flower stalks regardless of the daylength after experiencing cold weather for 4-6 weeks. Some leeks form an onion-like bulb instead of the familiar white leaf base when grown during very long, warm days.

Leeks can be overwintered under mulch in many areas where winters are not extremely cold. In far northern regions with severe winters, the plants must be dug in the fall, overwintered in a root cellar, and planted the next spring in a prepared bed. Leeks will stay in good, plantable condition for many months when stored at 32° F. and 80-90% humidity.

Leek varieties are easily crossed by insects. Isolation of one mile is recommended for seed production. Bagging with hand-pollination, alternate day caging, and caging with introduced pollinators can all be used to ensure pure seed crops. These pollination techniques are explained in detail in Section I.

Leeks that are left in the ground during the winter will often produce side shoots known as leek pearls. These pearls can provide an emergency method of preserving a variety that has been damaged or cross-pollinated. Leek pearls are genetically identical to their parent plants, and can therefore be used as leek sets and grown to maturity for seed, if the seed crop from the parent plants has been contaminated.

Leek seeds are more tightly encased in their seedpods than onion seeds. Therefore leeks do not shatter as readily as onions, so immediate harvest of the dry seed heads is not as critical. Seed may be threshed and winnowed as described in the introductory pages of the Amaryllidaceae family.

SEED VIABILITY

Leek seed will retain 50% germination for three years when stored in cool, dry, dark conditions.

Allium cepa - Common Onions and Multipliers

Botanists believe that the onion originated in Iran and Pakistan. Onion carvings and seeds have been found in Egyptian tombs dating back to 3200 B.C. Greeks and Romans wrote about onions as early as 400 B.C. and held festivals during onion harvest. By the Middle Ages, onions had been transported throughout northern Europe and were used as both food and medicine.

Flower stalks and seed heads of common onions (*Allium cepa*, Cepa Group).

Onion bulb formation is dependent on daylength or photoperiod. Onion varieties are classified according to the photoperiod required for bulbing: short day varieties require 12 to 13 hours of daylight; intermediate varieties require 13.5 to 14 hours; long day varieties require 14.5 to 15 hours; and a few very long day varieties require 16 or more hours of daylight. Onions tend to bulb more quickly during warm days, however temperatures over 104° F. can actually retard bulbing.

Despite these daylength classifications, onion bulbing is really a response to the length of the night, not daylight. Locations closer to the equator have shorter summer days than, for example, some areas of Alaska that have 20 hours of light on some June days. Thus, short day onions grow to full bulb size during the 12 hours of light available in the southern regions of the United States. Intermediate varieties bulb well in the nation's midsection, and long day types grow well in the northern regions. Gardeners in the mild winter regions of the intermediate zones often grow long day onions from spring to summer, and short day varieties from summer to fall.

BOTANICAL CLASSIFICATION

Onions belong to the genus *Allium* and species *cepa*. *A. cepa* includes several groups or subspecies.

The Aggregatum Group includes all of the multicentric onions which divide vegetatively. Shallots, multiplier onions and potato onions are all examples of the Aggregatum Group.

Biennial onions that produce seed comprise the Cepa Group.

The Proliferum Group includes the top setting onion which are commonly known as Egyptian onions, tree onions or walking onions.

POLLINATION, CROSSING AND ISOLATION

All varieties of seed-producing onions can be crossed by insects. Some of the top setting onions (*Allium cepa*, Proliferum Group) produce fertile flowers which can contaminate nearby seed-producing onions. There can also

Egyptian onion (*Allium cepa*, Proliferum Group) with sprouted bulbils.

occasionally be some crossing between seed-producing onions and some varieties of *A. fistulosum*. Seed-producing onions do not cross with chives or leeks.

Isolation of one mile is adequate for seed purity. Bagging or various caging techniques can be used when more than one variety is grown in the garden. These techniques are described in the introductory pages of the Amaryllidaceae family and also under each applicable species.

SEED PRODUCTION, HARVEST AND PROCESSING

Seed-producing onions are biennial and require two growing seasons to produce seed. Onion bulbs that are going to be replanted for seed production can be harvested after the first season. Only the best bulbs should be stored for replanting in the spring. This is referred to as the seed-to-bulb-to-seed method. In some mild winter climates, onions can be left in the ground to overwinter.

When using the seed-to-bulb-to-seed method, the onions are harvested after the first growing season when the tops begin to dry. The bulbs are then dried or cured for 10-12 days. Avoid drying the bulbs in the sun where temperatures exceed 75° F. or the bulbs will sunburn and spoil in storage. After curing the onions, remove the dry tops or braid into strands. Recent studies suggest that most varieties will keep for 3-6 months at 32 to 45° F. or at 77 to 95°, and at 60-70% humidity. The worst possible storage temperature is 60 to 70°, which is about room temperature. At a relative humidity of 40% or lower and a temperature of 37° F., some onion varieties can be stored for 10-12 months.

Onions will begin to sprout only after a period of rest, which varies from variety to variety. During this rest period, the bulbs will not sprout even when exposed to optimal growing conditions. Following the rest period, the onions enter a dormant phase. During this period of dormancy, the onions will sprout if the temperature and humidity are in the proper range.

During the next spring, the best, most true-to-type onions are replanted for seed production. As the days get longer, each onion will form a seed stalk and a flower head which contains hundreds of tiny flowers. As the seeds form, the flower and plant begin to dry. The seeds are encased in tiny pods which shatter easily. Onion seeds should be harvested as soon as the seeds are mature and the pods start to dry. The seed heads can be bent over into a sack and cut from the stalk to avoid losing any seeds during harvest.

The seed heads should be placed in a protected area, away from direct sunlight, to complete drying. Onion seeds fall free of the seedpods quite easily once the pods are dry. The remaining seeds can be removed with a commercial seed thresher. Other successful seed removal techniques include jogging in place on the seed heads, rubbing them over a wire mesh screen, or rubbing the seed heads together. Winnowing the seeds in a light wind will remove any remaining seedpods and debris.

SEED VIABILITY

Onion seeds will retain 50% germination for two years when stored in cool, dry, dark conditions.

_____ Lesser Grown Amaryllidaceae _____

Allium fistulosum - Japanese Bunching Onion

Japanese bunching onions have been used like green onions for centuries in China and Japan. They do not have a well-developed bulb, but definitely have the hollow, tube-like leaves of an onion. Seed heads are formed after a cold period, although some varieties will form topsets. Different varieties of

Japanese bunching onion (*Allium fistulosum*).

Allium fistulosum can be insect cross-pollinated and occasional crossing can also occur between *A. fistulosum* and *A. cepa* varieties.

Allium sativum - Garlic and Rocambole

Garlic is grown vegetatively from the cloves formed in each bulb. Several layers of sheath leaves surround each of the cloves. Each clove contains two mature leaves and a vegetative bud. The outer leaf is a dry sheath with an aborted blade. The second leaf is quite thick and also has an aborted leaf blade. The vegetative bud has a bladeless sprout leaf and one or two foliage leaves which remain at rest after the bulb is mature.

Rocambole, also known as serpent garlic, forms an elongated stalk that twists in a circular loop as it grows. Both the top setting bulbils and the underground cloves can be eaten or replanted. The cloves are usually pre-ferred for replanting, however, because the top sets may take two seasons to produce full-sized bulbs.

After harvest, garlic bulbs enter a period of rest similar to onions. Following this rest period, garlic cloves begin a period of dormancy. During this dormancy period, sprouting will occur when the temperature and humidity reach the proper range.

In mild climates, garlic is usually planted in the fall and allowed to grow during the cool conditions of winter. This allows the plants to grow to good size before bulbing begins during the lengthening days of spring. In cold climates, fall-planted garlic will remain dormant under mulch until the spring thaw, but still produces bigger bulbs than garlic planted in spring. Garlic harvest begins when the plant's partially dry top bends over. Garlic bulbs are usually dried for one week prior to storage, but never in direct sunlight.

After curing, garlic may be stored in paper bags or hung in braids. Bulbs that are to be used for planting stock will keep for 6-8 months when stored in the dark at 35-40° F. and 60% humidity. Higher temperatures can cause rough bulbs and early sprouting. Garlic bulbs are broken apart into individual cloves which are planted.

Allium schoenoprasum - Common Chives

Common chives look like tiny clumps of onions. The plants are perennial and grow for years. Each year some of the plants will produce purple-flowered seed heads which are insect-pollinated. Several different varieties of chives are stored in USDA collections. These varieties are distinguished from each other mainly by plant height and flower color variations. Seed catalogs in the United States offer generic chives only, with no mention ever made of any varietal distinctions. Different varieties grown near one another would be insect cross-pollinated. Common chives do not cross with garlic chives or any other common allium species.

Allium tuberosum - Garlic Chives

Garlic chives look like miniature leeks with flat leaves, and taste like very mild garlic. The plants flower freely in late summer. Their white flowers, which are often used as a

Garlic chives (*Allium tuberosum*).

garnish, are insect-pollinated.

Garlic chives are also called Chinese chives, as well as a myriad of names in various Chinese dialects. If different varieties exist and were grown near one another, they would be insect cross-pollinated. Garlic chives do not cross with common chives or with any other allium species.

THE BRASSICACEAE FAMILY

The Brassicaceae family (formerly known as the Cruciferae family) is quite large and includes over 350 genera. Cabbage and broccoli usually come to mind when brassica is mentioned, but some very important flowers, condiments and herbs are also members of the family. Garden cress, watercress, radish, horseradish and turnip all share family ties with the more common cole crops.

At times the vernacular associated with Brassicaceae becomes difficult to decipher. Many gardeners refer to broccoli, kale, cabbage and Brussels sprouts as cole crops. Another name, mustards, is sometimes used to refer to the entire family or just to the mustard species. Even the authoritative *Hortus Third* still lists Brassicaceae and Cruciferae as alternate names for one another.

Since recorded time, various forms of Brassicaceae have been savored by mankind. In Rome about 201 B.C., Cato described several different kinds of kales and cabbages. Chinese cabbages and mustards appear in artwork and literature dating many centuries before Christ. Perennial wild cabbage can still be found growing on the coasts of England and France.

Broccoli, a wild cabbage selected specifically for its flower buds, is thought to have been developed in Italy. Continual selection for the best edible shoots and flower buds has resulted in the broccoli varieties grown today. Similar selections have resulted in the development of many of the other cole crops.

FAMILY TAXONOMY

Seedlings of the Brassicaceae family all look very much alike and often are impossible to tell apart. The flowers are also quite similar, each having four

Brassicaceae in the Garden		
Genus	**Species**	**Common Name**
Armoracia	*rusticana*	horseradish
Brassica	*hirta*	white flowered mustard
	juncea	Indian mustard, mustard greens
	napus	rutabaga (Swede turnip), Siberian kale, rape
	nigra	black mustard
	oleracea	broccoli, Brussels sprouts, cabbage, cauliflower, collards, kale, kohlrabi,
	rapa	turnip, broccoli raab, Chinese cabbage, Chinese mustard
Crambe	*maritima*	sea kale
Eruca	*sativa*	rockett (roquette)
Lepidium	*meyenii*	maca
	sativum	garden cress
Raphanus	*sativus*	radish
Rorripa	*micrrophyla*	large leaf watercress
Rorippa	*nasturtium*	watercress

petals that form a cross. The outdated, though still commonly encountered family name, Cruciferae, was derived from this cross-like petal formation of flowers.

POLLINATION CHARACTERISTICS AND TECHNIQUES

The Brassicaceae family can be a difficult one for the garden seed saver. All members within each of the species cross with one another. This means

---

Facing Page: Checking for ripe pods on seed stalks of cabbage (*Brassica oleracea*).

that varieties of broccoli, Brussels sprouts, cabbage, kohlrabi, collards, cauliflower and kale will all cross with each other. The flowers are perfect, but require insects for pollination. Many varieties exhibit self-incompatibility similar to self-sterility in fruit trees, which is nature's way of ensuring diversity. The pollen of self-incompatible varieties cannot grow properly in a flower on the same plant. It will grow normally, however, when moved by an insect to a flower on another plant.

It is never a good idea to save seed from just one plant, but it would be impossible to do so in many of the Brassicaceae genera due to self-incompatibility. Insects must carry pollen from one plant's flower to a flower on another plant, not just one flower to another on the same plant. Therefore, the larger the group of plants, the better the pollination and seed production will be. Finally, to confuse matters even further, some summer or East Indian cauliflowers and some Brussels sprouts will self-pollinate.

To ensure seed purity it is necessary to isolate different varieties by 1/2 mile, use caging with introduced pollinators, or use alternate day caging. Spun polyester is an ideal caging material, because it allows air, water and light to pass through to the plants while restricting insect travel.

Alternate day caging requires the construction of a cage for each of the varieties. Each morning an alternate cage is removed, and each evening the cage is replaced. This method allows insects to pollinate each variety for one day and excludes insects the next. Seed production is restricted due to the lack of daily pollination.

Caging with artificial insect introduction requires the use of trapped flies or newly hatched bees. This method sounds far better than it works. Flies trapped with rotten meat can be introduced into the cage, but there is no guarantee that they will visit enough flowers to ensure adequate pollination. Caging with introduced pollinators is described in detail in Section I.

GENERAL PRODUCTION AND PROCESSING TECHNIQUES

Always select healthy plants that perform well in your area when saving seed. Plants that have excessive insect damage or are stunted, that show off-color foliage or produce poorly should not be saved for seed production. Weather and insect damage will not affect the genetic makeup of a plant but will affect the quality and quantity of the seeds.

Brassicaceae seedpods must develop fully while still attached to the growing plant. Plants pulled before they are completely mature and stored in hopes of further pod development produce little viable seed. As the seeds approach maturity, the pods begin to dry out and turn light brown. The seedpods of all cole crops have a tendency to shatter. The ripest seedpods will be located at the bottom of each seed stalk and should be hand-harvested as they dry. Progressive collection of the pods can be made over several weeks. If hand harvesting is too time-consuming, cut the entire stalk when the largest number of pods are dry but have not shattered. Maturing seed stalks may need to be netted or bagged to protect the seed crop from birds.

Continue to dry the stalks away from the direct sun. Many of the seedpods will shatter, while others will need to be broken by hand, or by jogging in place on top of a seed bag, or with the use of a seed thresher. The wind, a hair dryer or a fan can be used to winnow the seeds. Be sure to cover the area used for winnowing with a tarp or sheet. If a strong gust of wind accidentally causes seeds as well as chaff to be blown out of the winnowing container, the tarp will recover many of the seeds. Always be careful, however, to completely shake out the tarp when switching from one variety to the next.

Brassicaceae seeds do not normally require any further processing. However, if black rot (*Xanthomonas campestris*) or black leg (*Phoma lingam*) or black leaf spot (*Alternaria brassicae* and *A. brassicola*) is a problem, the seeds can be hot water treated to reduce incidence of the disease. The technique for hot water treatment of seeds is described in detail in Section I.

_____ *Brassica napus* - Rutabaga, Siberian Kale and Rape_____

Rutabagas (known as Swede turnip in England) appeared in Europe during the Middle Ages. Some gardening books indicate that rutabagas are the result of a cross between a turnip and a cabbage, but this could not be verified in any of the references cited. Rutabagas do not grow well in areas where summer temperatures exceed 75° F. for long periods of time. There are two common forms of rutabagas, one with white flesh and another with yellow flesh.

BOTANICAL CLASSIFICATION

Rutabagas belong to the genus *Brassica* and the species *napus*. Previously Sturtevant incorrectly classified rutabagas as *B. rapa* along with turnips. In more recent taxonomic references (*Hortus*, Yamaguchi, George), rutabagas and turnips have been correctly separated into different species.

Some residual name confusion still exists, however, especially with very old varieties. The names Swede turnip, Finnish turnip or Lapland turnip all refer to vegetables belonging to *B. napus*. Some varieties of agricultural or fodder turnips, however, may be *B. napus* while others are *B. rapa*. Additional research and testing are needed to separate all known varieties of rutabagas and turnips into their correct species.

Brassica napus is commonly divided into three subspecies. Napobrassica Group includes rutabagas which are grown for their roots. Pabularia Group includes rutabagas grown for their foliage, such as Siberian kale and Hanover Salad. The third group includes the rape varieties. Rape is grown as an oil seed, for birdseed and for animal forage.

POLLINATION, CROSSING AND ISOLATION

Rutabaga flowers are self-fertile and are capable of self-pollination. Varieties grown within one mile of each another are easily cross-pollinated by insects. Rutabagas will also cross with some varieties of agricultural turnips or fodder turnips, and with all varieties of winter rape.

To ensure seed purity it is necessary to isolate all varieties belonging to *Brassica napus* by one mile. If two or more varieties are grown within close proximity, caging is necessary. Various caging methods are described in the introductory pages of the Brassicaceae family.

SEED PRODUCTION, HARVEST AND PROCESSING

Rutabagas are biennial, producing seed during their second growing season. The plants are frost tolerant and, if well mulched, can be left in the ground under a snow cover. In areas with extremely cold winters, however, the roots should be dug after the first few frosts. Trim the tops to 2". Rutabagas will keep 2-4 months when stored in sawdust or moss at 32-40° F. at 90-95% humidity.

Rutabagas produce seed stalks 3' tall or more. The plants flower prolifically and are very attractive to bees. The seedpods, which form after the flowers begin to fade, are green initially, but turn tan as the seeds mature and the plant begins to dry. The seedpods shatter beginning with the pods lowest on the stalks. Several hand pickings will result in the greatest seed harvest. If harvesting by hand is too time-consuming, cut the entire stalk when the greatest number of seedpods are dry but have not yet shattered.

Continue to dry the stalks and seedpods away from direct sunlight. Many of the seedpods will shatter. The remaining pods will need to be broken by hand, with a seed thresher, or by jogging in place on a bag of seedpods. Winnowing will remove small pieces of seedpods, leaves and other remaining debris.

Rutabaga seeds do not normally require any further processing. If black rot diseases are a problem, the seeds can be hot water treated to reduce incidence of the disease. The technique for hot water treatment of seeds is described in Section I.

SEED VIABILITY

Rutabaga seeds will remain viable for five years when stored under ideal conditions.

Brassica oleracea - Cabbage

Cabbage is the fourth most produced vegetable in the United States. While we may eat a lot of cabbage, very few of the hundreds of known varieties are still grown. Today's headed cabbage was selected from a wild perennial cabbage that still grows along the coasts of England. Cabbages have evolved into a variety of head shapes and growth habits through centuries of climatic and human selection.

In the 1800s headed cabbages were divided into five categories determined by the shape of the heads: flat, round, egg or sugar loaf, elliptic, and conical. In addition, three colors are mentioned: white, green, and purple. *The Vegetable Garden* by Vilmorin lists 57 varieties that were available to growers in 1883. Today over 100 varieties are available to the home gardener, but many are just strains that have been "improved" with the wholesale storage market in mind. Many of the varieties listed by Vilmorin are still available in Europe and through seed importers in the United States.

BOTANICAL CLASSIFICATION

Cabbage belongs to the genus *Brassica* and the species *oleracea*. *B. oleracea* includes cabbage, cauliflower, broccoli, Brussels sprouts, kale, collards and kohlrabi. Cabbage belongs to a subspecies of *B. oleracea* known as the Capitata Group.

Cabbage is a biennial and must undergo "vernalization" (a period of cold temperatures) in order to flower. In some regions where winter temperatures do not drop below 28° F., it is possible to plant biennial Brassicas in the fall and harvest seed the following summer. In colder areas of the country, cabbage plants must be dug carefully in the fall and stored between 32 and 45° with moderate humidity. The plants are then set out in a prepared garden bed in early spring. The plants can also be dug and transplanted into pots that are kept in a greenhouse, until being planted out in the spring.

POLLINATION, CROSSING AND ISOLATION

Cabbage flowers must be insect-pollinated or hand-pollinated to produce viable seed. Most cabbages are self-incompatible. The pollen is viable, but is unable to grow in a flower on the same plant. Pollen carried by insects to a flower on another plant will grow normally. Because the insects must carry pollen from one plant to another, instead of just from one flower to another on the same plant, the larger the group of plants the better the pollination and seed production.

All *B. oleracea* varieties will cross with one another. To save seeds from more than one variety of *B. oleracea*, it is necessary to use caging techniques or isolate plants by a distance of one mile. Alternate day caging or caging with introduced pollinators can also be used. These techniques are described in detail in Section I.

SEED PRODUCTION, HARVEST AND PROCESSING

In cold winter areas, late season storage cabbages are best used for winter storage. Choose firm, solid heads and trim off loose outer leaves.

Dry, completely ripe cabbage seedpods (*Brassica oleracea*).

Dig the plants very carefully and trim the root system to 12" leaving some lateral roots. The roots can be covered with damp sawdust and the entire head can be wrapped in newspaper. Cabbage will keep for 2-4 months when stored between 32 and 40° F. at 80-90% humidity.

Cabbage varieties are commonly classified by seasons. Varieties such as Golden Acre and Copenhagen Market are grown as early crops. Midseason varieties include Greenback, King Cole, Roundup, Market Prize and Red Head. Autumn or storing cabbages include such varieties as Danish Ballhead, Rio Verde, Market Prize and Green Winter.

Growing cabbage for seed is one of the most interesting seed saving experiences. In early spring of the second growing season, cut a shallow "X" in the top of the head. This will allow the emerging seed stalk to push up through the cabbage a bit more easily. The seed stalk actually pushes the head open and uncurls itself as it rises out of the head. It is a vegetable birth in the most graphic sense. The stalk will grow 3-4' tall before branching out. For further information on seed production and processing, refer to the information in the introductory pages of the Brassicaceae family.

Cabbage seeds do not normally require any further processing. However, if black rot diseases are a problem, the seeds can be hot water treated to reduce incidence of the disease. The technique for hot water treatment of seeds is described in Section I.

SEED VIABILITY

When stored under ideal conditions, cabbage seeds will remain viable for four years.

Brassica oleracea - Broccoli and Cauliflower

Cauliflower and broccoli varieties are available in purple, green, and white. Prior to the turn of the century, purple broccoli was more common than green broccoli. Broccoli was described in garden literature long before cauliflower. In Italy the name broccoli originally referred to the tender shoots produced by various kinds of overwintered cabbages. The shoots were highly regarded and were grown in the royal gardens. Broccoli ceased to be a cabbage as gardeners selected and cultivated plants which produced the tenderest shoots in the greatest abundance. Centuries of selection resulted in varieties similar to the sprouting broccoli of today. As this selection continued, some plants exhibited white curds and were slowly developed into what is now known as cauliflower.

BOTANICAL CLASSIFICATION

Broccoli and cauliflower belong to the genus _Brassica_ and the species _oleracea_. _B. oleracea_ is a very large species whose different vegetable members can be grouped into eight subspecies according to physical characteristics. Broccoli and cauliflower are members of the Botrytis Group. Always remember that these groups will cross readily with one another, because they are all _B. oleracea_.

POLLINATION, CROSSING AND ISOLATION

Broccoli and cauliflower will cross with all other varieties within the huge _B. oleracea_ species, which includes all cabbages (except Chinese cabbage), Brussels sprouts, kale, collards and kohlrabi, as well as with each other. Beginning seed savers should restrict themselves to one variety of _B. oleracea_ per year. That means allowing just one variety of broccoli to flower, for example, and making sure that within a one-mile radius there are no flowering plants of Brussels sprouts, cabbages, cauliflowers, collards, kales or kohlrabis. Advanced seed savers may want to try methods of alternate day caging or caging with introduced pollinators, which are described in Section I.

SEED PRODUCTION, HARVEST AND PROCESSING

Broccoli and cauliflower are biennials and both must undergo vernalization in order to flower. In some regions where winter temperatures do not drop below 28° F., brassicas can be planted in the fall and seed is harvested the following summer. In addition, some of the shorter season broccolis, when planted in early spring, will flower and produce seed in one season.

In cold winter areas, broccoli and cauliflower plants are carefully dug in the fall and stored between 32 and 40° F. at 80-90% humidity. Even under the best conditions, however, the plants will quickly succumb to rot, often remaining in good condition for only 4-6 weeks. Broccoli cuttings can sometimes be rooted and grown in a greenhouse until planted out the next spring. Cauliflower seed production is generally limited to mild winter areas.

Seed producers in Japan have developed a new method for broccoli seed production. The plants are sown in the spring and the central head is harvested at least two months before a killing frost. The central head stump is cut to 4-6" above the ground. The resulting side shoots are cut when 4" tall, treated with a rooting hormone and planted in heated nursery beds. The rooted shoots are planted out the following spring. Since these rooted plant cuttings have undergone vernalization, they will bolt in the late spring and produce seed.

When broccoli and cauliflower are grown for seed, the heads should not be harvested for food. Some gardeners cut the central head of broccoli and only let the side shoots go to seed. While this does work, the seed crop is of lesser quality and quantity. The cauliflower head must be intact to produce a good seed crop.

Most broccoli and cauliflower is self-incompatible. To ensure a good seed set and to preserve as much genetic diversity as possible, a minimum of six plants should be used for seed saving. Twenty plants will provide a much greater genetic base.

Broccoli and cauliflower produce seed stalks 4' or taller. The yellow flowers are attractive to bees. For additional information on general production and processing techniques, see the introductory pages of the Brassicaceae family.

SEED VIABILITY

Broccoli and cauliflower seeds will remain viable for five years when stored under ideal conditions.

Brassica oleracea - Kale and Collards

Kale and collards may have been the first cultivated brassicas. Early Greek and Roman literature referred to kale-like plants. The first known reference to kale was written by Cato about 201 B.C.

Kale is highly prized in winter gardens and is remarkably hardy in areas with very cold, snowy winters. Ornamental kale, used in both flower and vegetable gardens, is edible and used in salads and as a garnish.

Collard greens and kale are opposites in some respects. Kale fades in the summer sun, but collards thrive on heat. A favorite vegetable in the southern United States, collards cooked with ham hocks or bacon drippings are a culinary institution. Collards are traditionally grown in mild winter areas, are extremely adaptable and can withstand temperatures as low as 10° F. The plants can be grown as perennials where weather permits.

BOTANICAL CLASSIFICATION

All collards and most kales belong to the genus *Brassica* and the species *oleraceae*. Botanically, kale is a bit confusing. Kales that belong to *B. oleracea* include Common, Scotch, Marrow-Stem, Borecale, Chinese, Tall, Cabbage, Tree, Decorative, Flowering, Kitchen, Ornamental, Cow and Curled. However, Siberian kale, Hanover Salad and Winter Rape kale are *B. napus*, along with rutabagas.

POLLINATION, CROSSING AND ISOLATION

Most kale and all collards will cross with all other members of *B. oleracea*, including cabbage, broccoli, Brussels sprouts, cauliflower, collards and kohlrabi. As just mentioned, the only exceptions are a few kales, including Siberian Kale and Hanover Salad, which are *B. napus* and will cross instead with rutabagas. Variety names have changed over time and are often confused. Several Siberian kales are available from seed companies, but it is not certain yet if these are all *B. napus*. Do not presume that a kale called Siberian will not cross with other varieties of kale belonging to *B. oleracea* or with

other members of the Brassicaceae family.

To ensure seed purity it is necessary to grow only one variety of any of the members of *B. oleraceae*. All varieties and types within the species will cross with one another. To save seeds from more than one variety within any brassica species, it is necessary to use caging techniques or to isolate different varieties by one mile.

SEED PRODUCTION, HARVEST AND PROCESSING

It is possible to eat kale or collards and save seeds from the plants as well. During the first season, small quantities of leaves can be harvested without affecting the seed crop. Kale and collards, which are biennials and produce seed during their second growing season, must undergo vernalization in order to flower. In some mild winter regions it is possible to plant biennial Brassicas in the fall and harvest seeds the following summer. Kale is extremely hardy and will overwinter in many areas. In areas with extremely cold winters, the plants should be dug, trimmed and stored in sawdust or sand. Kale plants stored between 32-40° F. at 80-90% humidity will only have a limited life of 1-2 months. Any stored plants that do make it through the winter are set out in a prepared bed in early spring.

Both kale and collards produce seed stalks that are 5' or taller. The plants flower prolifically and are very attractive to bees. Additional information on production and processing techniques is presented in the introductory pages of the Brassicaceae family.

Neither kale nor collard seeds normally require any further processing after harvesting and cleaning. However, if black rot diseases are a problem, the seed can be hot water treated to reduce incidence of the disease. Hot water treatment of seeds is described in detail in Section I.

SEED VIABILITY

Kale and collard seeds will remain viable for four years when stored in a cool, dry, dark location.

_____ *Brassica rapa* - Chinese Cabbage and Chinese Mustard _____

All types of Chinese cabbage and Chinese mustard are thought to have originated in China and Eastern Asia where they have been cultivated since the fifth century A.D. Chinese cabbage and Chinese mustard readily cross with one another. Selection and crossing, both intentional and accidental, have occurred thousands of times during the last 16 centuries. Distinct types have evolved due to local adaptations as well as traits which were specifically selected. Many of the varieties grown in Asia are not available in the United States. The varieties that are available here often have different names depending on the country from which they were imported. In addition, attempts to Romanize the Chinese dialect name has resulted in numerous English translations for the same variety.

BOTANICAL CLASSIFICATION

All Chinese cabbages and Chinese mustards belong to the genus *Brassica* and the species *rapa*. Some attempts have been made to change the common name from Chinese cabbage to Asiatic cabbage. The vegetables are found throughout Asia, so Asiatic cabbage would be more appropriate.

Many references go into great detail, grouping Chinese cabbages into various subspecies. Lengthy debates over different plant characteristics and growth habits have arisen as various taxonomists have developed different

classifications for these proposed subspecies. Herklots, Tsen and Lee, Sun, and Bailey have all done a great deal of work on subspecies classifications.

Most references place Chinese cabbages and Chinese mustards into one of three groups. Chinensis Group includes nonheading varieties of Chinese mustard, celery mustard and pak-choi. Pekinensis Group includes heading Chinese cabbage, celery cabbage and pe-tsai; and the Perviridis Group includes all spinach mustards. It is important to remember that these varieties are all members of the same species, *B. rapa*, and cross readily regardless of subspecies classification.

Confusion surrounding variety names in *B. rapa* is rampant. What one person buys as Chihli cabbage may be what someone else thinks of as Shantung cabbage. A patient, dedicated group of people with a lot of time is needed to grow, document and compile data on the vast array of *B. rapa* varieties available in this country.

POLLINATION, CROSSING AND ISOLATION

Chinese cabbages and Chinese mustards, which are both *Brassica rapa*, will cross with each other as well as with any turnip varieties, which are also *B. rapa*. Remember that this species also includes broccoli raab, a type of turnip grown for its flower stalks. Chinese mustard varieties will not cross with common mustard, which is a weed in many areas of the United States, or with varieties grown for mustard seeds, or with mustard greens.

Most Chinese cabbages are self-incompatible. Insects must move pollen from one plant's flower to a flower on another plant to produce viable seed. Thus larger groups of plants improve pollination and seed production. No fewer than six plants should ever be grown for seed production.

To save seed from more than one of any of the brassica species, it is necessary to use caging techniques or to isolate the different varieties by one mile. Reemay is an ideal caging material which does not restrict air, water and light to the plants, but does restrict insect travel. Alternate day caging or caging with introduced pollinators, as described in detail in Section I, can also be used.

SEED PRODUCTION, HARVEST AND PROCESSING

When growing Chinese cabbage or Chinese mustard for seed, some of the outer leaves can be harvested without significantly affecting the seed harvest. Always select plants that exhibit the desired characteristics for seed production. Do not use plants for seed production if they bolt prematurely or are of a different color, size or shape from the rest of the population.

Chinese cabbages and mustards are primarily biennial and normally require two growing seasons to produce seed. However, they may go to seed in a single season, if planted in early spring. Such plants have already experienced short days and cool spring temperatures and may bolt when the long, hot days of summer arrive. There is a danger, however, that this shortened method may actually amount to selecting for premature bolting.

In areas with extremely cold winters, Chinese cabbage will need to be overwintered in a root cellar and then replanted the next spring. Before the first killing frost, choose mature, solid plants and carefully dig the roots with some of the root ball and soil attached. Carefully pack just the roots and the attached soil in damp sand, while leaving the head exposed. Chinese cabbage will store 2-4 months at 32-40° F. and 90-95% humidity.

Chinese cabbages and Chinese mustards will produce seed stalks 3' or taller. The plants prolifically produce yellow flowers that are very attractive to bees. After the flowers fade, seedpods form which are initially green but turn tan as the seeds mature. As the plants begin to dry, the pods begin to shatter, starting with ones that are lowest on the stalks. Several hand pickings will result in the greatest seed harvest. If harvesting by hand is too time-consuming, cut the entire stalk when the greatest number of seedpods are dry but have not yet shattered.

Techniques for drying, cleaning and winnowing Chinese cabbage seeds are presented in the introductory pages of the Brassicaceae family.

SEED VIABILITY

Chinese cabbage seed remains viable for 5 years under ideal conditions.

Brassica rapa - Turnip and Broccoli Raab

Grown since prehistoric times, turnips have been savored in every European and Asian culture. Tiny white turnips shaped like eggs are currently popular. In times past the varieties of choice were the types with larger roots, which were noted for their storage capabilities. These larger types account for much of the name confusion between rutabagas and turnips. Rutabagas, which are sometimes called Swede turnips or Finnish turnips, belong to a different species, *Brassica napus*, from the common garden turnips of today.

BOTANICAL CLASSIFICATION

Turnips belong to the genus *Brassica* and the species *rapa*. *B. rapa* was sometimes referred to as *B. campestris* in some early taxonomic texts. Some varieties of agricultural or fodder turnips may actually be rutabagas, *B. napus*, and would therefore cross with rutabagas but not with turnips. It is unlikely, however, that such varieties would be available to most seed savers.

Turnips are grouped into two subspecies. Varieties grown for their roots are members of the Rapifera Group. Broccoli raab, rapa, Italian turnips and other varieties grown for their flower stalks are members of the Ruvo Group.

Turnips are grown as annuals for their fleshy roots and leafy greens. The root shapes vary greatly and include flat, long, and globe shapes. The flesh color of the roots is usually white or yellow. Skin colors range from white, cream, yellow, red, and purple to black. Flower color usually correlates with the flesh color of the roots. Plants with white fleshed roots usually produce bright yellow flowers. Yellow-fleshed varieties have flowers with pale orangish yellow petals.

POLLINATION, CROSSING AND ISOLATION

Different varieties of turnips will cross with each other as well as with all other members of *B. rapa*. This includes all Chinese cabbages, Chinese mustards and any turnips that are grown for their flower stalks such as broccoli raab. Turnips will not cross with any other brassica species. Most turnips are self-incompatible. Insects must carry pollen from a flower on one plant to a flower on another plant for pollination.

To ensure seed purity, isolate different varieties of *B. rapa* by one mile. Alternate day caging or caging with insect introduction can be used when two or more varieties are grown near one another. These caging techniques are described in Section I.

SEED PRODUCTION, HARVEST AND PROCESSING

Most turnips produce seed biennially and must undergo vernalization in order to flower. In some mild winter regions it is possible to plant turnips in the fall and harvest seed the following summer. In colder areas of the country, the crops must be overwintered in a root cellar. Carefully dig the turnip plants before a heavy freeze, trim the tops to 2" and store in cartons of sawdust, sand or leaves. Turnips will keep 2-4 months when stored at 32-40° F. and 90-95% humidity. The stored roots are set out in a prepared garden bed in early spring. The plants can also be transplanted into pots and kept in a greenhouse until spring. Some of the earlier maturing varieties of turnips have annual seeding characteristics and may be grown to seed in one season.

Turnips produce seed stalks 3' or taller. Flowers appear prolifically and are very attractive to bees. After the flowers fade, seedpods form which are initially green but turn tan as the seeds mature and the plant begins to dry. The seedpods shatter beginning with the pods lowest on the stalks. Several hand pickings will result in the greatest seed harvest. If harvest by hand is too time-consuming, then cut the entire stalk when the greatest number of seedpods are dry but have not yet shattered.

Additional drying of the stalks can be continued in a protected location away from direct sun. Many of the seedpods will shatter. Others will need to be broken by hand, with a seed thresher, or by jogging in place on top of a seed bag. The seeds can then be winnowed in the wind or with a hair dryer or fan.

Turnip seeds normally do not require any further processing. However, if black rot diseases are a problem, the seeds can be hot water treated to reduce incidence of the disease. The technique for hot water treatment of seeds is described in detail in Section I.

SEED VIABILITY

Turnip seeds remain viable for five years when stored under ideal conditions.

Raphanus sativus - Radish

The little red morsels that today's gardeners call radishes have an impressive history. Radishes were considered so important in ancient Egypt that their pictures were inscribed on many pyramid walls. Greeks presented offerings to Apollo which included turnips made of lead, beets of silver and radishes of gold. Often thought to be native to Asia, radishes appear in artwork and legends in the eastern Mediterranean which date back to 2000 B.C.

Radishes are available in nearly every size, shape and color. Oriental or daikon radishes stay tender and crisp even when grown to more than 20" long. French gardeners favor small red, white or pink radishes which are eaten with butter and French bread.

In India radishes have been developed which are grown for their large seedpods. One variety, Rat Tail radish, has seedpods that grow more than 12" long. The immature, green seedpods are often used as a green vegetable, incorporated into curries or made into pickles.

BOTANICAL CLASSIFICATION

Radishes belong to the genus _Raphanus_ and species _sativus_. _R. sativus_ is commonly grouped by growing season. Radiculata Group includes the annual small red and white varieties. Longipinnatus Group contains the long white daikon types common in Asia. Rat Tail radishes belong to the Caudatum Group.

POLLINATION, CROSSING AND ISOLATION

Radishes are insect-pollinated and will cross with all varieties of wild and domesticated radishes. They will not cross with any other members of the Brassicaceae family.

Most radishes are self-incompatible. The pollen is viable, but cannot grow in a flower on the same plant. Pollen carried by insects to a flower on another plant will grow normally. Because the insects must carry pollen from one plant to another and not just from one flower to the other, the larger the group of plants the better the pollination and seed production.

Any two radish varieties must be separated by 1/2 mile or grown using the caging techniques described in Section I. Wild radishes are common in some rural regions. Care must be taken to remove all wild plants or to isolate seed crops from the wild types.

SEED PRODUCTION, HARVEST AND PROCESSING

It perhaps goes without saying that radishes can't be eaten and saved for seed too. However, the green, immature seedpods can be eaten in small quantities with only a minimal effect on the seed harvest, since radishes are prolific seed producers.

Radish seed stalks grow 3' or taller. White or purple and white flowers appear prolifically and are very attractive to bees. After the flowers fade, the seedpods form. The pods are green at first, but turn tan as the seeds mature and the plant begins to dry. The seed stalks are harvested when the stalk and pods are dry.

Radish seeds are dried and cleaned using techniques similar to other members of the Brassicaceae family. It is a bit harder to remove their seeds from the seedpods, however, so plan on spending more time and getting fewer seeds than from other family members. Gently pounding the pods with a large hammer or a wooden maul will help break open pods that do not yield when rubbed by hand. Radish seeds require no further processing.

SEED VIABILITY

Radish seeds will remain viable for five years when stored in a cool, dry, dark location.

Daikon radishes (*Raphanus sativus,* Longipinnatus Group).

_____ Lesser Grown Brassicaceae _____

Armoracia rusticana - Horseradish

Horseradish is grown from root cuttings and does not produce seeds in most regions of the United States. When harvested, the large roots are dug for market and the small side roots and crowns are saved for replanting. The pungent flavor found in horseradish is caused by allyl isothiocyanate, a sulfur compound.

Horseradish is extremely hardy and will overwinter in the ground in most regions. The roots may also be dug before the ground freezes. The roots should be trimmed and the tops cut to 3" above the crown before storing in damp sand, sawdust or leaves. Horseradish roots will keep 4-6 months when stored at 32-40° F. and 90-95% humidity.

Brassica hirta - White Flowered Mustard

Brassica hirta varieties have white flowers and are used as spicy salad or cooked greens. The seedpods are small and contain three or four seeds. White flowered mustards are cultivated in the Mediterranean as an oil seed crop. They have been naturalized in North America and may be found growing as common weeds. *B. hirta* is not the seed from which the commercial condiment "mustard" is made. White flowered mustards are self-incompatible and require insects for successful pollination. *B. hirta* varieties do not cross with any other brassica species.

Brassica juncea - Indian Mustard and Mustard Greens

Brassica juncea includes brown mustard, Indian mustard, leaf mustard and mustard greens. The flowers are bright yellow. Some varieties have become a common weed in North America. Southern mustard or curled mustard is a member of the Crispifolia Group; varieties within this subspecies are commonly grown for mustard greens. Varieties in the Foliosa Group have very large, flat leaves and are often used as greens. Longidens Group, often found growing as weeds, has long, narrow leaves with prong-like teeth. Multisecta Group varieties have finely divided leaves and also occur as weeds.

Regardless of these groups or subspecies, all varieties of *B. juncea* will cross with one another. Varieties grown for seed must be isolated from other cultivated and weedy types by 1/2 mile. Varieties grown in close proximity can be caged. *B. juncea* varieties are self-compatible and self-pollinating. Seed is saved using techniques similar to rutabagas.

Brassica nigra - Black Mustard

Brassica nigra varieties produce the millions of seeds required to make the condiment mustard. Although recipes vary, all mustards begin with *B. nigra* seeds in whole, split or ground form. Growing *B. nigra* for the making of mustard is no more difficult than saving the seeds of any other brassica species.

B. nigra varieties have bright yellow flowers and often grow 6' tall. The flowers are insect-pollinated and do not cross with any other brassica species. The plants may be found growing as weeds, so care must be taken to isolate seed crops from weedy types. Isolation of 1/2 mile will ensure seed purity. Seed saving techniques are the same as those used for turnips.

Brassica oleracea - Brussels Sprouts

Botanically, Brussels sprouts are not really baby cabbages, but for culinary purposes the analogy is perfect. Brussels sprouts grow slowly over a long season and require nearly six months to develop the 3' plants commonly seen in garden magazines and seed catalogs. Despite frost and snow, their fresh garden flavor is maintained well into the winter months. The edible heads or sprouts appear during the first growing season and the seed forms during the second season.

Brussels sprouts are biennial and belong to the genus *Brassica* and the species *oleracea*, and also to the Gemmifera Group. They are self-incompatible and require insects for pollination. Brussels sprouts will cross with any of the groups that make up *B. oleracea*, which include all varieties of cabbage, cauliflower, broccoli, kale, collards and kohlrabi. They will not cross with any other brassica species. Plants grown for seed must be isolated from other *B. oleracea* varieties by one mile. When grown in closer proximity, caging techniques used for other *B. oleracea* varieties can be used.

Brussels sprouts will only keep in storage for a very limited time. The plants succumb to rot quickly and only last 4-6 weeks when stored between 32-40° F. at 80-90% humidity. Harvest and seed cleaning techniques are similar to those used for cabbage.

Brassica oleracea - Kohlrabi

Kohlrabi is the common name for *B. oleracea* varieties which belong to the Gongylodes Group. Kohlrabi is sometimes referred to as stem turnip because of the turnip-like enlargement of the stem. The swollen stem resembles a cabbage heart in flavor. Although not widely grown, kohlrabi is versatile and a quick grower. Both white and purple varieties are ready for harvest in seven to eight weeks.

Kohlrabi is a biennial and will cross with all varieties of *B. oleracea*. Kohlrabi plants are dug after frost and the leaves are removed. The roots are clipped to 4-6" and then stored in damp sand or sawdust. The best roots are planted out the next spring for seed production. Seed saving techniques are the same as those used for cabbage.

Crambe Maritima - Sea Kale

Sea kale is a perennial and requires care similar to rhubarb or asparagus. Plants grown from cuttings are ready for harvest one or two years sooner than those started from seeds. Sea kale seeds are not difficult to start and may be the only way to secure the plants.

Sea kale is native to the coasts of western Europe. In early spring the plants are covered with an inverted bucket or pot to completely exclude all light. The young stalks become blanched and tender, are cut like asparagus, cooked until tender in salted water, and served with butter or hollandaise. Sea kale is an especially attractive plant and is a nice addition to any edible landscape or flower garden.

Sea kale flowers have a distinctively pleasant odor and are very attractive to insects. Different varieties can be cross-pollinated by insects. Isolation distances are not available but, judging by the types of insects that visit the flowers, the 1/2 mile distance used for other species of Brassicaceae should be sufficient for seed purity. The seed stalks grow about 2' above the plant. Sea kale continues to produce leaves and remains green as the seed stalks dry. Each seed is enclosed in a round seedpod. Care must be taken to avoid smashing the seeds when the seedpods are removed. For home storage and seed trading, it is easiest to store the seeds in the seedpods.

Eruca sativa - Rocket (Roquette)

Rocket, also known as rocket salad or roquette or roka or gargeer, has been grown throughout history. The ancient Romans are known to have used its leaves. In India the pungent seeds add spice to many native dishes. Rocket is currently enjoying a resurgence of popularity as a salad green. In most parts of the United States, rocket is grown in the early spring or in the late fall and winter. Hot temperatures and long days cause the leaves to become extremely hot with a hint of bitterness. For most gardeners, rocket is an acquired taste at best.

Rocket is usually planted by broadcasting the seeds. The plants are pulled or snipped beginning when they have six true leaves. The flowers are self-sterile and require insects for cross-pollination. Rocket does not cross with any other genus or species within the Brassicaceae family. Different varieties of rocket will cross with one another and must be isolated by 1/2 mile for seed purity. Seed pollination, harvest and storage techniques are similar to those used for Chinese cabbage.

Turkish rocket, *Bunias orientalis*, is a perennial that is indigenous to Central Europe and Siberia. Further information or seed sources for Turkish rocket are unavailable.

Lepidium meyenii - Maca

Maca grows wild at high elevations in the Peruvian Andes and is used for both food and medicine. The frost resistant plants are widely cultivated throughout the central highlands of Peru. Maca forms a rosette of 12-20 leaves. As the outer leaves die, new ones form in the center of the plant. The roots resemble turnips and range in color from cream, yellow, and purple to black. They are traditionally cooked in Peru by roasting in hot ashes. Peruvian Indians believe that frequent consumption of the roots will increase

Rocket (*Eruca sativa*).

fertility in human beings and animals. The roots have a tangy taste with a slight butterscotch aroma. There is no known source for maca seed in the United States.

Lepidium sativum - Garden Cress

Garden cress resembles its namesake, watercress, in flavor but not habitat. Garden cress does nicely in the home garden and requires care similar to other salad greens. Seed is broadcast thickly where the plants are to grow. Harvest begins at the six-leaf stage by snipping the tops or thinning the plants. Long days and hot weather cause the flavor to decline.

The flowers are very small and rarely visited by honeybees, but crossing between varieties is possible. Isolation distances for garden cress are not available.

The seeds can be harvested like turnips. Those seedpods left to shatter on their own will result in renewable, self-sown beds.

Other garden cress varieties that are available in many seed catalogs include common cress, broad leaf cress, French cress, curled cress, curly moss cress, land cress, mustard cress, upland cress and peppergrass.

Rorippa microphylla - Large Leaf Watercress
Rorippa nasturtium var. aquaticum - Watercress

Many garden books still indicate that watercress must be grown in running water. Numerous time-consuming methods have been devised so that home gardeners can provide running water in streamless gardens. Watercress is found naturally in streams, but only needs to be rooted in mud. Running or still water has nothing to do with the plant's ability to grow.

Common watercress is *Rorippa nasturtium var. aquaticum*. Large leaf watercress is *R. microphylla*. The two species do not cross with one another. Watercress is usually propagated by divisions or cuttings. Watercress from the grocery store will root and may be used as a source for plants. Seeds are produced in very small, curved seedpods that develop from tiny white flowers. The seedpods shatter easily and are difficult to find and harvest. The tiny dry pods can be rubbed between the hands or rolled lightly with a rolling pin to extract the seeds.

European growers name cress after the areas where it historically has been grown. English connoisseurs may prefer cress from Springhead or Waltham. It is not clear if such designations refer to distinct varieties.

THE CHENOPODIACEAE FAMILY

The Chenopodiaceae family includes several very widely grown vegetables. Beets, chard and spinach were noted in Aristotle's writings as early as the fourth century B.C. Orach is recorded in ancient Indian history. Although not well known in the United States, quinoa is an important grain crop in the Andes Mountains of South America. Lamb's-quarters and Good King Henry are common in English gardens and are gathered wild throughout Europe and America.

FAMILY TAXONOMY

Members of the Chenopodiaceae family are very diverse in growth habit and even in seed formation. Beet or chard seed is an aggregate containing several seeds formed in an irregular, dry, hardened, woody calyx. Other family members have "panicles" (flower clusters) of single seeds.

POLLINATION CHARACTERISTICS AND TECHNIQUES

Members of the Chenopodiaceae family are wind-pollinated. The pollen is light and can travel up to five miles depending on the variety, air temperature and wind speed. Commercial seed production relies entirely on isolation to keep the seed crop pure.

In the home garden it is possible to bag beets, orach and spinach, if the plants are grown very close together. As the seed stalks form, a wooden or metal support stake is placed in the center of the plants. The seed stalks are all bent in slightly to the stake and covered with a large, water-resistant paper bag. The seed stalks are then wrapped with cotton batting to cushion and seal the bottom of the bag. The batting prevents stray pollen and

Chenopodiaceae in the Garden		
Genus	**Species**	**Common Name**
Atriplex	*hortensis*	orach (mountain spinach)
Beta	*vulgaris*	garden beet, sugar beet, mangel, Swiss chard
Chenopodium	*album*	lamb's-quarters
	bonus-henricus	Good King Henry
	capitatum	beetberry
	quinoa	quinoa
Spinacia	*oleraceae*	spinach

insects from entering the bag from the bottom. The bag is stapled shut and then tied or taped around the batting to form a secure seal. In most areas the daily winds will be sufficient to mix the pollen inside the bag. Shaking the bags on windless days will help to ensure good pollination and seed set.

GENERAL PRODUCTION AND PROCESSING TECHNIQUES

Except for beetberry, Chenopodiaceae seeds are harvested dry and are usually stripped from the plants by hand while still in the garden. Some beet and prickly-seeded spinaches can be hard on the hands, making gloves a necessity. The plants and their fully mature seeds can be pulled to finish drying under cover in areas where summer rains occur.

Facing Page: A single giant leaf of Swiss chard (*Beta vulgaris*), a red-stemmed variety known as rhubarb chard, becomes a child's toy.

Beta vulgaris - Garden Beet, Sugar Beet, Mangel and Swiss Chard

Beets have been providing food for humans and animals since ancient Grecian times. Invading Roman armies took beet roots into northern Europe to provide feed for their horses. The tender green leaves and long-keeping roots made beets an excellent crop for northern European climates. Centuries of selection resulted in varieties that produced tender, abundant greens, which have become the chards of today. Other selections have produced tiny red table beets, and also the huge varieties that are used for stock feed and sugar production.

In 1700 the Prussians began searching for a way to produce sugar in their short, cold climate. Their attention centered on beets, and by 1775 a forage beet with 6% sugar content had been developed. Today's sugar beets often yield a sugar content of 20% and provide nearly half of the world's sugar.

BOTANICAL CLASSIFICATION

Beta vulgaris includes all forage, sugar and garden beets as well as the chards. Chard varieties are beets that are grown for their greens rather than for root production. _B. vulgaris_ is biennial, requiring two seasons to produce seed. Beets will not flower until

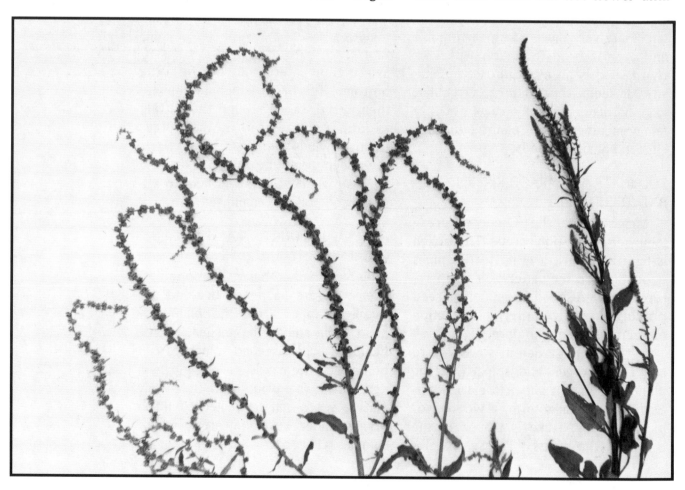

Garden beet (_Beta vulgaris_) flowers, right, and mature seeds, left.

their roots are mature and have been subjected to at least a month of cold temperatures. In mild winter climates, beets planted in the late summer will "bolt" (produce a seed stalk) during the following spring.

Sugar beets are usually white or cream colored and weigh from 8-15 pounds. Forage or mangel beets can grow much larger and are available in white, yellow, red, and red with white stripes. Table beets have been selected for their small size, sweet flavor, and for a variety of root shapes. Globe and round shapes are by far the most common. Cylindrical varieties are often preferred for canning and pickling because all of the slices are nearly the same diameter. Table beets are available in yellow, gold, pink, red, and red with white stripes.

The larger forage or mangel beets are rapidly vanishing from commercial catalogs and need immediate attention in order to be preserved. Rabbit breeders should be especially interested in growing mangel beets as a feed supplement and might provide a unique maintenance network.

POLLINATION, CROSSING AND ISOLATION

All beets and chards will cross with each other, no matter what their size or use. To make seed saving even more difficult, beets are wind-pollinated. Beet pollen is light and can travel up to five miles depending on the temperature and climate. Crop isolation or seed stalk bagging can be used to ensure seed purity. Isolation of two to five miles is required for absolute purity. In home gardens the bagging technique described on the Chenopodiaceae family pages can be used. A minimum of six beets should

be included in each bag or cage.

SEED PRODUCTION, HARVEST AND PROCESSING

As with other biennial root crops, two methods of seed production are commonly used with beets. The seed-to-seed method is the easiest, especially in mild winter areas. The beet seed is planted and the roots that are left in the ground over the winter produce seed the following year.

When using the seed-to-root-to-seed method, beet seeds are planted in the spring. The roots grow to maturity, are dug before the first killing frost, and are sorted for uniform color, size and shape. Be very careful not to nick or bruise the roots. The tops are cut leaving 2" of greens, and the root tips are trimmed to about 6". The roots are then packed into a layer of damp sand or sawdust, and the green tops are covered with sawdust, shredded newspaper or leaves. Beets will store for 4-6 months between 32-40° F. at 90-95% humidity. The best roots are replanted the following spring for seed production. Some gardeners cut the tops back to within 1" of the roots, while others believe that leaving the tops on provides an added source of nourishment for the roots.

Seed savers in mild winter climates usually use the seed-to-seed method. However, if there is any doubt about seed purity, use the seed-to-root-to-seed method so that the roots can be examined and any off-types can be rogued out.

Beet seed stalks can grow 4' tall and are usually harvested when the majority of the seed clusters have turned light brown. The fully mature seeds can be progressively stripped from the plant as they mature, or the entire seed stalk can be cut when the majority of the seeds are mature, and then dried further. The dried seed stalks can be threshed with a flail, but jogging in place on a bag of dried stalks is faster for large quantities. The seeds are then winnowed to remove any remaining pieces of stems and leaves.

Beet seeds have a different structure from other garden seeds. Each seed is actually a group of flowers that is fused together by the flower petals. This forms a multigerm cluster which usually contains two to five seeds. Plant breeders have recently developed single seeded clusters for some sugar beets, which eliminates the need for thinning.

Some seed companies break apart the seed clusters of garden beets for the same reason. Research suggests that this increases seed injury and reduces germination. Seed clusters can also be broken apart at home. Place the seeds in a bag and gently roll it with a rolling pin. Adjust the pressure until the clusters are broken apart but not crushed.

SEED VIABILITY

Beet seeds will retain 50% germination for six years when stored in a cool, dry, dark location.

Spinacia oleracae - Spinach

Spinach is known to have been cultivated in Europe since 1351. The species probably originated in central Asia and was mentioned in Chinese agricultural literature in the seventh century.

Spinach is a unique annual vegetable, because its plants produce either all male flowers or all female flowers. Spinach seed is either prickly or smooth, which corresponds to the plant's leaf shape. Prickly-seeded varieties produce flatter leaves, while smooth-seeded varieties generally are more wrinkled.

Seed-set in spinach is daylength sensitive, and long days will cause the plants to bolt to seed. Depending on the variety, plants will begin to bolt when daylight reaches 12.5-15 hours. In addition, plants exposed to alternating cold and hot temperatures will often bolt at even less than 12.5 hours of daylight. Crowded plants will bolt more quickly than those given ample space.

BOTANICAL CLASSIFICATION

Spinach belongs to the genus _Spinacia_ and the species _oleracea_. Different varieties of _S. oleracea_ have been selected for their resistance to bolting and for dark leaves that are rich in vitamins. Depending on climate and season, either cold tolerant or long day tolerant varieties can be grown.

The concentration of nitrate in spinach leaves can sometimes reach toxic levels. High nitrate levels usually occur when large amounts of ammonia fertilizers are used to produce the crop. Spinach also may contain high levels of oxalates which sometimes interfere with calcium intake in humans.

POLLINATION, CROSSING AND ISOLATION

Spinach is mainly wind-pollinated, which makes it difficult for home seed savers to grow more than one variety for seed without the use of bagging. Spinach pollen is very light and is carried for great distances by the wind.

Commercial spinach seed crops are separated by 5-10 miles. Spinach pollen is so fine that it easily penetrates mesh screen, but is severely restricted by spun polyester fabric. The bagging technique described on the Chenopodiaceae family pages can be used with some success.

As was stated earlier, spinach plants are either male or female. Always maintain a ratio of one male to two female plants, and also an absolute minimum of two male and four female plants per cage, which will result in good pollination and will retain a fair amount of genetic diversity within the population. The sex of spinach plants is hard to determine until the seed stalks have formed, which often results in less than ideal caging situations. Close plantings in wide beds will give the greatest chance that the necessary ratio of male to female plants will be growing in close proximity.

SEED PRODUCTION, HARVEST AND PROCESSING

In home gardens the outer leaves of the spinach rosette are often harvested as a cut-and-come-again vegetable. Commercially, the entire rosette is harvested. When spinach is being grown for a seed crop, a few of the outer leaves can be eaten without decreasing the quality or quantity of the seed.

Commercial spinach seed is usually dried in the field. In areas with prolonged summer rains, the plants can be pulled when the seed is fully formed but not yet dry. When possible, however, spinach seed is much easier to harvest directly from the plants in the garden. Prickly-seeded varieties are very abrasive, so heavy gloves are a necessity. Starting at the bottom of the plant, strip off the seeds and leaves in

Female spinach (*Spinacia oleracea*) plant with seeds, left, and flowering male plant, right.

an upward motion and let them fall into a basket or sack.

Seeds and leaves that are completely dry can be winnowed immediately after harvest. If still damp, let them dry for several additional days away from direct sunlight. Winnowing will then remove the remaining leaves and other debris.

Commercially produced prickly-seeded varieties are put through an abrasion process to smooth the seeds. This technique is not necessary and does not aid in germination.

SEED VIABILITY

Spinach seeds will retain 50% germination for five years when stored under ideal conditions.

_____ Lesser Grown Chenopodiaceae _____

Atriplex hortensis - Orach (Mountain Spinach)

Orach is also known as mountain spinach, French spinach, sea purslane and salt bush. The last two names refer to the plant's ability to withstand saline soils. The Greeks used orach as a medicine and later as a vegetable. Although not commonly cultivated in the United States, orach is widely grown in many parts of the world.

Orach can be used in place of spinach or chard in any recipe. The red variety is quite attractive and is sometimes planted in flower gardens. The three varieties that are available from seed companies include: red, green, and a light green that is sometimes called yellow.

Orach has tiny wind-pollinated flowers. Isolation or bagging will prevent cross-pollination between varieties. Orach plants bolt in response to lengthening days and are not truly biennial.

The seeds are enclosed in leafy membranes known as bracts which are easily stripped from the plants as they mature. The plants also produce some tiny black seeds without bracts, which are usually not fertile. After harvest the seeds are dried and stored.

Orach seeds will maintain 50% germination for six years when stored in cool, dry, dark conditions.

Orach (*Atriplex hortensis*) seed stalk, with leaves of red orach, top, and green orach, bottom.

Chenopodium album - Lamb's-Quarters

Lamb's-quarters is a weed in most temperate and tropical regions of the world. The leaves can be cooked like spinach or eaten raw. Southwest Indian tribes gathered the seeds and ground them into a flour for bread.

C. album is also sometimes called

pigweed or white goosefoot weed. Male and female flowers are produced on the same plant and can be either insect-pollinated or wind-pollinated. Different varieties, if available, would cross with one another.

Chenopodium bonus-henricus - Good King Henry

Until the beginning of the 1900s, Good King Henry was commonly grown in English kitchen gardens. Also known as fat hen plant, *C. bonus-henricus* is perennial and very hardy. Each spring its arrowhead-shaped leaves are used like spinach. The plants can be covered with an inverted flower pot in the early spring in order to blanch the stems which are then harvested and eaten like asparagus.

It is not known if different varieties of Good King Henry exist. If varieties do exist and were grown near one another, they would probably be crossed by either insects or wind. Tiny black seeds are harvested when the plant begins to die back in the fall.

Chenopodium capitatum - Beetberry

Beetberry is native to southern Europe where it is often considered a weed. The small plants produce numerous flower clusters on a short stem. Orangish red fruits develop around tiny, black seeds. The fruits are sweet but lack any real flavor. In some regions the fruits are called strawberry blite, although any resemblance to strawberries seems limited to color.

Beetberry is primarily wind-pollinated. Different varieties, if grown in close proximity, would most likely be cross-pollinated. Isolation distances are unavailable.

Mature seeds can be saved from fruits which are bright red or orange in color. The tiny, soft fruits are easy to crush with either fingers or the back of a spoon. The addition of a small amount of water will cause the pieces of the fruit to float and the seeds to sink. Pour off the water and pulp, drain the seeds and set out to dry. Care must be taken to ensure that the extremely small seeds do not pass through kitchen strainers.

Information on seed viability is unavailable.

Chenopodium quinoa - Quinoa

Quinoa is a native of the Andes Mountains of South American and has been the subject of much recent attention. Grown like orach, quinoa is well adapted to climates above 8,000' in the Andes. Most varieties are short day sensitive and do not produce seed until very late in the season when grown in the United States, although selections from the southern Andes are adapting well to comparable North American latitudes.

Quinoa's green or slightly greenish purple leaves are eaten like spinach. Many different varieties have developed in a vast range of altitudes throughout the Andes. Seed colors include white, ivory, pink, red, and purple. Quinoa seed is very bitter and must be soaked, washed and rubbed in several changes of water before being boiled for cereal or added to stews.

Quinoa's flowers are perfect. Different varieties grown near one another would probably be crossed by insects or the wind. Quinoa is not related to nor does it cross with amaranth.

THE COMPOSITAE FAMILY

Compositae is sometimes referred to as the salad family. Indeed, the family's claim to fame is lettuce. Millions of tons of lettuce are produced and consumed worldwide each year. Other salad vegetables include the chicories, endives and some of the daisies.

A flower garden would never be the same without daisies, but neither would the vegetable garden. Sunflowers, Jerusalem artichokes and shingiku are delicious and add color to any garden. For most gardeners, a big yellow sunflower represents happiness. Perhaps sunflowers take us back to our childhood when all flowers were drawn with rays and big happy faces.

FAMILY TAXONOMY

The Compositae family is immense and has been divided into groups on the basis of such characteristics as the presence or absence of milky or colored sap, corolla type, morphology of anthers and styles, etc. Compositae members that are used as vegetables make up a very small portion of this family's more than 20,000 species. Only 11 of those species are commonly used as vegetables worldwide.

POLLINATION CHARACTERISTICS AND TECHNIQUES

Compositae flowers are perfect and most are self-compatible. However, many species require insect or mechanical agitation in order for the pollen to reach the stigma. Several studies indicate that plants which are freely visited by insects have a greater number of viable seeds.

Compositae flowers are produced on a seed stalk that grows upward from the center of the plant. Although the flowers are perfect, they are also

Compositae in the Garden

Genus	Species	Common Name
Arctium	*lappa*	gobo (Japanese burdock)
Chrysanthemum	*coronarium*	shungiku
Cichorium	*endivia*	endive, escarole
	intybus	chicory (witloof chicory)
Cynara	*cardunculus*	cardoon
	scolymus	artichoke (globe artichoke)
Helianthus	*annuus*	sunflower
	maximiliani	edible rooted sunflower
	tuberosa	Jeruselum artichoke (sunroot)
Lactuca	*sativa*	lettuce, celtuce
Polymnia	*sonchifolia*	yacon
Scorzonera	*hispanica*	black salsify (scorzonera)
Tragopogon	*porrifolius*	salsify
	pratensis	wild salsify

designed to attract insects. A few varieties are self-incompatible and do require insects for pollination.

Most home seed savers either isolate or hand-pollinate different varieties within each species. It is also possible control pollination in the Compositae with caging, alternate day caging, and caging with introduced pollinators. These techniques are explained in detail in Section I.

PLANT SELECTION

At every stage of development, seed savers should check to make sure that

---

Facing Page: In order to obtain maximum seed yield, lettuce (*Lactuca sativa*) must be harvested daily over a 12-24 day period.

each plant is true-to-type. Remove any plants that are off color, shape or size. If any of the biennial Compositae bolt during the first season, remove the plants and do not save their seeds. Biennial plants that bolt prematurely usually do not produce full-sized, properly formed plants. Including bolters in a population of plants used for seed production increases the chances of many more poorly formed plants in future crops.

GENERAL PRODUCTION AND PROCESSING TECHNIQUES

All of the seeds in the Compositae family are harvested dry. Birds are readily attracted to Compositae seeds and can ruin a seed crop before it is ready for harvest. Some of the bagging and caging techniques described in each of the following vegetable sections will keep that damage to a minimum. The seeds can be harvested directly from plants that are left standing in the garden. It is usually more convenient, however, to cut the entire seed stalks and store them in feed sacks for threshing.

When the stalks are dry, many of the seeds will fall off. The remainder can be removed by jogging on top of the seed heads, or by using a flail or small seed thresher. Winnowing is usually necessary to remove any remaining leaves and debris.

_____ *Cichorium endivia* - Endive and Escarole _____

Endive has been used by the Egyptians for many centuries and is thought to have spread to northern Europe by 1200 A.D. The use of endive plants was described in English cookbooks in the 16th century and in an American recipe book in 1806. Historically endive has been used as a cooked vegetable, but today the leaves are most often used in salads.

Endive grows as a loose head of leaves with ruffled or serrated edges. The outside leaves are green and slightly bitter. The inner leaves, which are partially protected from light, are somewhat milder. Escarole, a smooth-leaved form of endive, has more of a heading tendency and is usually less bitter. Both types can survive light frost and extended periods of temperatures in the low 30s. The sugar stored in the plant gradually increases during cool weather, which results in improved quality and reduced bitterness.

BOTANICAL CLASSIFICATION

Endive and escarole belong to the genus *Cichorium* and species *endivia*. *C. endivia* does not include the Belgian endives or witloof chicory, which are both *C. intybus*. Endive is closely related to the chicories and probably developed from a chance cross of two wild chicory species. Endive differs distinctively from chicory, however, being fully self-compatible and self-pollinating.

The standard commercial endive variety is Green Curled Ruffec, which has curled, deeply-cut leaves. Salad King is larger and more tolerant to both heat and cold. Pink Star and Red Endive have anthocyanin in the midribs which causes the leaves to appear pink.

Full Heart Batavia is the most common variety of escarole, but Florida Deep Heart matures slightly earlier. A large number of imported varieties are available in the United States. Most bear the name of the region where they originated. Studies indicate that there are few, if any, differences in leaf color and shape between most varieties.

POLLINATION, CROSSING AND ISOLATION

Endive flowers, which are perfect and self-pollinating, open at first light and close by noon. Endive varieties cannot be crossed by chicory, but chicory can be crossed by endive. In 1953, studies with chicory and endive determined that two separate species classifications were appropriate. One endive and one chicory were planted next to one another. Insects freely visited both plants. The seeds produced by each plant were grown the following season. All of the seeds from the endive plant produced endive plants, proving that self-pollination had occurred and that crossing with chicory had not.

Different varieties of endive can be crossed by insects and should be either separated by 1/2 mile or caged to ensure seed purity. Endive flowers bloom over a long period, so the cage must be left in place from the first bloom until the last.

SEED PRODUCTION, HARVEST AND PROCESSING

Endives are biennial, but will bolt to seed during the first season if exposed to cool temperatures and short days. Such bolting often occurs when seeds are sown very early in the season. The plants begin to produce seed stalks as the days lengthen and the temperatures increase.

In mild winter climates, endives are usually planted in the fall. Light leaf harvest during the first growing season will not significantly harm either flower or seed production. Endive may be overwintered in the ground under a mulch in many regions of the United States. In climates where the ground freezes solid, the roots are dug before a hard frost. The tops are trimmed to 2" above the crown, and any small or secondary roots are clipped off. The endive roots are then stored in soil or sand and will keep for three months or more at 32-40° F. and 80-90% humidity.

Endive, left, and escarole, right, both *Cichorium endivia*.

The best roots are replanted in the spring for seed production.

Once the majority of the flowers have set seedpods, withhold water and let the seed stalks dry. Crush the base of a dry flower to check on the seed development. The individual seeds are tightly enclosed and require a good bit of prying to remove. The seeds are ready to harvest when they appear to be dry and are firm.

Two methods of small scale seed cleaning can be used. It is easiest to break the completely dry seedpods off of the stalks one at a time, and then store them in small glass containers without further cleaning. Entire pods can be planted, but thinning will be necessary when the plants appear. The pods can also be broken open to free individual seeds.

To obtain cleaner seeds, place the seed stalks in a feed sack on a concrete floor and pound the pods with a large hammer or wooden maul. For larger quantities, an I-Tech seed cleaner crushes the pods quite efficiently (see "Seed Cleaning Equipment" in Section I). The seeds will then need to be winnowed or screened to remove any remaining dust or debris.

SEED VIABILITY

Endive seeds will remain viable for eight years when stored in a cool, dry, dark location.

Cichorium intybus - Chicory (Witloof Chicory)

Chicory is an important salad vegetable throughout Europe. Over half of the chicory grown is in the form of witloof chicory or Belgian endive. The roots are dug, trimmed, and forced to sprout in underground pits or in dark, air-conditioned rooms. The "chicons" (blanched chicory sprouts) are harvested and used alone as a salad ingredient or as a lightly cooked vegetable.

Chicory production is concentrated in France, Holland and Belgium. Red chicory, favored in Italy and commonly referred to as radicchio, has found a place in the American gourmet market. Most chicories are quite bitter and are used in small quantities in salads or as garnishes.

Chicory root is well known as an addition to or substitute for coffee. After a full season of growth, the roots are dug, cleaned, cut into chunks, roasted until nearly black and then ground into a powder. Chicory roots become crisp and very light in weight when thoroughly roasted. Roots that are not roasted completely will gum up the blades of a blender or food processor.

Asparagus chicory, a type that is little known in the United States, sends up new shoots in the spring from roots that have wintered over. The shoots can be blanched by wrapping with paper or covering with an overturned flower pot. The shoots are cut when 4-6" long and are prepared like asparagus.

BOTANICAL CLASSIFICATION

All chicories belong to the genus _Cichorium_ and the species _intybus_. Some varieties of _C. intybus_ have escaped from cultivation and have become weeds in many temperate climates. Their light blue flowers open at first light, close by noon and are easy to spot in any landscape.

POLLINATION, CROSSING AND ISOLATION

Chicory flowers are perfect, but are also self-incompatible and require insect cross-pollination. Pollen from one flower will not successfully grow in another flower on the same plant. Insects must move pollen from one plant to the flowers on a different plant. Chicory plants will accept pollen from endive plants, which, of course, will ruin the chicory seeds. All chicory varieties will cross with one another. Cultivated varieties will also cross with any of the wild chicories growing nearby. An isolation distance of 1/2 mile will ensure seed purity.

One chicory variety and one endive variety can be grown for seed if the endive is caged. Alternate day caging can be used when two or more chicory varieties are grown in close proximity. Chicory plants produce abundant flowers over a long period of time. Alternate day caging can be used for up to five varieties. The seed yields will be reduced, but will still be sufficient for most home seed savers. Alternate day caging is discussed in detail in Section I.

Hand-pollination of chicory is also possible. The evening before the flowers are to open, bag or tape the flowers on as many different plants as possible. Early in the morning remove the bags or tapes and gently rub the flowers from two different plants together. If the plants are near one another, this can be done without picking the flowers. Just bend the stalks until the flowers touch. If that is impossible, pick several flowers to use during the hand-pollination process. Rebag or retape the flowers, and also mark each of the hand-pollinated flowers, possibly with a brightly colored piece of yarn.

Bags can be removed after the flowers fall off. If tape was used, it will fall off with the petals. If additional seeds are desired, hand-pollination can be repeated over several days. During harvest, exercise great care to pick only those blossoms that were hand-pollinated.

SEED PRODUCTION, HARVEST AND PROCESSING

Chicory varieties are biennial, producing seed during their second growing season. In mild winter climates the plants can be left in the ground. A light harvest of leaves during the first growing season will not harm either flower or seed production.

In climates where the ground freezes solid during the winter, the roots should be dug before a hard frost. The tops are trimmed to 2" and any small or secondary roots are removed. Endive roots will keep for three months or more when stored in sand or soil at 32-40° F. and 80-90% humidity.

The best roots are replanted in the spring for seed production. Once the majority of the flowers have set seedpods, withhold water and let the seed stalks dry. Crush the base of a dry flower to check on the seed development. The individual seeds are tightly enclosed and require a good bit of prying to remove. The seeds are ready to harvest when they appear dry and are firm.

Two methods of seed cleaning are used for small scale seed production. Break the completely dry flowers off of the stalks one at a time, and store them dry in a small glass container without any further cleaning. Entire pods can be planted, but thinning is necessary. The pods can also be broken open to free individual seeds.

To obtain cleaner seeds, place the seed stalks in a feed sack on a concrete floor and pound the pods with a large hammer or wooden maul. For larger quantities, the I-Tech seed cleaner is quite efficient (see Section I). After crushing the pods, the seeds will need to be winnowed or screened to remove dust and debris.

SEED VIABILITY

Chicory seeds will remain viable for eight years when stored in a cool, dry, dark location.

Cynara cardunculus - Cardoon

Cardoon is a 4' grayish green perennial thistle with soft-lobed leaves and beautiful bluish purple flowers. Unlike globe artichoke, cardoon's blossoms are not eaten, but the midribs of the plant's leaves are an Italian delicacy. Cardoon is native to southern Europe and is widely grown in France and Spain. Though not common in America, cardoon is easily grown and should be included in vegetable gardens and edible landscapes.

Cardoon requires some special garden preparation. In mild winter climates, cardoon is savored from November through February when there are few other garden chores and the preparation seems worth the time. Six weeks prior to harvest, tie the 4' stalks together about 6" from the top with a heavy twine. Pile leaves or hay against the stalks or wrap the plant with heavy paper to exclude all light. After this blanching period, the entire plant can be cut. Good results are also obtained by cutting only the leaf stalks near the center.

BOTANICAL CLASSIFICATION

Cardoon belongs to the genus _Cynara_ and the species _cardunculus_. _C. cardunculus_ is nearly nonexistent in the United States, where almost no choice of varieties is available. In contrast, Vilmorin described five varieties of cardoon that were commonly available in the Paris markets in 1885. Prickly Tours was described as the most spiny but also the most sought after in Paris. Smooth Solid was free of spines and produced a large plant with broad ribs and green leaves. Long Spanish was very large with broad leaves whose ribs were not as solid as other varieties. Artichoke Leaf was free from spines, had large, dark green leaves and ribs that were not very solid. Red Stemmed had red-tinged ribs which were also not very solid.

POLLINATION, CROSSING AND ISOLATION

Cardoon is easily grown from seeds. Individual cardoon flowers are self-sterile, having anthers that release pollen five days before the stigmas are receptive. At any given time, however, some of the anthers on the flower head will be releasing pollen and some of the stigmas will be receptive. Bees are readily attracted to cardoon's purple flower heads and quickly become covered with heavy pollen. Cardoon varieties will cross with artichokes.

If two or more varieties are grown for seed, bag the blossoms on as many different plants as possible just before they open. Homemade bags of spun polyester or heavy paper bags work well to protect the blossoms from contamination. A soft brush is used to agitate the blossoms once a day, which ensures that pollen will travel down the style and pollinate the ovule.

SEED PRODUCTION, HARVEST AND PROCESSING

The flower heads are cut from the stalks when the flowers are completely open and begin to show white, downy seed plumes. The flower heads should be stored in a large bag in a dry location away from direct sunlight. When the ends of the stalks are dry and the flower heads are brittle, place one flower head at a time into a feed sack or canvas bag. Lay the sack on a rigid surface, preferably concrete. Pound the base of the blossom with a hammer, allowing the down to float out of the bag. The seeds are heavy and will remain in the bag. The seeds should be removed from the bag after each flower is cleaned to avoid crushing them.

SEED VIABILITY

Cardoon seeds will remain viable for seven years when stored under ideal conditions.

Cynara scolymus - Artichoke (Globe Artichoke)

Artichokes are a delicacy worldwide and an important agricultural crop along the coasts of southern Europe and the western United States. The grayish green thistle-like plants produce flowers whose immature buds are eaten. Artichoke plants thrive in cool, sunny coastal climates and can tolerate temperatures into the low 30s. When produced under less than perfect weather conditions, however, the buds will be much smaller than those seen in grocery stores. In areas where freezing temperatures occur, the plants are trimmed back and the roots are dug for winter storage.

BOTANICAL CLASSIFICATION

Artichokes are a member of the genus _Cynara_ and the species _scolymus_. Individual plants of _C. scolymus_ will grow 5' tall and 3-5' in diameter. Artichoke leaves are usually spineless.

POLLINATION, CROSSING AND ISOLATION

Artichokes do not usually come true from seed and are generally not propagated in this manner. Instead, plants that produce the greatest number of tight, tender flower buds are divided after flowering. Seeds are sometimes used to produce a wide variety of new plants, and the best of these are saved and divided.

Individual artichoke flowers are self-sterile, because their anthers release pollen five days before the stigmas are receptive. At any given time some of the stigmas on the flower head will be receptive to the pollen that is being released. The large purple flower heads are quite attractive to bees. Artichokes will cross with cardoon varieties.

For selective breeding purposes, the individual flowers can be bagged to prevent crossing. It is necessary to agitate or brush the tops of the blossoms once a day to ensure that the pollen travels down the style and pollinates the ovule. In mild winter climates, artichoke plants that have gone to seed have propagated huge populations of pernicious weeds. If seeds are not going to be harvested, the artichoke

The large, thistle-like purple flowers of globe artichoke (*Cynara scolymus*).

flowers should be destroyed. Preventing the plant from producing seeds also channels more energy into the next crop of flower buds.

SEED PRODUCTION, HARVEST AND PROCESSING

Artichoke flower heads are cut when completely open and beginning to show their white seed plumes. Store the flower heads in a dry location away from direct sunlight until dry and brittle. Place one of the dry flower heads in a feed sack or canvas bag on a concrete surface. Pound the base of the blossom with a hammer and allow the down to float out of the bag. The seed is heavy and will remain behind, but should be removed from the bag after each flower is processed to avoid crushing.

SEED VIABILITY

Artichoke seeds will remain viable for seven years when stored under optimum conditions.

Helianthus annuus - Sunflower

North and South American Indians used sunflower plants in their entirety. The stalks were used for bean poles and animal fodder, and were peeled into thin sheets for use like paper. Immature leaves, flower petals and roots were all cooked as vegetables. Mature leaves were used as a tobacco substitute and for animal feed. Some tribes even used the empty seed compartments in the flower head as containers for dye and paint. Many Indian varieties have retained tribal references in their names, such as Apache Brown Stripe, Hopi Black Dye and Tarahumara White.

Sunflowers are grown commercially for oil and for seed. Oil seed sunflowers have been specifically selected for high oil content. The large seeded varieties, such as Mammoth Russian and Large Gray Striped, are preferred for snacks. In home gardens, sunflowers are often grown as flowers and for bird seed.

BOTANICAL CLASSIFICATION

Cultivated annual sunflowers are members of the genus *Helianthus* and the species *annuus*. Wild populations of *H. annuus*, which are native or introduced throughout much of North America, will cross with any other *H. annuus* cultivar. In addition, cultivated sunflower varieties are often found growing wild, usually spread by birds and animals that have visited commercial fields. These cultivated escapees will also cross with cultivated varieties.

A whole host of other annual and perennial species of Helianthus is native to North America, including wild Jerusalem artichokes. None of these, however, will cross with *H. annuus*.

One of the perennial sunflowers, *H. maximiliani*, is sometimes cultivated for its very thin but tasty roots. Maximilian sunflower is being evaluated at The Land Institute in Salina, Kansas for its seed-bearing potential in perennial polycultures, and has also been used recently in various permaculture applications.

POLLINATION, CROSSING AND ISOLATION

Sunflower heads can have from 1,000 to 4,000 individual florets. These individual florets are perfect and usually open for two days. On the first day the anthers release pollen into the anther tube. On the second day the stigma pushes up, and its two lobes open and are receptive to, but out of reach of, its own pollen. Insects, mainly bees, move the pollen around causing fertilization.

It takes five to ten days for all of the florets on a single flower head to open. A typical flower head usually has dried florets around its outside edge, followed by a ring of receptive stigmas, then another ring of pollen shedding florets, and unopened florets in its center. Some varieties are self-incompatible, requiring the transfer of pollen from one plant to another. Other varieties are self-compatible, so insects must only move the pollen from floret to floret on the same flower head.

To maintain seed purity, different varieties must be isolated by 1/2 mile to three miles depending on the size of the populations of sunflowers being grown in the area.

Hand-pollination, which is time-consuming but not difficult, requires that the flower heads be bagged before the first florets open. Each day for ten days, remove the bags from two adjacent plants and gently rub the surfaces of the flower heads together. Continue down the row of plants, unbagging and rebagging the flowers as you proceed. This method will effectively pollinate both self-incompatible and self-compatible varieties.

SEED PRODUCTION, HARVEST AND PROCESSING

When the sunflower head is completely filled out and the flower petals have fallen off, the head can be cut and dried in a protected area. Protection from birds is crucial. Blue jays will actually fly into rooms through open doors to steal sunflower seeds.

The seeds can be removed from the flower heads when they are no longer soft or damp. To clean large numbers of flowers, rub sunflower heads across a 1" x 1" welded wire screen placed over a five-gallon plastic pail. Cut the wire 12" larger than the diameter of the pail and mold the wire down over its sides. Place the container between your knees, which will hold its wire top in place. Rub the sunflower head roughly against the wire and the seeds will fall into the container below.

Using your thumbs and index fingers, grasp each end of a shelled sunflower seed and try to bend it. Seeds which snap in two instead of bending are sufficiently dry for storage. Most seeds will need some additional drying. Place a 1" layer of seeds in baskets or containers and finish drying in a warm area away from direct sunlight.

SEED VIABILITY

Sunflower seeds will remain viable for seven years when stored in a cool, dry, dark location.

Helianthus tuberosa - Jerusalem Artichoke (Sunroot)

Jerusalem artichoke is native to America and was taken to Italy by Champlain. How the English managed to corrupt "girasole articocco," its Italian name, into Jerusalem artichoke is an etymological mystery. The plant has nothing to do with Jerusalem or artichokes. In the diaries of their travels, early explorers noted various Indian tribes using Jerusalem artichoke as a vegetable.

Jerusalem artichoke, sometimes known as sunroot, has not been the most popular garden vegetable. The knobby protuberances make the roots difficult to clean. Jerusalem artichoke roots are extremely hardy. Pieces of unharvested tubers resprout in the spring and are almost impossible to eradicate. Many gardeners have tried Jerusalem artichokes with enthusiasm, only to spend the next several years wishing they hadn't.

BOTANICAL CLASSIFICATION

Jerusalem artichoke belongs to the genus _Helianthus_ and the species _tuberosa_. _H. tuberosa_ should not be confused with white Jerusalem artichoke, _Bomarea edulis_, which is a member of the Amaryllidaceae family.

Jerusalem artichoke varieties include a wide range of shapes and colors. Golden Nugget is shaped like a carrot and has yellow flesh. Smooth Garnet has red skin and white flesh. Fuseau and Long Red are shaped like sweet potatoes. The knobby tubers of French Mammoth White are commonly available in grocery stores.

The towering, sunflower-like plants of Jeruselum artichoke (*Helianthus tuberosa*).

Although some varieties of Jerusalem artichoke will flower, any seed produced is usually sterile. The plants are traditionally grown from tuber pieces. The roots will overwinter in the ground in most regions, or can be dug, the soil brushed off, and stored in plastic bags or damp sand. Jerusalem artichoke roots will keep for two months or more at 32-40° F. and 90% humidity.

Lactuca sativa - Lettuce and Celtuce

Today's cultivated lettuces probably originated from wild lettuce, *Lactuca serriola*, which was used as a medicinal herb. Lettuce was grown in Egypt about 4500 B.C. and its likeness is carved into the walls of many tombs. The Greeks and Romans also made frequent culinary use of lettuce.

Wild lettuce (*Lactuca serriola*) before flowering.

Lettuce is used primarily as a fresh vegetable in salads and on sandwiches. Occasionally lettuce is used as a cooked vegetable and, in some areas of the world, is even used as a tobacco substitute.

BOTANICAL CLASSIFICATION

All varieties of garden lettuce belong to the genus *Lactuca* and the species *sativa*. Some insect crossing does occur between *L. sativa* and *L. serriola*, a wild species, but the extent of such crossing continues to be debated. Some growers think that any crossing between the two species is minimal, while others claim to have seen such crosses at distances that exceed 150'. When crosses do occur, their offspring have intermediate characteristics and are often bitter.

L. sativa and *L. serriola* are thought to have evolved from chance hybrid populations. Crossing between *L. sativa* and an unknown third species may have produced *L. serriola*, or *L. sativa* may have evolved from a cross between *L. serriola* and an unknown third species. Differences between the two species have been further enhanced by the constant cultivation and selection of *L. sativa* varieties.

There are six types of lettuce: crisphead, butterhead, cos, leaf, stem and Latin. Crisphead types (more commonly known as head lettuce) are the ones usually available in grocery stores. The heads are tightly folded with crisp, greenish white leaves.

Butterhead varieties have small, loose, green heads and soft-textured leaves. Butterheads are the most popular lettuces grown in northern Europe. One group of butterhead varieties produces firm heads during lengthening days of summer, while another kind was developed for winter greenhouse production.

Cos or romaine lettuce has elongated leaves that form an upright loaf-shaped head. The outer leaves are dark green with heavy ribs. Cos varieties are very popular in the United States, southern Europe and Mediterranean countries.

Leaf lettuce varieties lack heading tendencies and produce a rosette of leaves. Leaf lettuces are often grouped by leaf shape and color. Numerous green and red varieties, including many beautiful heirlooms, are available to the home gardener.

Asparagus lettuce, also known as celtuce or stem lettuce, is grown for its succulent, thick stem and tender leaves. The plant is thought to have originated in China, where it is used both raw and cooked.

Latin lettuce, grown mainly in the Mediterranean and South America, has elongated leaves that form a loose head. Common varieties of Latin lettuce include Gallega, Criolla Verde, Criolla Blance and Madrilene. Gallega was the first identified source of resistance to lettuce mosaic virus.

POLLINATION, CROSSING AND ISOLATION

Lettuce flowers form in heads of 10-25 individual florets. Each floret is one celled and produces one seed. All of the florets in a head open on the same

Mature seed stalks of lettuce (*Lactuca sativa*), left, and wild lettuce (*L. serriola*), right.

day, usually in the morning. The style emerges through the anther tube and is pollinated by pollen grains along the sides of the style. Shortly after opening, the florets close and never reopen.

Bees and other hairy insects visit lettuce flowers and cause some crossing between different varieties. Many growers claim that lettuce varieties do not cross at all, while others report up to 5% crossing in varieties grown side by side. Lettuce varieties exhibit many different flower characteristics which greatly affect the chances of crossing. Some flowers are open for as little as 30 minutes, others for several hours. Most commercial seed companies require that different varieties be separated by 25', while USDA publications suggest at least 12' of separation between varieties.

Caging will ensure absolute seed purity when two or more varieties are flowering at the same time. Just before the flowers open, wrap seed heads with spun polyester or put a wire cage in place. The fabric or cage can be removed when the plants stop flowering and begin to dry.

SEED PRODUCTION, HARVEST AND PROCESSING

A few outer leaves of each lettuce plant can be picked without affecting the quality or quantity of the seed produced. Lettuce will bolt to seed in response to lengthening days.

The seed stalks of head lettuce varieties often have difficulty pushing up through the heads. Slitting the top of the head or twisting the head may promote the emergence of the seed stalk. If no effort is made to assist the plant, head rot brought on by heat and humidity often proves fatal. Some gardeners strike the top of the head sharply with their open palm, which supposedly fractures each leaf base where it attaches to the stem without damaging the seed stalk. After the head is struck, the leaves are removed. In commercial fields the heads are often slit halfway open with a knife. Probably the most reliable method is to simply peel the leaves away to expose the emerging stalk.

Lettuce seeds ripen irregularly and are ready for harvest from 12—24 days after flowering. To obtain the maximum amount of seed, the plants should be harvested daily during that period by shaking the seed heads into a large grocery sack which is then stored each night in a dry area. Label the sacks clearly to avoid any mixups when working with more than one variety. If maximum yield is not essential, the entire plant can be cut when the greatest percentage of seeds is ripe and placed head first into a bag. When the lettuce seed heads are totally dry, grasp the cut ends of the stalks and shake the heads vigorously within the sack. Rubbing the seed head between your palms will result in additional seed falling into the sack.

More than half of the seed volume will be white lettuce feathers and chaff. The seeds and chaff are about the same size and weight, so attempts at winnowing often result in lots of seed being lost. Use a fine mesh screen that will allow the seeds to pass through but will restrict the feathers. Shake the screen gently while lightly blowing the feathers to the far edge of the screen. The seeds collected below the screen will be clean enough for most home seed savers.

Further cleaning can be accomplished by a reverse screening. Select a screen that is slightly too small for the seeds to pass through. Pour the seeds and remaining chaff on the top of the screen and gently rub the mixture with the palm of your hand. The clean seeds will remain on top of the screen, while the small chaff and the remaining feathers will pass through.

SEED VIABILITY

Lettuce seeds will remain viable for three years when stored in a cool, dry, dark location.

Scorzonera hispanica - Black Salsify (Scorzonera)

Scorzonera has all but disappeared from American gardens, but is still quite common in Europe. A full season is required to produce large carrot-sized roots with smooth, oyster-flavored white flesh and contrasting black skin. Scorzonera's foliage is quite attractive and very much at home in the flower garden. Plants that are not dug for fall and winter use will send up a bouquet of yellow daisy-like flowers the following spring.

Scorzonera roots remain tasty and tender even when the flower stalks appear, and can be grown for a second year before harvest. The distinctive oyster-like flavor is contained in the skin of the roots. If the skin is peeled while being prepared for cooking, much of the flavor will be lost. New spring shoots produced by unharvested roots can be cut and used like asparagus. Young leaves can also be used like lettuce in salads.

BOTANICAL CLASSIFICATION

Scorzonera is a member of the genus _Scorzonera_ and the species _hispanica_. _S. hispanica_ is also known as black salsify, Spanish salsify, viper's grass and black oyster plant.

POLLINATION, CROSSING AND ISOLATION

Scorzonera does not cross with any other vegetable. Few, if any, varieties are available in the United States. Most seed companies just sell scorzonera, with no variety name specified. Scorzonera flowers are perfect, but different varieties could be crossed by insects. Isolation of 1/2 mile will ensure seed purity. When two or more varieties are grown in close proximity, caging can be used. Scorzonera can also be found growing wild in some parts of the United States. Always check the area for wild varieties before relying on isolation.

SEED PRODUCTION, HARVEST AND PROCESSING

Scorzonera is biennial, requiring two seasons to produce seeds. The roots can be mulched and left in the ground in most areas of the country. In climates where the ground freezes solid in the winter, plants are carefully dug, tops clipped to 3" and roots stored in damp sawdust. The roots will keep 2-4 months when stored at 32-40° F. and 90% humidity. For maximum seed production, the early spring shoots should not be eaten.

Scorzonera plants send up a seed stalk of beautiful yellow daisy-like flowers during their second season. As these flowers fade, seeds form inside each flower base. When fully mature, the base of the flower will begin to flatten and the seed will float away in the wind. Seeds must be collected daily for maximum harvest. Once each day, remove the seeds from the freshly opened seed capsules. Break the fluff away from the seeds, and then set the seeds aside for further drying.

Scorzonera seeds should be dried away from direct sunlight for two or three days. Seeds that break in half are ready for storage. If the seeds bend instead of breaking, further drying in a warm, dry location is needed.

SEED VIABILITY

Scorzonera seeds will remain viable for two years when stored under optimum conditions.

Tragopogon porrifolius - Salsify and *T. pratensis* - Wild Salsify

Salsify is a European native, where it is commonly referred to as havrerod or haverwortel. A few named varieties do exist. The roots and flower buds have been savored since at least the 13th century. The plant sends up a seed stalk of beautiful bluish purple flowers during its second season of growth. The flowers remain open until noon and have earned a place in the English flower garden as John Go To Bed At Noon flowers.

Salsify, sometimes called vegetable oyster, is easy to grow and is eaten in three different forms. When grown from a spring sowing, the roots are mild and taste slightly of oysters. Roots left to overwinter produce tasty asparagus-like shoots in the spring. Also the unopened flower buds can be used as a green vegetable in the early spring. They are traditinally served lightly sauteed in butter. Salsify is a very versatile vegetable and has been unjustifiably ignored by most gardeners.

BOTANICAL CLASSIFICATION

Salsify belongs to the genus *Tragopogon* and the species *porrifolius*. Another species, *T. pratensis*, is a common weed that is sometimes referred to as wild or yellow-flowered salsify.

POLLINATION, CROSSING AND ISOLATION

Salsify has escaped from the garden and become a weed in many areas. These garden escapees should not be confused with *T. pratensis*, known as yellow-flowered salsify, which is also a weed. Bluish-purple flowered salsify, *T. porrifolius*, does not cross with the yellow-flowered species.

Most seed companies sell only Mammoth Salsify, or just salsify with no variety name specified. The flowers are perfect, but different varieties of the same species can be crossed by insects. Isolation of 1/2 mile will ensure seed purity. When two or more varieties of the same species are grown in close proximity, caging must be used. Always check for any blue-flowered escapees growing in the wild before relying on isolation.

SEED PRODUCTION, HARVEST AND PROCESSING

T. porrifolius and *T. pratensis* are both biennial and require two growing seasons for seed production. In most regions of the country, salsify roots can be mulched and left in the ground over winter. In areas where the ground freezes, and the roots would be damaged, the plants are dug, tops are trimmed to 3", and roots are stored in damp sawdust. Salsify roots will keep 2-4 months at 32-40° F. and 90% humidity. The best roots are then replanted in the spring. Two or three flower buds on each plant can be harvested for eating without significantly reducing the seed production.

Salsify seeds are very easy to save, and germinate readily. As the flowers fade, the seeds form inside their bases. When fully mature, the seed capsules will begin to flatten and the salsify seeds will float away in the wind. Once a day, remove seeds from the newly opened seed capsules.

Break the fluff away from the seeds, and set the seeds aside for further drying. Salsify seeds should be dried for two or three days away from direct sunlight. When the seeds break in half, they are ready for storage. If the seeds bend instead of breaking, further drying is needed.

_____ Lesser Grown Compositae _____

Arctium lappa - Gobo (Japanese Burdock)

Gobo is a native of Siberia and is grown extensively in Japan. The tender root can grow to 36" in length and is used as an ingredient in many Japanese dishes. The leaves also can be eaten like spinach.

The plants are biennial and can tolerate both high and very low temperatures. After a period of vernalization, gobo produces a flower stalk. The flowers are self-pollinating, but different varieties of gobo can be cross-pollinated by insects. Caging can be used when two or more varieties are being grown for seed. Isolation of 1/2 mile will also ensure seed purity.

In some areas of Japan and in the western United States, gobo has escaped from the garden and become a weed. Gobo will not cross with *Arctium minus*, another weed found throughout the United States and also called burdock or dock.

Gobo seeds will remain viable for five years when stored under ideal conditions.

Chrysanthemum coronarium - Shungiku

Shungiku, sometimes called garland chrysanthemum, is a very common vegetable in Japan. There are three distinct types based on their leaf structure: narrow, finely parted and dark; medium sized; broad and pale green. The narrow leaf varieties do well in cold climates, while those with broad leaves are better adapted to warm climates. Their tender shoots and new leaves are harvested continually for use in salads and stir-fry dishes.

Shungiku plants produce beautiful yellow chrysanthemum-like flowers following vernalization. The flowers are self-pollinating. Insects freely visit the flowers and will cross different varieties of shungiku that are growing within 1/2 mile of each other, but bagging or caging are effective preventions. Shungiku does not cross with annual garden chrysanthemums, *C. carinatum*, or with perennial chrysanthemums. The method used to save shungiku seed is similar to lettuce.

Polymnia sonchifolia - Yacon

Yacon plants are grown in the Andes Mountains of South America for their crunchy, sweet tubers. The plants are not daylength sensitive and will grow in the mild climate areas of the United States. Unfortunately, the small daisy-like yellow flowers rarely set seeds. Yacon is propagated from small offshoots and tuber cuttings. Yacon cuttings and plants are available from some botanical gardens and tropical nurseries in the United States.

SEED VIABILITY

Salsify seeds will remain viable for four years when properly stored.

THE CUCURBITACEAE FAMILY

The Cucurbitaceae family in its many and varied forms has been feeding the world since the beginning of recorded history. The remains of cucumbers and gourds have been found in archaeological excavations dating two centuries before Christ. Various members of Cucurbitaceae can be found in every country of the world and in every culture both past and present.

Members of the Cucurbitaceae family have origins in many different regions of the world. They are some of the first plants used by mankind and have been widely dispersed throughout the world. Only the *Cucurbita* genus (squash) is thought to have originated in the warm regions of North, Central and South America. Cucurbits provided an important part of the diets of the Inca and Maya civilizations.

FAMILY TAXONOMY

Cucurbitaceae have easily identified tendril-bearing vines and alternate leaves. Most of the cultivated members of the Cucurbitaceae family are tender, heat-loving annuals. The perennial exceptions are *Sechium edule*, *Cucurbita ficifolia* and *Cucurbita foetidissima*.

POLLINATION CHARACTERISTICS AND TECHNIQUES

All members of the Cucurbitaceae family rely on insects for pollination. Each plant produces both male and female flowers. Insects, especially honeybees, randomly move pollen from

Facing Page: A small sample of the incredible variety of fruit shapes and colors found in squash (*Cucurbita spp.*).

Cucurbitaceae in the Garden

Genus	Species	Common Name
Benincasa	*hispida*	wax gourd (winter melon)
Citrullus	*vulgaris*	watermelon, citron
Cucumis	*anguria*	West Indian gherkin (burr cucumber)
	melo	muskmelon, cantaloupe, honeydew, casaba, Armenian cucumber (snake melon), Asian pickling melon, pocket melon (vine pomegranate), vine peach (mango melon)
	metuliferus	jelly melon (African horned cucumber)
	sativus	cucumbers (except Armenian cucumber, burr cucumber and African horned cucumber)
Cucurbita	*ficifolia*	Malabar gourd (chilacayote)
	foetidissima	calabazilla
	maxima	squash (vars. - banana, buttercup, hubbard, turban)
	mixta	squash (vars. - green striped cushaw, white cushaw, wild Seroria squashes, silver seeded gourds)
	moschata	squash (vars. - butternut, cheese, golden cushaw)
	pepo	squash (vars. - acorn, crookneck, scallop, small striped and warted gourds, spaghetti, zucchini)
Cyclanthera	*pedata*	caihua (achoecha)
Lagenaria	*siceraria*	hard shelled gourd
Luffa	*acutangula*	angled luffa
	aegyptiaca	smooth luffa
Momordica	*balsamina*	balsam apple
	charantia	balsam pear (bitter melon)
Sechium	*edule*	chayote (vegetable pear)
Sicana	*odorifera*	cassabanana
Trichosanthes	*anguina*	serpent gourd

flower to flower and from plant to plant. All members of the Cucurbitaceae family will accept pollen from other varieties within the same species. In other words, any two (or more) varieties within the same species must be prevented from crossing in order to save pure seed. The progeny of any uncontrolled crosses produces plants and fruits that are widely varied and bear little resemblance to their parents. To prevent such random pollinations, insects must be kept from visiting the flowers selected for seed saving and the pollen must then be transferred by hand.

During the process of hand-pollination, pollen from a male flower is transferred to a female flower of the same variety. If male and female flowers from the same plant are used for hand-pollination, the process is known as "selfing." Plants are generally "selfed" whenever seed purity is in question or when specific plant characteristics are being selected. When male and female flowers are taken from different plants of the same variety, the process is referred to as "sibing" and results in a greater degree of genetic diversity.

Seed savers must first be able to differentiate between male and female blossoms in order to hand-pollinate a member of the Cucurbitaceae family. Female blossoms sit atop a small, immature fruit (ovary), while male blossoms are attached only to a straight stem. This structural difference is most easily seen in squash which have large, easily manipulated flowers. Watermelons, muskmelons, cucumbers and chayote have very small flowers whose sex is more difficult to identify.

A morning and evening inspection of the plants and their blossoms will be required each day. Seed savers must learn to identify blossoms that are still green (immature), or are about to open, or have already opened. Blossoms that are almost ready to open will begin to show some color along their seams and the tip of the blossom may begin to break apart. Flowers that have already opened will be wilted and are of no use for making pollinations.

Male and female blossoms that will open the next morning must be taped shut in the evening and then relocated the following morning. The only exception to this evening/morning schedule is *Lagenaria siceraria*, the hard-shelled gourds, whose white blossoms open in the evening and bloom during the night. Male and female blossoms of *L. siceraria* must be located and taped shut in the morning and hand-pollinated during the evening of the same day.

Sometimes blossoms that were taped shut 10-12 hours earlier are difficult to relocate. Brightly painted stakes or surveyor's flags are often used to mark the row and can even be placed next to the taped flowers. Another trick is to stick a piece of masking tape on the leaf above the taped flower. Also, always try to walk in the same pattern each evening and morning. If the flowers were seen while walking east to west in the evening, walk in that same direction in the morning. The taped flowers are less likely to be hidden from view by leaves if the orientation is the same.

The next morning after the dew has dried, pick the male flower and several inches of its stem. Remove the tape from the male blossom and carefully tear off all of the flower petals. Next, gently remove the tape from the female

Left: Male squash blossoms, taped to prevent insect contamination and then stripped of petals for use in hand-pollinations. Right: Immature fruit (ovary) at the base of a taped female squash blossom.

flower, which will slowly open. When untaping flowers, be sure to work quickly. Bees have been known to fly into an untaped flower that has just been pollinated, before it can be taped shut again. If that occurs, the flower cannot be used for seed saving.

Hold the petal-less male flower by its stem like a brush and gently rub pollen onto each section of the stigma of the female flower. Pollination will be more successful if several male flowers are used to pollinate each female flower. Now retape the female flower and tie a brightly colored marker around its stem, possibly a piece of yarn or plastic surveyor's ribbon. Markers must be strong and durable enough to withstand water, heat, sunlight and birds looking for

Left: Tape and tips of female blossom are gently removed.   Right: Pollen covered anthers of the petal-less male flower are used as a brush to transfer pollen onto the stigma of the female flower.

nesting materials. If the markers get lost, at harvest time there will be no way to tell which fruits were hand-pollinated and contain pure seed. Poultry bands, available from hatcheries and animal feed stores, work well as markers and come in many colors and sizes. The brightly colored plastic bands expand, stay put and are reusable.

Each species within the Cucurbit-aceae family has slightly different physical characteristics and requires slight variations in the hand-pollination technique, which are detailed in the following sections. Any plant, no matter what species, is attempting to produce only a limited number of fruits. Although the plant will continue to produce flowers after those fruits are set, the later blossoms will be

Left: Female blossom is retaped to prevent insect contamination. Right: Hand-pollinated fruit is marked with surveyor's tape and covered with the used male flower as an additional insect barrier.

aborted unless those fruits are damaged or removed. Hand-pollination is most successful early in the season during the formation of the "crown fruit" (first fruit to be set) and the few additional fruits that follow. If the plant has already set numerous fruits that were not hand-pollinated, those fruits can be removed. The plant will then begin producing new flowers, which provides another chance for hand-pollination. This technique only works, of course, if the new fruits still have time to mature before frost.

PLANT SELECTION

Genetic diversity within a population is best preserved by growing as many plants of a variety as possible. Six plants of each variety should be considered a minimum, and growing a population of 12-20 plants will maintain a greater amount of diversity.

GENERAL PRODUCTION AND PROCESSING TECHNIQUES

Cucurbitaceae must be grown to full maturity before being harvested. A study at Arizona State University determined that the point at which the greatest number of fertile seeds occurs is 20 days after the fruit is fully mature. During the 20 days after the fruit is picked, the seeds continue to increase in size and to gain strength. If the fruit is picked when immature, its seeds gain some weight during that period, but will never gain the full strength displayed by mature seeds. The study was repeated using several different species and seemed to hold true for all cucurbits. Seed savers should always remember to take advantage of this 20-day period during which the seeds actually improve in the fruit after harvest.

After this post-harvest ripening period, the fruits are cut open and the seeds are removed. The flesh and seed attachments are cleaned off, either by washing the seeds in a strainer or by putting the seeds through a fermenta-tion process. Fermentation is recommended for cucumbers and can be used with other genera as well. Some studies indicate that fermented Cucurbitaceae seeds have a slightly higher germination rate. The fermentation process probably destroys a germination inhibitor or fungi that are present. Fermentation techniques are explained in detail in the section on cucumbers.

The seeds are then rinsed and dried on a rigid surface away from direct sunlight. Seeds should never be dried in an oven, since damage begins to occur at temperatures above 95° F. Avoid drying seeds on napkins, paper towels or other paper products, because the paper sticks to the dry seed and is difficult to remove. Seeds are easily dried on plastic or glass plates and on cookie sheets.

Cucurbitaceae seeds that will break in half are dry enough for storage. If the seeds bend instead of breaking, continue the drying process. Place the completely dry seeds in an airtight container which should be stored in a cool, dry, dark area or frozen for long-term storage.

Citrullus vulgaris - Watermelon and Citron

With hybridization, watermelons have become nearly rindless and uniformly sweet. The old-fashioned watermelons our great-grandparents grew had plenty of seeds for spitting, a thick protective rind that was used for watermelon pickles, and were just as sweet and delicious as modern varieties.

Citron is practically unknown to the home gardener. While just as easy to grow as watermelon, citron is not eaten fresh. Its flesh is made into preserves, sweet pickles and candied fruit.

Both watermelon and citron are indigenous to South Central Africa. In times of extreme drought, watermelons have been used by man and beast as a source of uncontaminated water. Immature watermelons can also be prepared like summer squash, and watermelon wine is common in some areas of Africa.

BOTANICAL CLASSIFICATION

Watermelons and citron belong to the genus *Citrullus* and the species *lanatus*. *C. lanatus* are frost tender, vining annual fruits that require warm temperatures and a long growing season.

Watermelon flesh can range in color from white to ivory, light yellow to dark orange, and light pink to blood red. The seeds can be white, yellow, reddish, brown, black, or mottled with brown and black. The colors and patterns of the rinds are too varied and numerous to mention.

The rind of citron is usually green with either white or greenish white flesh. The seeds are bright green, red, or dull gray. Citron fruits keep for six months and can be processed after summer canning chores have slowed.

POLLINATION, CROSSING AND ISOLATION

All varieties of watermelon will cross with each other and with citron. Isolation of 1/2 mile is recommended to prevent cross-pollination by insects, usually honeybees. When more than one variety is grown in close proximity, hand-pollination is necessary.

General techniques for hand-pollination are described in the introductory pages of the Cucurbitaceae family. Hand-pollination of watermelons is relatively easy, even though the flowers are rather small. Watermelon and citron pollinations are usually successful 50-75% of the time, if conditions are favorable and the plants are not under stress. In early maturing watermelons, this percentage can be increased if the very first female flowers are selected for hand-pollination. The number of fruits set by late maturing varieties, which drop nearly 90% of their first flowers, is much higher if the second flush of flowers is hand-pollinated. The success rate can also be increased if each female flower is pollinated with two or more male flowers, because in some varieties the males don't produce very much pollen.

Sometimes it is difficult to tell which watermelon flowers are going to open the next morning. Go ahead and tape any flowers that appear to be ready. When the tape is removed the next morning, the flowers that are ready will pop open. When a female flower is located that is ready to open, usually the second flower back along that vine is a male flower that will also open the next morning. The tiny, circular, ridged, pollen-bearing structures in the center of the male flower are its anthers, which look like a tiny fuzzy yellow ball once the pollen starts to shed. Male flowers which lack that appearance are not mature enough for pollination.

SEED PRODUCTION, HARVEST AND PROCESSING

Many gardeners have trouble determining just when a watermelon is ripe. Counting the number of days from planting works only in those rare seasons when the weather is fairly normal. The plink, plank, plunk method of thumping is popular, but seldom reliable. Watching for the light-colored patch, where the watermelon touches the ground, to change to the next darker shade works with some varieties. Probably the most reliable sign of ripening occurs when the small tendril directly opposite the fruit's "peduncle" (stem attachment) changes from green to brown and becomes dry. Commercially, watermelons are plugged and their juice is checked against a refractive index. Good quality watermelons that are ready for harvest should have a soluble solids reading of 10.5% at the center or core of the fruit.

Children are great at saving watermelon seeds. When the watermelon is ready to eat, the seeds are also mature. Try donating watermelons to a teacher at a local elementary school with the following instructions. Gather a large group of children on the lawn, provide each child with a cup for the seeds, and make everyone promise to spit the seeds into their cup. When tummies and cups are full, collect the seeds in a bowl, add a squirt of mild dishwashing soap and wash the seeds gently. Washing will remove the sugar and saliva that remain on the seeds. Then pour the seeds into a strainer and rinse thoroughly.

Citron has hard flesh and the seeds must be picked out by hand. If the melon is also to be used for processing, remove the center of the melon with the greatest seed concentration. The remainder of the flesh will be nearly seedless. Pick the seeds out one by one and rinse thoroughly. It is also possible to leave the citron melons out to rot. After the flesh and rind are soft, put the fruits in a wheelbarrow or large container and chop them up with a shovel or hoe. The seeds will sink when water is added, and the debris is then poured off. Repeat the process until most of the seeds are clean. Put the seeds in a strainer and rinse. Drain the seeds and dry as with other Cucurbitaceae.

SEED VIABILITY

Watermelon and citron seeds will remain viable for six years when stored in cool, dry, dark conditions.

Cucumis melo - Melons

Melons are thought to have originated in tropical West Africa, where more than 40 wild species have been found. A secondary center of origin occurs in the areas surrounding Iran, south central Russia and some regions of Southeast Asia.

In the United States only the sweet varieties of _Cucumis melo_ are referred to as melons. Throughout Asia, however, numerous other melon varieties are grown for pickling. After the seed cavity is emptied, the thin flesh and rind are brined or made into fresh condiments. The fruits are also used like summer squash in various ethnic dishes.

In addition to Asian pickling melons, a now neglected small group of melons was also once grown for the fragrance of the fruits. Before daily bathing became popular, European ladies carried Queen Anne's pocket melons in the pockets of their gowns. The sweet fragrance emitted from the melons helped mask less desirable odors.

BOTANICAL CLASSIFICATION

Melons belong to the genus _Cucumis_ and the species _melo_. All varieties of _C. melo_ will cross with one another, but do not cross with watermelons or any other Cucurbitaceae family members.

There are seven recognized groups or subspecies within _Cucumis melo_. Cantalupensis Group includes medium-sized fruits with hard, rough or scaled rinds. These are the true cantaloupes whose mature fruits do not slip from the vine and do not have netted skin.

True cantaloupes are commonly grown in Europe, but are seldom seen in the United States. Members of the Cantalupensis Group should not be confused with the netted muskmelons that are common throughout the United States.

Chito Group includes mango melon, orange melon, garden lemon, melon apple and vine peach. Members of this group all have small leaves, yellow or orange fruits about the size of a lemon or orange, and are primarily used in Asia for making pickles.

Members of the Conomon Group have smooth, oblong or club-shaped fruits and are widely grown in Asia. This group includes all of the Asian pickling melons which are prized for their crisp flesh and usually made into pickles.

Queen Anne's pocket melon, also known as vine pomegranate or plum granny, belongs to the Dudaim Group. Their fruits are about the size of oranges and are very fragrant.

Armenian cucumbers, also called snake melons, belong to the Flexuosus Group and can be eaten or processed like cucumbers. Most gardeners mistakenly think that this group is related to cucumbers, but they are melons and will cross only with *Cucumis melo*.

Christmas melons, honeydew melons, crenshaw melons and casaba mel-

Armenian cucumber (*Cucumis melo,* Flexuosus Group), although grown and used like cucumbers, is botanically a melon and will cross with all other varieties of *C. melo,* regardless of group.

ons comprise the Inodorus Group. Their rinds may be smooth or wrinkled, with flesh that is either green or white.

Muskmelons and Persian melons belong to the Reticulatus Group. The common muskmelon with its netted rind and firm orange flesh is characteristic of the Reticulatus Group, which will often slip from their stems when ripe.

It is important to remember that these groups, which are sometimes called subspecies, are used only to describe plants within a species that have similar characteristics. All of the varieties within all of the groups mentioned above belong to *Cucumis melo*, and will therefore all cross with one another.

POLLINATION, CROSSING AND ISOLATION

Melons are the most frustrating species of Cucurbitaceae for seed savers. Melon plants rely on bees and small flies for pollination. Despite multiple insect visits to each flower, melons abort 80% of the female blossoms, plus hand-pollination is even less effective than insect pollination. There is no way to tell which flowers the plant is going to abort, so only about 10-15% of the hand-pollinated blossoms will develop into fruits.

Melon seed can be successfully saved using one of three methods. The easiest way, although not always practical, is to use isolation with 1/2 mile recommended between varieties. Caging with introduced pollinators is commonly used at research stations and universities, which often employ a beekeeper who maintains small, specially constructed hives built into the sides of the cages. Such techniques are complex and expensive, and are sel-

dom used by home gardeners. The third option is to pollinate the fruits by hand.

Hand-pollination is not difficult, but is very time-consuming. The flowers are tiny and require a delicate touch. Careful observation is required to identify male and female blossoms that are ready to open. Using small pieces of masking tape about 1/4" wide and 1 1/2" long, tape flowers closed in the early evening. When wrapping the narrow strips of tape around the tips of the female flowers, pinch the tape together beside the flower but leave the two tip ends of the tape apart. That will make it much easier to untape the female flower the next morning. Always be careful to not break the tiny stem off of the male flower when tearing off its leaves. That happens very easily and makes the blossom awkward to manipulate, but a piece of masking tape can be used in place of the stem.

The following morning after the dew has dried, gently remove the tape from the female flower. Pick the male flower and remove the tape and its petals, then gently rub the pollen from the anthers of the male flower onto the stigma of the female flower. Retape the female flower and mark the stem with colored yarn or a poultry band. If the melon's stem attachment is still green after three days and the tiny fruit has slightly enlarged, chances are good that the pollination was successful.

The success rate with hand-pollinated melons can be slightly improved if pollinations are made using the first female flowers that bloom, which are the most likely to set fruit. Each time that the plant sets a fruit, more of the subsequent flowers are going to abort. Fruits that are not hand-pollinated should be removed, which will keep the plant blooming and improve the chances for successful hand-pollinations.

SEED PRODUCTION, HARVEST AND PROCESSING

Melon seeds are mature when the fruits are ready to eat. Slightly over-ripe fruits have 2-10% more mature seeds, but are not very palatable. Most home gardeners appreciate being able to eat the fruits as well as save the seeds.

Melons should be cut open carefully. The seeds of many varieties will simply fall out, while others are attached to the cavity of the melon or to a soft core and will need to be scooped out. In any case, have a bowl ready. Work the seeds between your fingers to free them of any attachments and pulp. Add enough water to allow the hollow seeds and the attachment fibers to float. Pour off the water and debris, repeating the process until only clean seeds remain. Pour the seeds into a strainer and rinse thoroughly under a stream of cool water to remove any traces of sugar. Dry the bottom of the strainer on a dish towel to remove as much moisture as possible. Then dump the cleaned seeds onto a glass or plastic plate or onto a cookie sheet to dry.

SEED VIABILITY

Melon seeds will remain viable for five years when stored in cool, dry, dark conditions.

Cucumis metuliferous - Jelly Melon

Jelly melon, an obscure exotic fruit, was recently rediscovered in New Zealand where it is now being grown as an export crop. The oval fruits, which are beginning to appear in American supermarkets as tropical oddities, usually grow to 3" x 5" and are covered with sharp horns or projections. Jelly melon's eye-catching orange rind contrasts strikingly with its chartreuse green flesh. The fruits can be juiced like oranges or eaten fresh like melons, with a flavor that is often likened to a mixture of bananas and limes.

BOTANICAL CLASSIFICATION

Jelly melon, which belongs to the genus *Cucumis* and the species *metuliferous*, is also sometimes known as African horned cucumber or hedgehog gourd. At this time only one variety of jelly melon is available in the United States, however, other varieties are likely to exist. *C. metuliferous* does not cross with any other Cucurbitaceae.

Jelly melon is best grown on trellises to save garden space and prevent fruit rot. The vines resemble cucumbers, but are more rampant and spiny. Jelly melons will grow to maturity anywhere cucumbers can be grown for seed. Fully mature fruits will keep at room temperature for up to six months and contain four times the vitamin C of an orange.

A few words of caution about jelly melon might be appropriate. Some authorities are concerned about the potential for jelly melon to escape and become a noxious weed. Jelly melon plants are definitely killed by frost, but might be able to self-sow. Anyone who has seen the fruit's sharp spines and rampant vines can appreciate this concern.

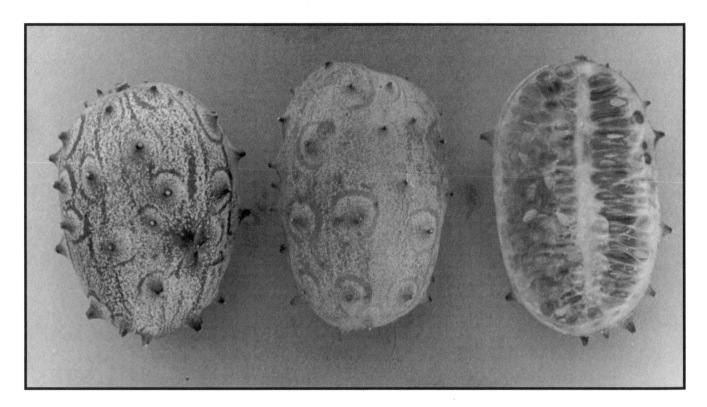

Jelly melon, sometimes known as African horned cucumber (*Cucumis metuliferus*).

POLLINATION, CROSSING AND ISOLATION

Jelly melon vines produce both male and female flowers which are insect-pollinated. The isolation distances used for cucumbers, 1/2 to 1 mile, should ensure complete seed purity if more than one variety is grown. Hand-pollination, described in the introductory pages of the Cucurbitaceae family, is also possible.

SEED PRODUCTION, HARVEST AND PROCESSING

Jelly melons are mature and ready for harvest when the fruits turn bright orange. Undamaged fruits keep up to six months, and seed cleaning can be initiated at any time. Carefully cut the melon open and scoop the jelly capsules into a blender or food processor. Process briefly, just until the capsules are broken. Each capsule will yield one tiny seed.

The seed capsules can also be fermented to free the seeds. Depending on the temperature, the fermentation process will take from two to five days to break down the seed capsules. During this time the aromas emanating from the bowl will grow increasingly worse and some mold may form over the top of the mixture. Stir the mass twice each day. The fermentation process should be stopped when most of the seeds have settled to the bottom of the bowl and the seed cases are floating on the top of the mixture.

After either blending or fermenting, add as much water as possible, stir the mixture and allow the good, clean seeds to settle to the bottom. Gently pour off the debris and hollow seeds. Add more water and repeat the process until only clean seeds remain. Pour the seeds into a strainer and rinse thoroughly under running water. Wipe the bottom of the strainer on a towel to remove as much moisture as possible, and dump the seeds onto a cookie sheet or dish to dry.

Stir the seeds twice daily to ensure even drying. Never dry seeds in direct sunlight or in an oven, because damage begins to occur at temperatures above 95° F. The seeds are dry enough for storage when they break or snap in half. If the seeds bend instead of breaking, more drying is needed. Store the completely dried seeds in an airtight container in a cool, dry, dark area or freeze them for long-term storage.

SEED VIABILITY

Information on seed longevity for jelly melon is not available.

Cucumis sativus - Cucumber

Botanists believe that cucumbers are descendants of a wild cucurbita found in the Himalayas. Cucumbers in various forms are found in pictures and carvings from India dating about two centuries before Christ. Today the largest and most widely varied populations of indigenous cucumbers are still found growing in India.

Cultural preferences for various shapes, colors and sizes strongly govern the agricultural production of cucumbers. Round cucumbers are prized in Asia, as are very long varieties. Americans generally favor 8" dark green types. The cornichon, a tiny cucumber grown for pickling, is a favorite in France. Specially bred varieties that do not require pollination to produce fruits are commonly grown in European greenhouses. Such fruits are referred to as parthenocarpic and are seedless. Of the choices available to seed savers, there is a color, texture and shape to suit every need and preference.

Cucumber bitterness is a subject that generates much speculation among home gardeners. Bitterness is caused by compounds called cucurbitacins, and the amount of the compound found in the fruit is genetically controlled. Some gardeners believe that bitterness is the result of a lack of water and can be corrected by watering the plant more often. While it is true that the concentration of this compound can be slightly influenced by the amount of water the plants receive, bitterness is not caused by a lack of water. Bitterness is also not caused by crossing with melons or squash, which is not botanically possible. Cucurbitacins are toxic to humans, but bitter fruits are not palatable and are rarely eaten. Plants that produce bitter fruits should not be used for seed saving.

BOTANICAL CLASSIFICATION

Cucumbers belong to the genus _Cucumis_ and the species _sativus_. West Indian gherkins, Armenian cucumbers, snake melons and serpent gourds are all commonly referred to as cucumbers because of similar usage, but do not belong to _C. sativus_ and will not cross with cucumbers.

Although shapes and sizes vary considerably, varieties grown for commercial pickling have an ideal length-to-diameter ratio of three-to-one. Slicing varieties have usually been selected for a longer length. All varieties can be used for both pickling and slicing, but many home gardeners feel that the best pickles are made from drier-fleshed cucumbers. Varieties with

Some of the myriad shapes, colors and sizes exhibited by cucumbers (*Cucumis sativus*).

crisp, juicy flesh are usually chosen for slicing.

Cucumber vines vary in size and suitability for trellising. In general, smaller vines with lighter colored fruits do better on the ground. Trellised cucumbers often sunburn in hot summer climates, but in very humid regions, trellising is often preferred because it reduces some mildew problems.

The cucumber varieties commonly grown in the Unites States are moderately daylength sensitive. Studies indicate that the greatest number of female blossoms are produced on days with 11 hours of daylight. This occurs in the early and late summer and helps explain why some gardeners complain of a midsummer cucumber shortage.

POLLINATION, CROSSING AND ISOLATION

All cucumbers, *Cucumis sativus*, will cross with one another. Armenian cucumbers, also known as snake melons, are used like cucumbers but are really melons, *Cucumis melo*, and will cross with muskmelons and cantaloupes. West Indian gherkin, *Cucumis anguria*, and serpent gourd, *Trichosanthes anguina*, are both used similarly, but will not cross with cucumbers.

Cucumber varieties must be isolated by 1/2 mile. Many gardeners prefer to grow several different varieties of cucumbers, which poses no problem for the seed saver who is adept at hand-pollination. The success rate for hand-pollinated cucumbers is usually about

85%. Slightly higher rates are possible if two or more male flowers are used to pollinate each female blossom. Cucumber flowers are 1/2-1" in diameter. Each female blossom sits atop a tiny immature cucumber, while the male blossom is just attached to a straight stem. After a bit of practice, blossoms that will open the next morning become easy to identify. The hand-pollinating technique, described in the introductory pages of the Cucurbitaceae family, works well without any special modifications.

Hand-pollination has the best chance of being successful during 11 hour days when the vines produce the greatest number of female flowers. Cucumber plants will abort their fruits during periods of drought and excessively high temperature, so hand-pollination should not be attempted during those times.

SEED PRODUCTION, HARVEST AND PROCESSING

Cucumbers that are being saved for seed must be grown to full maturity and allowed to ripen past the edible stage. The fruits will be large and beginning to soften. Depending on the variety, the fruits will change from green to white or deep yellow or orange.

Each cucumber that is successfully hand-pollinated will yield hundreds of seeds. Fully mature cucumbers, when cut from the vine and kept for about two weeks, have a slightly greater number of viable seeds. Sometimes hand-pollinated cucumbers will mature but have few if any seeds when cut open. Such blossoms either received an inadequate amount of pollen, or that variety may have a parthenocarpic tendency and is capable of developing fruit without fertilization.

After harvest, carefully cut open the cucumbers and scoop the seeds into a large bowl. Each cucumber seed is encased in a gelatinous sack that is most easily removed by fermenting the seeds. Add about as much water as seeds but not too much or fermentation will be slowed. Then set the bowl away from direct sunlight in a protected location to ferment. Depending on the temperature, fermentation will take from one to three days. At 90+° F., 24-36 hours should be sufficient. During this period, the aromas from the bowl will be less than pleasing and some mold may form over the top of the mixture. Stir the mass twice a day. Fermentation is complete when most of the seeds have settled to the bottom of the bowl and the seedcases are floating on top of the mixture.

Now stir the mass while adding as much water as possible, which allows the clean seeds to settle to the bottom. The debris and hollow seeds will float and can be gently poured off with the excess water. Repeat this process until only clean seeds remain. Then pour the seeds into a strainer, wipe the bottom of the strainer on a towel to remove as much moisture as possible, and dump the seeds out on a cookie sheet or dish to dry.

SEED VIABILITY

Cucumber seeds will remain viable for ten years when stored under ideal conditions.

Cucurbita spp. - Squash, Malabar Gourd and Calabazilla

Cucurbita ficifolia - Malabar Gourd (Chilacayote)
C. foetidissima - Calabazilla
C. maxima - Squash
C. mixta - Squash
C. moschata - Squash
C. pepo - Squash

Various members of the genus _Cucurbita_, known collectively as squash, have been used for many centuries by Native Americans throughout the North and South American continents. The number, sizes, shapes and colors of the varieties once grown are astounding. Many Native American varieties have been overlooked by home gardeners who are often interested only in meal-sized winter squashes. Our ancestors, however, prized larger squashes for their ability to feed large numbers of people. Squashes were also used as edible mixing bowls, water containers, and for livestock feed.

Summer squash, winter squash and pumpkin are three commonly used terms that have left more than a few people confused. All squashes and pumpkins can be eaten when young and tender, and also when mature. Varieties that have been selected for outstanding keeping qualities and dry flesh are known as winter squash. Others that have young, tender skin and few seeds are referred to as summer squash. The difference between pumpkins and winter squashes can be even more confusing. In the United States, small, round, orange squashes used for pies and jack-o'-lanterns are commonly referred to as pumpkins. However, the term pumpkin is also a frequently used name for certain types of large, orange, field pumpkins. Actually, all pumpkins are squash. Pumpkins are not even a "subspecies" (group).

BOTANICAL CLASSIFICATION

Squashes belong to the genus _Cucurbita_ and to one of six different species. Each of the six species has specific stem, leaf, flower and seed characteristics which are described below. An extensive listing of all of the known squash varieties within each species has also been included, so that gardeners can make an isolated planting that includes one variety from each of the species without having to resort to hand-pollination.

Cucurbita maxima

Squash varieties that belong to _C. maxima_ have very long vines, huge, hairy leaves and soft, round, spongy, hairy stems. The thick seeds are white or tan or brown with cream-colored margins and thin cellophane coatings.

The following varieties all belong to the species _C. maxima_ and will cross with each other: All Gold, Alligator, American Indian, Amish Pie Pumpkin, Araucana, Argentine Primitive Pumpkin, Argentine Summer, Arikara, Asuncion, Atlantic Giant, Atlas, Australian Butter Pumpkin, Autumn Pride, all of the **BANANAS** (Blue, Chinese, Giant, Hartman, Orange, Pink, Pink Jumbo), Banquet, Bay State, Belgium Pumpkin, Big Max, Big Moon, Big Red, all of the **BUTTERCUPS** (Blue, Branscomb, Branscomb White, Burgess, Bush, Russian, Verda's), California White Pumpkin, Candy Roaster, Cherokee Indian Pumpkin, Criolo, Crown Prince, Doe, Emerald, Equadonantian, Essex, Essex Hybrid, Estampes, Flat White Boer, Forragero, Francis Bellew's Candy Roaster, Genuine Mammoth, German Green Pumpkin, German Sweet Potato, Gilmore, Ginny's Large, Gold Nugget, Golden Delicious, Goldpak, Golzar, Greek Small Orange Pumpkin, Green Delicious, Greengold, Guatemalan Blue, Herman's Delight, Hillbilly, Hokkaido Green, Hokkaido Orange, all of the **HUBBARDS** (Baby, Baby Blue, Black, Chicago, Chicago Warted, Golden, Green, Green Improved, Kitchenette, Large Blue, Little Gem, Minnesota, Sugar, True, Warted, Warted Green, Warted Improved), Hungarian Mammoth, Hungarian Mammoth (Cornell Strain), Iran, Ironclad, Iron Pot, Japanese, Jarrahdale, Kabule, Kara Kabak, Kentucky, Kindred, King of Giants, King of Mammoths, Kuri Blue, Kuri Red, La Calabaza (Philippine), La Kalabaza, Large Moroccan, Large Yellow Paris, Large White Manteca, Leningrad Giant, Mammoth Chile, Mammoth Gold, Mammoth King, Mammoth Orange Gold, Mammoth Whale, Marblehead, all of the **MARROWS** (Autumnal, Boston, Orange, Prolific, Warted), Mexican Indian, Mexigold, Mooregold, Mohawk, Ni-es-pah Long, Old English, Old Humbolt, Old Winter, Orange Giant, Orange New Guinea, Pikes Peak Pumpkin, Pink Giant Pumpkin, Plymouth Rock, Quality, Queensland Blue, Rainbow, Red Chestnut, Red Estampes, Red Skin, Roaster, Rouge Vif d'Etampes, Shanghai, Siva Stambolka, Show King, Sibley, Silver Bell, Smooth Green Pie, South American, Stambolka, Sweetbush, Sweetkeeper, Sweetmeat, Tokyo, Tri-Star, Triamble, all of the **TURBANS** (American, Golden, Turk's), Umatilla Marblehead, Valenciano, Victor Watten, Vojicka, Vounicheo Blue, Vounicheo Orange, Warren, West Virginia Big, Whangaparoa, White African, White Pumpkin, Winnebago, Yakima Marblehead, Yugoslavian Pie Pumpkin, Zapallo Poloma.

Cucurbita mixta

Varieties that belong to C. *mixta* have spreading vines and large, hairy leaves. The fruit's stem, which flares out only slightly where it attaches to the fruit, is hard, hairy and slightly angular. The leaves of C. *mixta* are slightly lighter green than C. *moschata* with rounded leaf tip and hardly any indentations along their sides. The white or tan seeds have a pale margin and cracks in the skin coat on the flat sides of the seeds which are covered with a thin cellophane coating.

The following varieties belong to the species C. *mixta* and will cross readily with each other: Big White Crookneck, Black Sweet Potato, Chirimen, Cochita Pueblo, the **CUSHAWS** (Albino Hopi, Australian, Gold Striped, Green Striped, Hopi, Longneck, Neckless, Old Fashioned, Solid Green, White, White Crookneck, Winter) [the only exception is Golden Cushaw which is C. *moschata*], Gila Cliff Dweller, Hindu, Indian Vining Zucchini, Japanese Pie, Jonathan, Large White New Mexico Cliff Dweller, Mixta Gold, Mrs. Morris' Potato Pumpkin, Pennsylvania Crookneck, all of the wild Seroria Squashes, all of the Silver Seeded Gourds, Tennessee Sweet Potato, Woodrey Sweet Potato.

Cucurbita moschata

C. moschata varieties have spreading vines and large hairy leaves. The fruit's stem, which flares out quite noticeably where it attaches to the fruit, is hard, hairy and slightly angular. The flower has large, leafy, green sepals at its base. The leaves of *C. moschata* are slightly darker green than *C. mixta*, and have a pointed leaf tip and slight indentations along their sides. Each of the small, beige, oblong seeds has a dark beige margin.

The following varieties all belong to the species *C. moschata* and cross readily: African, African Bell, Aizu Gokwuase, Alagold, Borinquen, Butter-

bush, all of the **BUTTERNUTS** (Baby, Early, Eastern, Hercules, Mexican, Ponca, Puritan, Waltham, Western), Calabaza (or Cuban Squash), Calhoun, Cangold, Chirimen, all of the **CHEESES** (Cutchoque Flat, Flat Warty, Large, Long Island, Tan, Wisconsin), Citrouille d'Eysines, Cuban, Dickinson, East India Big Red, Florida Buff Pie, Fortuna, Futtsu Kurokawa, Golden Cushaw, Hawaiian, Hercules, Honduran, Kentucky Field, Kikuza, La Primera, Long Keeper, Longfellow, Mediterranean, Melon Squash (or Tahitian Squash), Mexican, Neck, New Jersey, Old Time Tennessee, Papaya, Patriot, Peraora, Ponca, Priester Crookneck, Sequalca,

Typical seeds of the four squash species. Top to bottom: *C. pepo, C. maxima, C. mixta* and *C. moschata*.

Showell Sweet Potato, Shumway's Tennessee Sweet Potato, Sweet Red, Tahitian Squash (or Melon Squash), Tamala, Upper Ground Sweet Potato, Virginia Mammoth, White Rind Sugar, Wisconsin Canner.

Cucurbita pepo

Varieties belonging to *C. pepo* have prickly leaves and stems, especially when mature. The fruit's stem is hard and has five sharply angular sides. The seeds are cream colored and each has a white margin. Included within this species are the soft-shelled striped and warted gourds found in grocery stores at Thanksgiving and nearly all of the commonly grown summer squashes.

The following varieties belong to the species *C. pepo*: All of the **ACORNS** (Des Moines, Ebony, Ebony Bush, Golden, Jersey Golden, Royal, Table King, Table King Bush, Table Queen, Table Queen Bush, Table Queen Ebony, Table Queen Mammoth, White), Amish Field Pie Pumpkin, Austrian Bush Summer, Baby Pam Pumpkin, Bahce, Bela Sakaska, Bicolor Spoon, Big Red California Sugar, Black Beauty, Bloomfield Pumpkin, Bulgarian Summer, Buscholkurbis Naked Seed, Casserta, Chestnut, Cheyenne Bush, Chiefini, Cinderella, Citrouille de Touraine, all of the **COCOZELLES** (Green, Vining), Connecticut Field, Cornfield Pumpkin, Cozini, Connecticut Sweet Pie, all of the **CROOKNECKS** (Dwarf Summer, Early Summer Golden, Early Summer Yellow, Golden, White Summer), Crystal Bell, Cupid, Delicata, Dumpling, Early Cheyenne Pie, Early Prolific, Early Prolific Straightneck, Eat All, Erken, Eskandarany, Fordhook, Fordhook Bush, Fort Berthold, French White Bush, Gem, Gills Golden Pippin, Golden Centennial, Golden Custard, Golden

Oblong, Gririt, Halloween, Howden, Huicha, Hyuga Black, Idaho Gem, Ingot, Jack-o'-Lantern, Japanese Pie (from Abundant Life), Kahcona, King of Mammoth, Kline Pumpkin, Kumi Kumi, Lady Godiva, Large Yellow Paris, Lebanon, Little Boo, Lunghissimo Bianco di Palermo, Mammoth Gold, Mandan, Marego, Maryland Pie Pumpkin, Midwest Sweet Potato, Mihoacan, Miniature Pumpkin, Naked Seeded, New England Pie Pumpkin, Oaxacan, Oaxacan Bicolor, Oaxacan White, Oland, Omaha, Omaha Pumpkin, Panama, Pepinos, Perfect Gem, Pie Pumpkin, Prostate, Royal Bush, all of the **SCALLOPS** (Benning's Green Tint, Early White Bush, Early Yellow Bush, Long Island White Bush, Mammoth White Bush, Patty Pan, St. Pat, Summer Bush, Yellow Golden), Showell, Small Sugar Pumpkin, Spaghetti Squash, Spookie, Stickler, Straightneck, Streaker, Sugar Pie, Sweet Dumpling (or Vegetable Gourd), Sweetnut, Table Gold, Tarahumara Indian Pumpkin, Tatume, Thelma Sanders Sweet Potato, Thomas Halloween, Tricky Jack, Triple Treat, Tuckernuck, Uconn, Uncle Herman, all of the **VEGETABLE MARROWS** (English Vegetable, Green Bush Improved, Long White, True & Tender, Vegetable, White Bush, White Vining Vegetable), Vegetable Spaghetti, Wilbur Field Pumpkin, Winter Luxury, Winter Luxury Pie, Winter Nut, Woods Prolific, Woods Earliest Prolific, Youngs Beauty, all of the **ZUCCHINIS** (Black, Black Beauty, Burpee's Fordhook, Burpee's Golden, Dark Green, Gold Rush, Gray, Green, Round, Yellow, White Egyptian), Zikusa, and any of the small decorative striped and warted gourds.

Cucurbita ficifolia

Varieties that belong to *C. ficifolia*

have very flat, black or gray seeds. The plants are perennial in warm winter climates and produce fruits with greenish cream mottled skin that keep for three years. The fruit's flesh is crisp and used in Mexico for making candy.

Cucurbita foetidissima

C. foetidissima varieties have light gray, arrowhead-shaped leaves that emit a disagreeable odor when brushed. The plants are perennial in frost-free areas. The 4" diameter fruits are not eaten, but the seeds are pressed as a source for oil.

POLLINATION, CROSSING AND ISOLATION

Squashes are divided into six different species: *Cucurbita maxima*, *C. mixta*, *C. moschata*, *C. pepo*, *C. ficifolia* and *C. foetidissima*. Different varieties within the same species will cross easily, but crossing does not occur between the different species. Therefore, one variety from each of the six different

Note: The general rule of inter-species incompatibility in squash has worked well for most seed savers for many years. A recent study, however, has proven that some crossing can occur between *C. moschata* and *C. mixta* (which some researchers have suggested be renamed *C. argyrosperma*), when *C. mixta* is the female parent and *C. moschata* provides the pollen. The study focused on certain Mexican cushaws and wild squash, however, and the possible extent of such crossing in garden varieties is not clear. Hand-pollination should probably be used to ensure absolute purity when *C. mixta* and *C. moschata* are grown in close proximity.

species (one from each group listed above) can be grown together without cross-pollination problems. Different varieties within the same species must be separated by 1/2 mile or must be hand-pollinated, so be sure to check neighbors' gardens for varieties that

could ruin your isolated plantings.

Squash is easy to hand-pollinate even for the beginner, because the blossoms are large and easy to identify. The female blossom sits atop a tiny immature squash, while the male blossom is just attached to a long, straight stem. In the early evening, identify male and female flowers that will open the following morning unless sealed shut. Such blossoms will begin to show a yellow flush of color, especially along their seams, and the different sections of the flower may start to break open at the tip. Use 3/4" masking tape to securely tape the tips of the blossoms shut. Morning dew will sometimes cause cheap brands of tape to burst open, so be sure to select a brand that is extra sticky.

To ensure a greater amount of genetic diversity, choose male and female blossoms from different plants of the same variety. If there is any question about the seed's purity, however, male and female blossoms on the same plant should be used.

Wait until after the dew dries the next morning, because the female flower will need to be retaped after being hand-pollinated, and the wet tape doesn't stick very well. Locate the male and female flowers that were taped shut the previous evening. Pick the male flower including a good-sized chunk of its stem which will be used as a handle. Remove the tape from the male flower and carefully tear off all of its petals. Some gardeners hold the male flower between their teeth, so that both hands are free to untape the female flower. Next, carefully tear off just the tip of the female flower including the tape. Then, as if in slow motion, the female flower will open wide.

Holding the petal-less male flower

by its stem like a brush, swab the pollen-covered anthers of the male flower onto each of the sections of the stigma of the female flower. The success rate of hand-pollinations can be increased by using two or more male flowers on each female flower. If more than one male flower is to be used, be sure to prepare all of the male flowers before removing the tape from the female flower. That way there will be less chance of bees contaminating the female flower while it is exposed.

After the pollination process is complete, retape the female flower and mark the fruit's stem with a marker. Sometimes an especially brittle flower will split along one of the large seams that run from the tip of the flower to the tiny fruit. If that should happen, keep taping closer and closer to the fruit until the hole along the seam is covered. The entire blossom can be covered with tape and the technique will still work. Be careful, however, not to damage the small, sensitive neck between the tiny fruit and the base of the flower, which will cause the fruit to abort.

In some areas of the United States, bumblebees and some solitary bees will chew through the sides of taped flowers to gain access to the pollen, which causes crossing even though the flower was hand-pollinated. If this becomes a recurring problem, female flowers can be covered with 2" wide masking tape. The tape should form a band around the entire flower. Petals from the male flowers used during the pollination process can also be draped over the top of the taped female blossoms. The petals will wilt down quickly over the female flowers, forming a double or triple layer that is more difficult for the bees to chew through.

SEED PRODUCTION, HARVEST AND PROCESSING

Winter squashes or pumpkins used for seed saving must be grown until fully mature. Hand-pollinated summer squashes must be left to grow until quite large with hard-shelled rinds that cannot be dented by a fingernail. Squashes have a greater number of viable seeds when cut from the vine and left to sit for three weeks or longer. This is easily accomplished with winter squashes, which are usually stored for 3-6 months before being used. When hand-pollinated squashes are stored along with the main crop which are to be eaten, the rinds of ones being saved for seed can be clearly marked with an indelible marking pen. Most summer squashes will not keep much beyond two months. Their seed should be removed three weeks or longer after harvest.

Winter squashes are often cut or chopped open to remove the seeds and prepare the flesh for eating. Summer squashes that are ready for seed saving can be smashed open with an ax or shovel. Be sure to exercise caution, however, because the squashes can easily roll out from under the smashing implement. Gather any scattered seeds and pick out those seeds still attached to the flesh. Rinse the seeds in a colander under a stream of water and remove any strings or debris. If squash flesh remains attached to the seeds, rub the seeds in a wire strainer under running water to loosen it. Drain the seeds and dry as with other Cucurbitaceae.

SEED VIABILITY

Squash seeds will remain viable for six years when stored in cool, dry, dark conditions.

Lagenaria siceraria - Hard-Shelled Gourd

Gourds have played a major role in the daily life of many cultures around the world. Although eaten in their immature stages, gourds have more importantly been made into bottles, bowls, ladles, churns, spoons, pipes, musical instruments, penis sheaths and planting tools. Since modern cultures seldom grow their own bowls, many of the hard-shelled gourds are becoming endangered.

Few American seed companies offer varieties of hard-shelled gourds. Members of the Seed Savers Exchange and The American Gourd Society, however, do make available a rich assortment of gourds. The names of just a few varieties currently being offered include Bushel Basket, New Guinea, Hercules, Long Neck Dipper, Dumbbell, Club, Powder Horn, Kettle, Dolphin, Trough, and the ancient-looking Dinosaur gourd.

BOTANICAL CLASSIFICATION

Hard-shelled gourds belong to the genus _Lagenaria_ and the species _siceraria_. Different varieties of _L. siceraria_ do not cross with any other Cucurbitaceae. The small, multicolored, striped and warted gourds seen in grocery stores around Halloween and Thanksgiving belong to _Cucurbita pepo_ and are discussed in the section on squash.

L. siceraria vines are rampant growers and are often trellised or tied along a fence to save space. The long-necked bottle or dipper gourds develop perfectly straight necks when hanging from a trellis. The necks of such gourds often curve or curl when the plants are grown on the ground.

Some _L. siceraria_ varieties are eaten like summer squash when very young. Various Italian varieties of Cucuzzi, also known as Longissima, are prized for their flavor and texture when immature. Most varieties of _L. siceraria_, however, are grown for their mature shell. Many hard-shelled gourds contain toxic amounts of bitter compounds called cucurbitacins which must be leached from the dry shells before the gourds are used for food storage containers. The American Gourd Society (Box 274, Mt. Gilead, OH 43338) offers pamphlets on gourd curing, carving, preservation and use.

POLLINATION, CROSSING AND ISOLATION

Lagenaria siceraria flowers are large, white and as thin as tissue paper. The female blossoms are attached to a tiny, immature gourd and are easily identified. Male blossoms have only a straight stem. The flowers open in the late afternoon or early evening, remain open during the night, and are pollinated primarily by crepuscular insects in the tropics. In more temperate zones, cucumber beetles and honeybees visit the flowers while they are open in the late afternoon.

Although _L. siceraria_ will not cross with any other Cucurbitaceae, different varieties within the species can easily be crossed by insects. An isolation distance of 1/4 to 1/2 mile is recommended. When more than one variety is grown in close proximity, hand-pollination is necessary. During the morning, male and female flowers that will open that evening are located and taped shut. The hand-pollination process takes place that same evening, when the blossoms would normally be opening.

Except for the reversal of the sessions, the hand-pollination technique for *L. siceraria* is the same as for squash. Carefully pick the male flower and remove the tape and white flower petals. Gently untape the female flower and rub the pollen from the anthers of the male flower onto the stigma of the female flower. Retape the female flower and mark its stem.

SEED PRODUCTION, HARVEST AND PROCESSING

All hard-shelled gourds must be grown to full maturity, which is best determined by examining the stem of the fruit. A gourd is ready for harvest when the fruit's stem changes from green to brown or yellow. Although mature, gourds at this stage still contain large amounts of water and should be placed in a cool, dry location with good ventilation until completely dry. During this drying period, the shell and the contents of the gourd dry so completely that the seeds will rattle when the gourd is shaken vigorously.

The seeds can be removed from mature gourds that are not completely dry, if the gourd's shell is not going to be used for other purposes. Fermentation is not necessary, and the seeds only need to be separated from the pulp and air-dried. The pulp of *L. siceraria* can be quite irritating. Wet pulp can cause minor cuts to become swollen and painful, and the dust from dry pulp can irritate the nose and respiratory tract.

To preserve the gourd for use or display, drill or cut a small opening in the stem or blossom end and remove the seeds through that opening. Gourds that will be made into bowls or storage vessels can be cut in half around the middle or a lid can be cut from the top portion. Shake the seeds out of the gourd and pull them free of any fiber or dry flesh. Seeds that snap in half when folded are sufficiently dry for storage. Seeds that bend instead of breaking need further drying.

SEED VIABILITY

Gourd seeds do not require any further treatment and will remain viable for six years when stored in cool, dry, dark conditions.

Sechium edule - Chayote (Vegetable Pear)

Chayote is grown in many tropical regions throughout the world. The first green shoots are harvested in the spring when 6-8" long and are eaten like asparagus. The leaves are used for animal fodder, the vines are woven into rope, and the mature roots are prepared like potatoes. Chayote fruits are seasoned, spiced or sweetened and are eaten in soups, salads, main courses, breakfast foods, custards and desserts.

In 1901 the USDA printed a bulletin entitled *The Chayote: A Tropical Vegetable* by O. F. Cook, Special Agent for Tropical Agriculture. The bulletin included black and white pictures of twelve different varieties of chayote that were being grown in Mexico, Central America and on various tropical islands. Mr. Cook recommended chayote as a useful and desirable crop for farmers in the southern United States. The bulletin also states that chayotes were in great demand in France in 1888 as a substitute for artichoke hearts, and that hats made from chayote vines were fashionable in Paris during the summer of 1900.

Despite Mr. Cook's recommendations, chayote farming never caught on in the United States. In frost-free areas the rampant perennial vines require trellising and frequent pruning. Although each plant is capable of producing 50-100 fruits, labor costs were apparently prohibitive even in 1901.

Chayote is an excellent perennial plant for large home gardens in regions of the United States where the ground does not freeze. Although frost will kill the plants to the ground, the roots will resprout each spring. Chayote can be grown as an annual in northern climates when started in a greenhouse 2-3 months before the last frost date. The roots can also be dug after the first frost and stored over the winter in moist sawdust at temperatures slightly above freezing.

BOTANICAL CLASSIFICATION

Chayote belongs to the genus *Sechium* and the species *edule*. *S. edule* does not cross with any other Cucurbitaceae. Of the varieties listed in Mr. Cook's article, only the one with spineless, green, pear-shaped fruits is commonly available in the United States. Other documented varieties include fruits that were round, pear-shaped, spineless, spiny, white, and green. The white varieties were described as more tender than the thicker skinned green types, but did not store as long and were easily bruised during handling. The spines on some of the wild varieties are capable of inflicting serious cuts during harvest. Chayote fruits are also known by such names as christophine, chuchu,

mirliton and vegetable pear.

POLLINATION, CROSSING AND ISOLATION

Chayote produces both male and female flowers on the same plant and is pollinated by insects. Some books suggest that two plants must be grown to provide for adequate pollination, but neither reduced set nor self-incompatibility was observed in solitary plantings of the pear-shaped, spineless, green variety.

Chayote varieties can be cross-pollinated by insects. Bees are strongly attracted to the flowers, which yield abundant nectar and appear late in the season. If more than one variety of chayote is grown, isolation of one mile is necessary to ensure absolute purity. Hand-pollination is possible, but the flowers are very small and difficult to identify and to tape.

SEED PRODUCTION, HARVEST AND PROCESSING

Each chayote contains a single seed which is enclosed within the fruit and cannot be separated from the flesh. Fully mature fruits, which can be recognized by their tough-looking skins, should be harvested for future plantings. The fruit should be wrapped individually in newspaper and stored in boxes, but never more than three fruits deep. A dark, cool area with a constant temperature of 35-40° F. will provide the best storage conditions. Less mature fruits are stored the same way and can be eaten throughout the fall and winter. The entire sprouted fruit is planted out the next spring with the large end buried just below the soil's surface.

_____ Lesser Grown Cucurbitaceae _____

Benincasa hispida - Wax Gourd (Winter Melon)

Wax gourd, also known as winter melon, is an important food crop in India and China. Seed is available in the United States under a variety of names including ash gourd, Chinese preserving melon, Chinese watermelon, gourd melon, tallow gourd and white pumpkin. At full maturity the fruits can weigh 100 pounds with a diameter of more than 10" and will keep for 12-18 months. The dark green skin is thin, hard and waxy. The flesh is very bland and releases a lot of water when cooked. Wax gourd is most famous as the main ingredient in winter melon pond soup, or dong gwa jong. The soup, which includes one or more spiced meats, mushrooms, chunks of seeded winter melon and many spices, is often served in the carved rind of the melon. In India, the fruits are cooked with sugar and made into a sweetmeat called heshim.

Fresh juice collected from the vines of the plants is said to be a beneficial treatment for nervous disorders and to expel tapeworms. Wax scraped from the melon skin has been used to make candles.

Fuzzy melon, a smaller variety of *Benincasa hispida*, is slightly larger than a cucumber and is covered with short white hairs. Fuzzy melon, which is also known as tseet gwa, has firmer flesh than wax gourd. Tseet gwa is used by Cantonese cooks to make a family-size version of winter melon soup, and also as a squash-like vegetable in stir-fry dishes. The fruits can be used in place of summer squash in any recipe.

All varieties of fuzzy melon and wax gourd will cross with one another, but will not cross with any other Cucurbitaceae. Isolation of 1/2 mile or hand-pollination will maintain seed purity.

Cucumis anguria - West Indian Gherkin (Burr Cucumber)

Many gardeners have planted West Indian gherkin mistakenly thinking it was a cucumber used for pickle making. Gherkin pickles are made from many different varieties of immature cucumbers processed in a brine and sweet syrup. Despite their name, gherkin pickles have nothing whatsoever to do with West Indian gherkin.

The decorative vines of West Indian gherkin produce spiny, green, seedy, 1-2" diameter fruits. The plant is also referred to as gooseberry gourd, goarseberry gourd and burr cucumber. Seeds are very difficult to secure and are not available from commercial seed companies in the United States.

Very young fruits of *Cucumis anguria* are edible when the spines are soft and the seeds are immature. Fully ripe fruits of West Indian gherkin will split open exposing the seeds. The plants rely on insects for pollination and will not cross with any other members of the Cucurbitaceae family. Isolation of 1/4 mile or hand-pollination will prevent crossing between varieties.

Cyclanthera pedata - Caihua (Achoecha)

Caihua fruits are eaten in Peru and Bolivia where the plants grow as cultivated weeds. The 10' plants have very small yellow or white flowers and produce 2" fruits with scattered prickles. *Cyclanthera pedata* does not cross with any other Cucurbitaceae species. There are no known sources of Caihua in the United States.

Luffa acutangula - Angled Luffa

Angled luffa, grown extensively in Asia, is sometimes referred to as Chinese okra or ridged gourd. The vine is delicate and has night-blooming yellow flowers. The seeds are black with a pitted surface and lack a rim on the margin. A single generic variety is sold in the United States, although several varieties are available in Asia. The immature fruits are eaten in curries in India and are used like summer squash in Asia. Mature dry fruits can be prepared for sponges. Although the ridges make it more difficult to scrape the dry flesh off of the fibrous core, the sponges are softer than those made from *L. aegyptiaca*.

It has generally been thought that *L. acutangula* does not cross with *L. aegyptiaca*. However, Charles Heiser, a noted authority on gourds, reports that a hybrid can be obtained when the pollen of *L. aegyptiaca* is applied to the stigmas of *L. acutangula*. The resulting seed will produce vigorous hybrid plants with good fruit set, but the fruits do not contain viable seed. Luffa seeds are saved like those of hard-shelled gourds.

Luffa aegyptiaca - Smooth Luffa

The immature fruits of smooth luffa can be eaten but are most often grown for the fibrous core inside the mature gourds. Different varieties of smooth luffa sponge are available in the United States and will cross with one another. Hand-pollination or isolation of 1/2 mile is recommended for complete seed purity. Black (or occasionally white) *L. aegyptiaca* seed is smooth with a distinctive rim or groove around the margin and lacks the pitting of *L. acutangula*. Smooth luffa preparation is discussed in a pamphlet available from The Gourd Society (see *Lagenaria siceraria* for their address). Luffa seeds are saved like hard-shelled gourds.

Momordica balsamina - Balsam Apple

Balsam apple is not usually used for food, but is probably edible if prepared like balsam pear. Historically, the fruits have been used to make a salve which is said to cure skin rashes. At maturity the fruits split open exposing red, fleshy seed capsules. Balsam apple does not cross with balsam pear or with any other Cucurbitaceae family member.

Momordica charantia - Balsam Pear (Bitter Melon)

Balsam pear is also known as bitter melon in the United States and by the Cantonese name foo gwa or fu kwa. The fruits are used throughout Asia in Indian curry, Ceylonese pickles, Indonesian salads and in Cantonese stir-fry dishes. The melons have warty skins, grow 4-10" long, and are quite bitter and firm in their immature stages. Fully ripe melons turn orange and soft. Cantonese cooks parboil immature balsam pears in several changes of water before using them in recipes, which removes much of the bitterness and allows the melons to absorb other flavors. Balsam pear shoots and leaves can be eaten as greens. Different varieties of balsam pear can be cross-pollinated by insects, so isolation or hand-pollination is required to ensure seed purity. Balsam pear does not cross with balsam apple or any other Cucurbitaceae species.

Sicana odorifera - Cassabanana

Cassabanana is a perennial vine found growing wild in the Gulf States of America. The orange, cylindrical,

24" fruits have a pleasing odor and are edible and somewhat sweet. The seeds are not commercially available and different varieties are not documented. The plants flower in response to shortening days and are very frost-sensitive. The large vines are inappropriate greenhouse specimens and will not produce fruit in areas with winter temperatures below 35° F.

Trichosanthes anguina - Serpent Gourd

Serpent gourd, also known as club gourd or snake cucumber or viper gourd, is about 36" long and 4" in diameter. The fruits are commonly grown in India and are eaten in curries. The plants are also found in Central America where the fruits are used like squash. Snake gourd requires a long growing season and is successful in climates where hard-shelled gourds can be grown to maturity. *Trichosanthes anguina* will not cross with members of the *Lagenaria* genera or with any other members of the Cucurbitaceae family. Different varieties of snake gourd will cross, so hand-pollination or 1/4 mile isolation is required to ensure seed purity.

THE LEGUMINOSAE FAMILY

Vegetables in the Leguminosae family rank second only to grains as the most important source of food for mankind. Leguminosae have been cultivated for over 6,000 years. Various species are thought to have originated in Africa, China, India, Indochina, Europe and South America. Grains and legumes, when eaten together, provide all of the essential amino acids needed by man. In addition to their value as food crops, species within the Leguminosae family provide forage crops, timber, fiber, dyes, tannins, gum resins, insecticides, flavorings and flowers.

FAMILY TAXONOMY

The Leguminosae family includes more than 600 genera and 12,000 species. Only about 25 species are commonly used for food in the developed world. Pisum (peas) and Phaseolus (beans) are important both as green vegetables and as dry food crops. Many other Leguminosae species are grown primarily for their dry seeds. The leaves, shoots and roots of some species also are used as minor vegetables.

The Leguminosae family has been reclassified many times by various taxonomists. Faboideae, Caesalpinioideae and Mimosoideae are now considered subfamily names of no botanical standing. Between the time that *Hortus Second* and *Hortus Third* were published, substantial changes in classification occurred. Some of the genus and species names included here will definitely conflict with taxonomical texts published before *Hortus Third*.

Some taxonomists classify legumes according to the position of the "cotyledons" (seed halves) during ger-

Facing Page: Various species and varieties of beans (*Phaseolis spp.*) and cowpeas (*Vigna unguiculata*).

Leguminosae in the Garden		
Genus	**Species**	**Common Name**
Arachis	hypogea	peanut
Cajanus	cajun	pigeon pea
Canavalia	ensiformis	jack bean
	gladiata	sword bean
Cicer	arietinum	garbanzo (chick pea)
Cyamposis	tetragonobus	cluster bean
Dolichos	lablab	hyacinth bean
Glycine	max	soybean
Lens	culinaris	lentil
Lupinus	mutabilis	tarwi
Pachyrhizus	ahipa	ahipa
	erosus	jicama (yam bean)
	tuberosa	potato bean
Phaseolus	acutifolius	
	var. latifolius	tepary bean
	coccineus	runner bean
	lunatus	lima bean (butter bean)
	vulgaris	common bean
	vulgaris	
	subsp. nunas	nunas (popping bean)
Pisum	sativum	garden pea, edible podded pea
Psophocarpus	tetragonolobus	winged bean, asparagus pea
Vicia	faba	fava bean (broad bean)
Vigna	aconitifolia	moth bean
	angularis	adzuki bean
	mungo	black gram
	radiata	mung bean (green gram)
	umbellata	rice bean
	unguiculata	cowpea
	unguiculata var. sesquipedalis	yard long bean (asparagus bean)

mination. "Hypogeal" refers to cotyledons which remain under the surface of the earth when the seedlings emerge. Peas, fava beans and runner beans all have hypogeal cotyledons. "Epigeal" cotyledons are pushed above the surface during emergence. *Phaseolus vulgaris*, common beans, have epigeal cotyledons.

POLLINATION CHARACTERISTICS AND TECHNIQUES

Leguminosae flowers are perfect, usually butterfly shaped and quite pretty. Leguminosae flowers are self-pollinating, but are occasionally crossed by honeybees and other insects. The flowers usually open between 7 a.m. and 8 a.m. and never close. The anthers "dehisce" (shed pollen) the evening before the flowers open. The pollen does not usually get transferred to the stigma until the flower is disturbed or tripped, usually by the wind. Insects, especially bees, also visit the flowers and can cause some amount of cross-pollination.

The extent of insect cross-pollination is hotly debated. The percentage of crossing is dependent upon the type of flower, the number of bees and other pollen carrying insects that are present, and whether or not there are other pollen and nectar sources in the area. Thus, it is possible to have considerable crossing in some populations in some areas, while other populations may show little or no crossing.

The distinctive seed coat patterns and the shapes of various Leguminosae seeds are sometimes used in attempts to prove the presence or absence of crossing. Leguminosae species also possess a wide variety of genetic characteristics that are not visible in their seeds, so statements about seed purity based solely on seed coat characteristics are not valid. Changes in seed coat color are just one indication of crossed seed.

Always remember, even if crossing has occurred that is capable of showing up visibly, the crossed seeds that are harvested will look exactly like the parent seeds. After a flower is crossed, the seeds that are produced will carry that cross unseen within them. Evidence of crossing only becomes visibly apparent when another generation is grown out from those crossed seeds, first appearing as variations within the population of plants and then in the seeds that are harvested. Therefore, always save and label seeds from each year's crop in separate containers. If crossing becomes visible in the seeds, remember that the previous generation of seeds is not pure either, even though it appears to be. Throw away the generation of seed which is visibly crossed, throw away the previous generation which is carrying the cross, and start over with seed from the generation before that, which should be pure.

Saving Leguminosae seed may require isolation, bagging or caging depending on the following factors. The larger the flower, the more likely it is to be visited by bumblebees and honeybees. When more desirable sources of pollen are available, bees are less likely to bother with legumes. Insects with smooth bodies are extremely inefficient at carrying pollen and are unlikely to cause crossing. Finally, insects that chew through the side of a blossom to extract nectar, do not usually come in contact with pollen and are very unlikely to cross-pollinate flowers.

In areas where other pollen sources are abundant, growers often claim that beans and other Leguminosae do not cross at all. However, growers in desert and mountain areas, where other pollen sources are scarce, have sometimes demonstrated up to 25% crossing. Many researchers claim that legumes are rarely visited by bees, but other studies have shown that various crops can be frequently visited by bees. Depending on the site and other available pollen sources, crossing can be rare or commonplace.

When attempting to prevent crossing, consider cages for bush plants and blossom bags for the taller varieties. Cages are easily made from spun polyester or window screen and need to be in place from first blossom until last. Blossom bagging, using spun polyester or a similar material, is more time-consuming. The bag must not block too much light or the flowers will not develop properly. Paper bags exclude far too much light and plastic bags trap too much heat and humidity.

Blossom bags must be tied carefully into place when the flowers begin to form along the "raceme" (flower cluster). The flowers can be examined through the bag, and the bag can be removed when the tiny pods begin to show. As the bags are removed, tag the racemes that were bagged so that those pods can be harvested separately for seed saving. String, tape or poultry bands all make good markers.

PLANT SELECTION

Always save seeds from healthy plants that appear true-to-type and bear heavily. Legumes should be rogued after the plants emerge, and during both flowering and pod formation. When the plants are about 6" tall, remove any that show off-type foliage or that are of an unusual height. Later, when the flowers appear, remove any plants with flowers that are not true-to-type for color, shape and number of flowers per node. Finally, remove any plants with newly formed pods that are not the typical shape, size and color. Seed should never be collected from plants which do not exhibit the characteristics of the variety.

GENERAL PRODUCTION AND PROCESSING TECHNIQUES

Legume seeds are usually left on the plant to dry, however sometimes fully mature but still green pods can be picked and then allowed to dry until crisp. Timing for green seed harvest is critical and should only be used as a last resort. A better method for green harvest, sometimes used when a nearly mature crop is about to be ruined by frost, is to pull the entire plant and hang it upside down in a warm area until the pods are dry. This method allows the seeds to continue to draw energy from the plant for several days, which results in higher quality seed. Depending on the climate, however, there can be some problems with pod damage from either extreme heat, freezing temperatures or molds.

Leguminosae seeds are enclosed in pods which split along both sides. Pods that are crispy dry can be broken open and the seeds will fall free. Although that sounds relatively simple, the actual process can be quite frustrating at times. The I-Tech seed cleaner (see Section I) does an excellent job on many Leguminosae seeds, but its success depends on having the right-sized screen. If I-Tech or another seed cleaning device is unavailable, any of the following methods can be used.

Feed Sack Method - Place the dry

pods in a feed sack or pillow case, and tape or tie the opening shut. Then either place the sack on the floor and jog in place on top of it, place the sack on a work bench and roll with a rolling pin, or hang the sack in a tree and beat it with a baseball bat or stick.

Tarp Method - Dump the dry pods onto a tarp and jog in place or beat with a flail.

Hand Method - Splitting the pods by hand and letting the seeds fall into a container is rather slow, but makes it easy to grade the seed quality and keep the seeds clean.

If the seeds need additional cleaning, place them in baskets or bowls. The seeds can be winnowed by pouring them from one basket to another during a stiff breeze. Vary the distance between the baskets according to the wind velocity. The chaff will be blown away as the seeds in the baskets become progressively cleaner. Sometimes unexpected wind gusts can blow seeds right out of the baskets. If the area is covered with a clean tarp or sheet, the seeds can be easily retrieved. Always be careful to avoid mixing, however, by flipping the tarp each time that a new variety is started. It is also possible to use a hair dryer or fan in place of the wind. Small fans from old vacuum cleaners or computers are very handy.

Leguminosae seeds are very susceptible to bean weevils, which can totally destroy stored seeds in a very short time. The adults lay eggs in the flowers or young pods. The larvae hatch inside the seeds and slowly eat their way out, leaving tiny round holes in the seed coat. The weevils usually emerge in the spring, mate and lay eggs in a new crop of blossoms. Weevils are almost always present in home-saved seeds and can destroy the seed if left unchecked.

To prevent weevil damage, freeze the dry seeds when they are ready for storage. If it isn't possible to get to threshing and winnowing right away, put the pods into an airtight container and freeze them. Weevil eggs are killed by three days at 0° F. Leguminosae seeds should be left in the freezer for five days, since all portions of the home freezer may not reach 0° F. When the seeds are removed from the freezer, let the airtight container set out overnight to reach room temperature. If the container is opened too soon, condensation will form on the cold seeds causing them to take on moisture. It is possible for the seeds to be recontaminated if left in an open container where weevils are present. If whole pods were frozen because you couldn't get to them right away, the seeds should be refrozen after being cleaned and winnowed.

Seeds that are not totally dry may be damaged by freezing, but a quick check can be made with a hammer. Put several seeds on a hard surface such as concrete and hit each one with the hammer. Seeds that shatter are dry enough for storage. Seeds that mash instead of shattering need further drying.

Most Leguminosae seeds maintain high germination rates over relatively long periods of time when stored under ideal conditions.

Arachis hypogea - Peanut

Gardeners have long been intrigued by the peanut's unusual growth habit. The flower stalk produces a fertilized ovary which is called a "peg." The peg grows downward penetrating 1-2" into the soil where the seedpods form.

A native of South America, the peanut is now grown throughout the temperate world. In the United States peanuts will grow to maturity as far north as New York State.

In June 1925, George Washington Carver published "How to Grow the Peanut and 105 Ways of Preparing It for Human Consumption." His recipes included mock veal peanut cutlets, baked peanuts and rice, peanut stuffing, peanut salad, peanut bisque, peanut bread and even peanut confections. Dr. Carver did, however, leave out one item. The tender shoots and leaves of the peanut can be used as a green vegetable.

BOTANICAL CLASSIFICATION

Peanuts belong to the genus *Arachis*

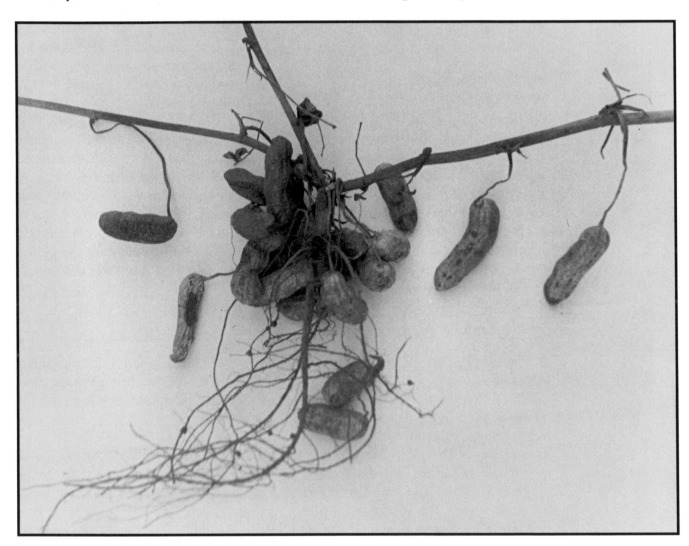

Peanut plant (*Arachis hypogea*) showing dried pegs growing downward to mature seedpods.

and the species *hypogea*. We refer to *A. hypogea* as nuts, but that is botanically incorrect.   Peanuts are seeds which grow in seedpods under the ground.

There are two distinct types of peanuts grown in the United States. The Virginia types have true runners, require a long growing season, and usually have two seeds per pod. Their seeds require a long rest period between harvest and germination. The Spanish and Valencia types are more erect plants, need a shorter growing season, and require no rest period between harvest and germination. Spanish peanuts usually contain two seeds per pod, while Valencia types have three to four.

POLLINATION, CROSSING AND ISOLATION

Peanut flowers are perfect and self-pollinating. The flowers are very attractive to bees and other insects, which can cause up to 35% crossing between varieties. Several researchers have noted that the percentage of cross-pollination relates directly to the protrusion of the stigma out of the "keel" (lower petals of the flower). A few of the very old varieties have flow-ers which impede self-pollinating and require insect-pollination. Peanut varieties should be isolated by one mile to ensure seed purity. Varieties grown in closer proximity to one another should be caged to prevent any crossing.

SEED PRODUCTION, HARVEST AND PROCESSING

Peanuts are harvested when the plants turn yellow at the end of the season. The whole plant is pulled out of the ground with the peanuts still hanging on the pegs. The plants are left to cure in the garden or in a frost protected enclosure for 2-3 weeks. After this drying period, the pods are stripped from the vines. Pods kept for seed should be thoroughly dry, but do not need any further treatment.

SEED STORAGE

Peanuts remain viable for four years when stored at 35° F. with 5% moisture. When stored in gunny sacks in outbuildings, however, peanuts lose 50% germination over a period of 12 months. If also exposed to sunlight during storage, peanuts lose the power to germinate even more quickly.

Cajanus cajun - Pigeon Pea

Pigeon peas are probably native to Africa and are commonly grown in India. Although not yet widely known in the United States, pigeon peas are very drought tolerant and adapt easily to a variety of climates. The plants are perennials, but are sensitive to frost.

Pigeon peas have a distinctively pleasant flavor. The young green pods are eaten like green peas and the immature shelled seeds are used like shelly beans. The entire plant is used for food in India, where it also provides forage and fodder for animals, firewood, thatching, and dry material for basket making.

BOTANICAL CLASSIFICATION

Pigeon peas belong to the genus *Cajanus* and the species *cajun*. *C. cajun* are branched, free-standing plants that grow 3-4' tall. The plants are very attractive and are often used in the back borders of flower gardens.

Pigeon pea varieties available in India are grouped by pod color. Flavus or tur varieties mature very early and have green, three-seeded pods. Bicolor or arhar varieties have purplish green pods which contain four to five seeds. Arhar varieties are daylength sensitive and mature during short, warm days.

POLLINATION, CROSSING AND ISOLATION

Pigeon peas are self-pollinating. The plant's flowers are small and seem to be difficult for insects to enter. Research indicates, however, that small bees are attracted to the flowers and can effectively cross-pollinate different varieties grown within 1/2 mile of each other. Blossom bagging or caging will ensure seed purity when two or more varieties are grown in close proximity. Pigeon peas do not cross with any other species.

SEED PRODUCTION, HARVEST AND PROCESSING

Pigeon pea pods are easily collected and are not difficult to shell. General information on shelling techniques is given in the introductory pages of the Leguminosae family. Pigeon peas are available through the Seed Savers Exchange and occasionally from Indian and Hindi food stores in larger cities across the United States.

SEED VIABILITY

Information on the decline of germination rates during storage was not available for pigeon peas.

Cicer arietinum - Garbanzo (Chick Pea)

Garbanzo is often referred to as chick pea in Europe and the United States. The plants are grown throughout the temperate world and are an important source of protein in many countries. Whole dried seeds are used like dry peas or beans, and the green pods and tender leaves are eaten as a green vegetable. In the United States the mature seeds are canned in brine and used in salads.

BOTANICAL CLASSIFICATION

Garbanzo is a member of the genus _Cicer_ and the species _arietinum_. _C. arietinum_ is also known as Indian bean, Egyptian pea and Bengal gram. The plants are bushy, upright annuals that grow 2' tall. The short, oblong, 1" pods contain one or two angular seeds.

The leaves and stems of the plants are covered with "glabular" (sticky) hairs. The hairs exude malic acid which is collected in India and used like vinegar or for medicine. In remote rural villages, Indian women wrap the plants in fabric each evening. The fabric is removed the following morning and the liquid is wrung out and collected in containers.

Garbanzos are attractive plants in any vegetable garden. Whenever the plants are touched, however, malic acid is deposited on clothing and skin. Some persons are bothered by rashes after contact with the plant.

POLLINATION, CROSSING AND ISOLATION

Garbanzo flowers are perfect and self-pollinating. Several research reports indicate that honeybees frequent the flowers and cross-pollination is common. Different varieties should be

Garbanzo (*Cicer arietinum*) foliage and seedpods.

isolated by 1/2 mile or caged to ensure seed purity.

SEED PRODUCTION, HARVEST AND PROCESSING

Water should be withheld from garbanzo plants after the seeds have set and flowering ceases. In regions with summer rains during harvest, the plants can be pulled and allowed to dry under cover. The dry plants are then threshed to free the seeds, which helps prevent skin irritations that might result from trying to pick the pods individually. The Leguminosae family pages describe various threshing and winnowing techniques.

SEED VIABILITY

Garbanzos maintain 60% germination for three years when stored in a cool, dry, dark location.

_____ *Dolichos lablab* - Hyacinth Bean _____

Hyacinth bean plants in full bloom are covered with beautiful flowers that spread perfume throughout the garden. The plants are relatively unknown in the United States and deserve a great deal more attention. Hyacinth beans are short-lived perennials in frost free areas, and tolerate both drought and poor soil.

Hyacinth bean pods have a distinctive, strong bean-like taste that is much appreciated in Southeast Asia and India. The flavor is sometimes a bit overwhelming when the pods are cooked alone, but is quite pleasant in combination with other vegetables. Unfortunately, the "anthazion" (colored layer) in the purple podded varieties is quite thin and disappears no matter how briefly the beans are cooked.

Full-sized immature seeds are sometimes used like shelly beans. The dry beans with colored seed coats contain cyanogenic glucosides in toxic amounts. Some references indicate that soaking dry seeds in several changes of water renders them edible, while other texts caution against eating the dry beans at all.

BOTANICAL CLASSIFICATION

Hyacinth beans belong to the genus *Dolichos* and the species *lablab*. *D. lablab* are also known as Bonavista beans, Lubia beans, Bovanist beans, Seim beans, Indian beans and Egyptian beans. Available varieties include those with white flowers and large light green pods, pink flowers and light green pods, pink flowers and dark

Immature pods, dried pods and dry seeds of hyacinth bean (*Dolichos lablab*) with light green podded variety, left, and purple podded variety, middle and right.

green pods, purple flowers and green pods, and purple flowers and purple pods.

POLLINATION, CROSSING AND ISOLATION

Hyacinth beans have large, perfect flowers which are very attractive to a wide variety of insects. The blossoms are certainly large enough for bees to work with ease, but are not really significant sources of pollen or nectar. Isolation or bagging should be used to ensure seed purity.

SEED PRODUCTION, HARVEST AND PROCESSING

Hyacinth bean pods are very difficult to shell. The large "hilum" (seed scar) is firmly attached to the pod, and the pod also shrinks tightly around the individual seeds as it dries. For large amounts of seeds, a mechanical seed thresher is highly recommended.

SEED VIABILITY

Information on the decline of germination rates during storage was not available for hyacinth beans.

Phaseolus coccineus - Runner Bean

Runner beans are native to Central America. Some runner bean varieties are daylength sensitive and may not flower during the first year of growth in northern regions. Immature runner bean pods are used like snap beans. The mature dry seeds are mealy and are used in some areas of Central America. Runner beans appear frequently in English gardens where the flowers, edible pods and green shelly beans are much appreciated.

Runner bean varieties are often included in the flower sections of seed catalogs because of their striking ornamental blossoms. Scarlet Runners have red flowers and light burgundy seeds with black blotches. Black Runners have a more intense red flower and seeds that are completely black. The variety known as Painted Lady has beautiful bicolored blossoms that are half white and half light red, with seeds that are similar to Scarlet Runners. White Runners have white flowers and white seeds.

BOTANICAL CLASSIFICATION

Runner beans belong to the genus _Phaseolus_ and the species _coccineus_. _P. coccineus_ varieties do not cross with any other bean species.

Runner beans are easily distinguished from other bean species by their unique growth habit. The plant's "cotyledons" (seed halves) remain underground as the vine emerges. The first growth that appears above the ground is the stem and first set of true leaves. To assist the rather weak, unprotected seedlings, the soil should be well prepared.

Runner beans also climb differently from most other species. Most beans twine counterclockwise when viewed from above, but runner beans twine clockwise. Be sure to take this into consideration when assisting the young plants on poles. The vines will either break or literally fall off of the pole if twined in the wrong direction.

POLLINATION, CROSSING AND ISOLATION

The flowers of runner beans are very large and open, and are quite attractive to honeybees, bumblebees and hummingbirds. There is often considerable crossing between different varieties of runner beans. Isolation of 1/2 mile will maintain seed purity. Two or more runner bean varieties grown in close proximity will require blossom bagging or caging for seed purity. Runner bean flowers are perfect but are unable to self-pollinate without being tripped by insects. To simulate insect tripping and ensure seed set, remove the blossom bag or cage and depress the bottom portion of each of the new flowers. Continue tripping the flowers each day until the desired number of seedpods are set. Blossom bagging techniques are discussed in the introductory pages of the Leguminosae family.

SEED PRODUCTION, HARVEST AND PROCESSING

Runner bean plants are perennial, but light frost will kill their foliage to the ground. Each spring the plant sprouts from tuberous roots which are poisonous if eaten. In areas where the ground freezes, the roots must be dug in the fall, stored over winter in slightly damp sand and replanted in the spring. Vines that grow from the tuberous roots produce flowers much earlier in the season than those started from seeds.

In short season climates, runner bean pods often do not have enough time to dry on the vine. The pods can be harvested when fully mature and just beginning to change color, then spread out and left to dry away from direct sunlight. The large pods are not difficult to shell by hand. When using other shelling methods, take extra care to avoid breaking the large seeds.

SEED VIABILITY

Runner bean seeds will retain 50% germination for three years when stored under ideal conditions.

_____ *Phaseolus lunatus* - Lima Bean (Butter Bean) _____

Large-seeded lima beans have been traced back to 5000-6000 B.C. in Huaca Prieta, Peru. Small-seeded varieties, also called sieva beans, date back to 300-500 B.C. in Guatemala and Mexico. Wild varieties of limas can still be found in many regions of Central and South America. Some of the wild types contain toxic amounts of cyanogenic glucosides and are considered to be poisonous, but can be rendered edible with repeated "leaching" (repeatedly adding and discarding water during cooking). Lima varieties available in the United States contain variable amounts of cyanogenic glucoside, but do not require leaching to be used as food. Some people cannot eat limas, however, and report being very sensitive to the compound.

BOTANICAL CLASSIFICATION

Limas are members of the genus *Phaseolus* and the species *lunatus* and will not cross with any other beans. Both bush and pole varieties are available in the United States. Baby limas or sieva limas are annuals and are sometimes classified as *Phaseolus lunatus var. lunonnus*. The large-seeded perennial limas, which are also referred to as potato limas, are sometimes classified as *Phaseolus limensis var. limenanus*. Neither the plant nor the root

of the large-seeded varieties can tolerate frost. These taxonomic classifications are simply attempts to group the members of the species by flowering times and by their annual or perennial tendencies.

POLLINATION, CROSSING AND ISOLATION

All varieties of both small-seeded and large-seeded limas will cross with one another. Limas have self-pollinating flowers which are filled with high quality nectar. Honeybees work the flowers intensely when the blossoms first open. In some areas beehives are moved into lima fields, not to benefit the beans, but to produce a fine, light-colored honey.

Different varieties of limas must be isolated by at least one mile to ensure seed purity. If two or more varieties are to be grown in close proximity, blossom bagging or plant caging is necessary. Bagging and caging techniques are discussed in the Leguminosae family pages and also in Section I.

SEED PRODUCTION, HARVEST AND PROCESSING

Lima pods that are left to dry on the vine shatter very easily and must be picked carefully. Close your hand around each seedpod before picking the pod off the vine. The dry pod will usually crack open in your hand. If bean weevils are a problem, the pods can be picked when fully mature but not yet dry. Spread the pods out and allow them to dry as quickly as possible before shelling. Continue drying the shelled beans until the seeds shat-

ter when struck with a hammer. Then freeze the seeds for 48 hours to kill the weevil eggs that are under the seed coat.

STORAGE

Lima beans will maintain 50% germination for three years when stored in cool, dry, dark conditions.

Phaseolus vulgaris - Common Bean

The easiest way to turn gardeners into seed savers is to show them a large assortment of beans. The beautiful shapes, colors and patterns of the seeds are enough to entice almost any gardener. Especially popular are the numerous bush and pole varieties of _Phaseolus vulgaris_, which include snap beans, string beans, wax beans, shelly beans, kidney beans and all kinds of dry beans. The immature pods of the most tender varieties are eaten as snap beans or green beans. When the beans swell to their maximum size but have not yet started to dry, the seeds are often shelled out and eaten as shelly beans. When left to dry on the vine, the seeds are known as dry beans or soup beans.

Many old-timers prefer bean varieties with strings, which they claim are more highly flavored and taste beanier than the modern stringless types. While this may be true, stringless varieties have brought beans to the forefront of the processed green vegetables. About $250 million of fresh, canned and frozen green beans are sold each year in the United States. Increased consumption has also meant increased monotony, as breeders and producers strive to develop the perfect processing bean. Consumers nationwide are all purchasing nearly identical

strains of Blue Lake or Kentucky Wonder at the grocery store.

BOTANICAL CLASSIFICATION

Common beans are members of the genus _Phaseolus_ and the species _vulgaris_. Members of the Seed Savers Exchange are maintaining more than 2,200 varieties of snap and dry beans. Many are heirloom varieties maintained by many generations of gardeners for their flavor, productivity and climatic adaptability.

POLLINATION, CROSSING AND ISOLATION

All _P. vulgaris_ flowers are perfect and self-pollinating. After reading the information on crossing in the Leguminosae family pages, decide what precautions will be needed to save seed in your area. Other local seed savers may prove to be good sources of information on bean crossing.

At the very least, do not grow different varieties of _P. vulgaris_ side by side if you intend to save seed. Also, never grow two white-seeded varieties next to each other, which would destroy any possibility of noticing possible crossing. For a more complete discussion of visible signs of crossing in beans, see the Leguminosae family pages.

SEED PRODUCTION, HARVEST AND PROCESSING

Most *P. vulgaris* varieties are easily harvested from the dry vines. The pods are also easy to clean using any of the methods described in the Leg-uminosae family pages.

SEED STORAGE

Bean seeds will maintain 50% germination for four years when stored in cool, dry, dark conditions.

_____ *Pisum sativum* - Garden Pea and Edible Podded Pea _____

Peas originated in the eastern Mediterranean. Carbonized seeds have been discovered in Switzerland that date back to about 7000 B.C. During this lengthy period of cultivation, a gradual separation of varieties occurred. Succulent sweeter varieties were selected for vegetable use, while starchy varieties were grown for dry use and fodder. In Asia, peas were further selected for succulent edible pods and tender shoots. Varieties with edible young leaves and vines have also been long prized in some Asian cuisines.

With the introduction in the late 1970s of Sugar Snap and its related varieties, peas have received a great deal of new attention. Their fat, sweet, edible pods do not require stringing or shelling. These peas are easily grown and have tempted many gardeners into trying other types of peas for the first time. Sugar Snap varieties are not new, however, and were quite popular in France in the 1800s. Vilmorin's 1885 edition of *The Vegetable Garden* documents seven distinct varieties of the edible podded peas.

BOTANICAL CLASSIFICATION

Peas belong to the genus *Pisum* and the species *sativum*. *P. sativum* does not cross with any other species of peas or beans.

Most of the peas that are grown as green vegetables have green or white seeds, white flowers and wrinkled seed coats. The smooth-seeded varieties, *Pisum sativum var. arvense*, are starchy and better adapted to cool weather than the wrinkled-seeded types. These varieties have violet flowers, angular seeds which are often a grayish color, and are grown for forage, meal and silage.

POLLINATION, CROSSING AND ISOLATION

Pea flowers are perfect and self-pollinating. Most references indicate that the flowers are pollinated before opening and that crossing is very minimal. In European countries, the required isolation distance for commercially grown seed stock is 100 meters.

Any crossing in peas that does occur would be very hard to notice, because of the similarities in varieties. Whenever there is little else to feed on, bees will visit pea flowers, which greatly increases the chances that crossing will occur. Pea varieties should be separated by a minimum of 50'. Blossom bagging or caging can be used to assure seed purity when it is necessary to grow different varieties side by side.

SEED PRODUCTION, HARVEST AND PROCESSING

Peas mature rather early in the summer and are usually allowed to dry on the vines. Both harvest and shelling are fairly easy. Suggestions for threshing are discussed in the Leguminosae family pages.

SEED VIABILITY

Pea seeds will retain 50% viability for three years when stored in cool, dry, dark conditions.

_____ *Vicia faba* - Fava Bean (Broad Bean) _____

Fava beans are one of the oldest legumes under cultivation and have been an important crop since the Stone Age. Favas were well known in the ancient cultures of Egypt, Greece, Italy and many Middle Eastern countries.

In some people, especially males of southern European ancestry, eating fava beans or inhaling fava pollen causes a potentially deadly reaction called favism. The symptoms include muscle weakness, paralysis and, in extreme cases, death. Favism is an inherited disorder usually associated with eating large quantities of fresh fava beans.

BOTANICAL CLASSIFICATION

Fava beans belong to the genus *Vicia* and the species *faba*. *V. faba* are also known as broad beans, horse beans, English beans, European beans, Windsor beans, field beans and tick beans.

Fava plants have rigid stems and an upright growth habit. Varieties range from 2-6' tall and have white flowers with dark purple or violet blotches. The pods vary from 2-12" in length and contain from one to several large seeds.

POLLINATION, CROSSING AND ISOLATION

Favas are self-pollinating, but bees are attracted to the large flowers and can cause a good deal of cross-pollination. An isolation distance of one mile is necessary to ensure seed purity. When varieties are grown in closer proximity, caging or bagging is required.

SEED PRODUCTION, HARVEST AND PROCESSING

Fava beans are usually picked from dry vines. The pods are moderately difficult to thresh. The seed's "hilum" (scar where the seed was attached to the ovary) is firmly fastened to the inside of the seedpod. Hand shelling is only recommended for small amounts of seeds.

SEED VIABILITY

Fava beans will maintain 50% germination for six years when stored under optimal conditions.

_____ *Vigna unguiculata* - Cowpea _____

Cowpeas migrated from Asia into Africa, and were brought from there to Jamaica and the southern United States by slaves. Cowpeas are eaten as immature pods, shelled green peas and dry peas. Most varieties have well-developed spots or eyes surrounding the "hilum" (seed scar). Varieties which have a black spot or eye around the hilum are commonly called blackeyed peas. Other varieties have eyes that are dark purple, brown or maroon.

BOTANICAL CLASSIFICATION

Cowpeas belong to the genus *Vigna* and the species *unguiculata*. The pods of *V. unguiculata* vary from 4-12" long. Cowpeas do not cross with any other Leguminosae species.

POLLINATION, CROSSING AND ISOLATION

Cowpeas are self-pollinating and the process is generally complete before the flower opens. The flower's receptivity to pollen is limited to the tip of the stigma and only for a short time. Pollen rubbed on the style will not induce fertilization.

Cowpea flowers are attractive to honeybees and bumblebees. The flowers are fairly tight and require a heavy insect to depress the flower's wings and expose the stigma. Honeybees do visit the flowers, but are probably not heavy enough to accomplish any fertilization. Bumblebees, however, are definitely capable of crossing the flowers.

Caging or blossom bagging might be used to ensure absolute purity when different varieties are grown side by side.

SEED PRODUCTION, HARVEST AND PROCESSING

Cowpea seeds are allowed to dry on the vines before harvest. The pods are easily shelled using any of the methods discussed in the Leguminosae family pages.

SEED STORAGE

Cowpea seeds will maintain 80% germination for four years and 50% for seven years when stored in cool, dry, dark conditions.

_____ Lesser Grown Leguminosae _____

Canavalia ensiformis - Jack Bean

Jack bean is an annual bushy plant from Central America. The pods grow 3" wide by about 10" long and contain 3-18 white seeds. Both the young pods and the immature seeds are reportedly used for food. Young pods grown in central California were very tough and not very savory, while the immature seeds were bland with a texture not unlike a very large fava. Mature jack bean seeds are poisonous. Jack bean flowers are large and attractive to bees. Different varieties grown in close proximity would most likely be crossed by insects. Jack bean seeds are unavailable from commercial companies in the United States.

Canavalia gladiata - Sword Bean

Sword bean is even larger than jack bean. The flat pods commonly grow 3" wide and 15" long. Each pod contains 5-10 dark red seeds. The shape of the slightly curved pod resembles a sword. Mature seeds rattle inside of the seedpods, which have been used as musical instruments.

Sword bean is a viny perennial that is native to tropical Asia and Africa. The vines and roots are very sensitive to frost. The immature pods and immature green seeds are eaten as vegetables. The vine is sometimes grown for animal fodder. As with jack bean, the mature seeds are reported to be poisonous. Information about possible different varieties of sword bean is unavailable and commercial sources do not exist.

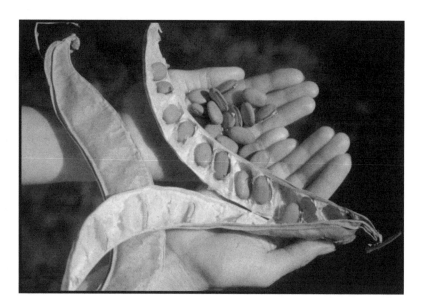

Sword bean (*Canavalia gladiata*).

Cyamposis tetragonobus - Cluster Bean

Cluster bean is native to India and found throughout Southeast Asia. The immature pods are eaten and the plants are used for animal feed. The seeds are very "mucilaginous" (slimy) when cooked.

Cluster bean plants are annual and form an attractive bush that grows about 3' tall. The pods contain 5-12 oval seeds which can be harvested about 120 days after planting.

In central California the plants produced tasty pods late in the season with little attention. The flowers are small in size and do not seem attractive to bees. Information on possible crossing between varieties is unavailable.

Glycine max - Soybean

The soybean, one of the world's oldest crops, has been grown in Asia for 5,000 years. An important source of plant protein, soybeans are also a valuable oil crop. Most soybeans are grown as large-scale agricultural crops for their dry seeds. However, the seeds of some varieties can be shelled out when green and are used as a cooked green vegetable.

Soybeans are daylength sensitive, but varieties have been developed for both long day and short day areas. Soybean flowers are self-fertile. The anthers "dehisce" (shed pollen) before the flowers open. In other words, pollination and fertilization are completed before the soybean flower is even open.

Soybean pods are allowed to dry on the plants before being harvested. The pods are brittle and sharp, so shelling is very hard on the hands. A seed cleaner, such as the I-Tech described in Section I, works well and is a necessity for large amounts of seeds.

Lens culinaris - Lentil

Lentil was probably one of the earliest domesticated crops. Both the immature pods and the dry seeds are used as staples in Indian cuisine. Lentil plants are very delicate in appearance. The plant's tiny flowers are self-pollinating and do not seem to be attractive to bees. The plants continue to produce pods over a long season, but do not tolerate long, hot days in full sun. The ripe pods shatter easily and need to be collected carefully for maximum harvest. Lentil seeds are easily shelled.

Lupinus mutabilis - Tarwi

Tarwi produces brilliant blue blossoms and seeds that contain 40% protein. The plant is widely grown in Peru, Bolivia and Ecuador, but its importance as a world food crop has been restricted because of alkaloids in the seeds. Indians in the Andes highlands remove the bitter alkaloids by soaking the seeds in running water for several days. Tarwi requires a long growing season but is very frost and drought tolerant. Different varieties grown within half a mile would be easily crossed by insects. Tarwi will also cross with some of the wild lupines found growing in the United States. Tarwi seeds are available from several companies in the United States.

Pachyrhizus ahipa - Ahipa

Ahipa, a relative of jicama, is a popular vegetable in Bolivia and Peru. The sweet, white tubers are eaten raw and in fruit salads, or are fried like potatoes. The plant's leaves, stem, seedpods and seeds are toxic and thought to contain large amounts of rotenone. Ahipa plants do not appear to be daylength sensitive and will not tolerate any frost. Ahipa produces lavender or white blossoms and needs a six-month frost-free season to develop seeds. Information about different varieties and the possibilities of cross-pollination is unavailable. There are no known sources for ahipa seed in the United States.

Pachyrhizus erosus - Jicama (Yam Bean)

Jicama, which grows wild in Mexico and Central America, has long climbing vines and large blue or white flowers. Each plant can yield up to seven turnip-shaped roots, but will only produce in the extreme southern regions of the United States. Jicama was grown successfully in central California, but only with a great deal of effort. The seeds were started in a greenhouse in January and the vines were set out on March 30 when all danger from frost had passed. The vines covered a square yard per plant, were grown in full sun with plenty of water, and only one 4" root per plant was harvested in late October. The flowers appeared late in the season and produced ripe but not dry seeds by harvest time. Both the seeds and seedpods are poisonous. Jicama seeds are available from several companies in the United States. Information on pollination and varietal crossing is unavailable.

Pachyrhizus tuberosa - Potato Bean

Potato bean is native to South America, where it grows wild. The roots are collected and are similar to jicama. The plants have irritating hairs which cause major skin rashes. Seeds are unavailable in the United States.

Phaseolus acutifolius var. latifolius - Tepary Bean

Tepary bean is a traditional food crop of Indians in the desert areas of the United States Southwest and northern Mexico. Teparies can be substituted for green beans, shelly beans or dry beans in recipes. Most tepary seeds carry bean common mosaic virus (BCMV) and will infect other beans that are grown nearby. BCMV is most commonly spread by aphids, but can also be spread by splashing rain or irrigation, by people moving through wet plants, or by infected seed and crop debris.

The extent of crossing between tepary bean varieties is dependent on the insects in the area (see the discussion in the Leguminosae family pages).

Teparies are drought tolerant and produce crops under extremely dry, hot weather conditions and on alkali soil. Seeds are saved similarly to other *Phaseolus* species.

Phaseolus vulgarus subsp. nunas - Nunas (Popping Bean)

Nunas is a type of common green

bean with one important difference - when heated the seeds pop like popcorn. Popped nunas taste slightly like roasted peanuts and are a favorite snack food in Ecuador and Peru. Nunas are grown like other pole beans. The flowers are more open than most *Phaseolus vulgaris* and can be more easily cross-pollinated by bees. The plants must be isolated from other *P. vulgaris* varieties by half a mile or caged to ensure purity. Seed is saved like other P. vulgaris varieties.

Some nunas varieties are daylength sensitive and will not produce pods before frost in most areas of the United States. Home garden trials of day-neutral nunas varieties are just starting, so seed should be available from U.S. seed companies within a few years.

Psophocarpus tetragonolobus - Winged Bean

Winged bean has been grown for centuries in Asia and India. Crops are quite successful in hot, humid regions where it is difficult to grow soybeans. The entire plant is used for food: immature pods are eaten like green beans; seeds are shelled and used like soybeans; tender shoots, flowers and leaves are eaten like pea vines; and the tuberous roots are used like potatoes. The plants are perennial, but frost kills the vines to the ground.

Winged bean does not grow well in hot, dry climates. The plants stayed alive in central California and managed to produce small amounts of foliage, pods and roots. Seed savers report excellent yields in Hawaii, where the plant is much better adapted.

The flowers of winged bean are perfect and self-pollinating. Winged bean will not cross with any other vegetable. Information on possible insect cross-pollination between different varieties of winged bean is unavailable.

Psophocarpus tetragonolobus - Asparagus Pea

Asparagus pea, one of ten subspecies of *Psophocarpus tetragonolobus*, forms a ground cover that is 3" tall and 12" in diameter. The flowers are brilliant red and very decorative in the spring. The peas resemble miniature winged beans and are eaten as a green vegetable when very young. As the pods mature, a cellulose layer forms that is impossible to chew. Asparagus pea pods can be shelled, but are small and not usually considered worth the trouble.

Asparagus pea is self-pollinating. The flowers are attractive to small insects and some crossing between varieties is possible. Within a period of 2-3 months in the very early spring, asparagus pea blooms, produces fruit, sets seeds and dies. The plants are unlikely to be blooming at the same time or in the same climate as winged bean. Information on possible crossing between these two subspecies is unavailable.

Vigna aconitifolia - Moth Bean

Moth bean, sometimes called mat bean, is widely grown in India. The green pods are used as a vegetable and the mature seeds are cooked like lentils. Moth bean is a short-day, warm season, drought tolerant plant. Seeds are not commercially available in the United States.

Vigna angularis - Adzuki Bean

Adzuki bean is probably a native of Japan, where bush varieties are quite popular. Vining varieties of adzuki are widely grown in China and Taiwan.

The plants are "hypogeal" (develop with their seed halves underground) and flower during short, warm days. Adzuki bean seeds are usually red and have white hilums. Seeds are available from several commercial companies as well as from Japanese groceries and specialty stores.

Vigna mungo - Black Gram

Black gram is an important crop in India. The immature pods are used as a green vegetable and the mature seeds are used like dry beans. Seeds may be available from some Indian groceries here in the United States.

Vigna radiata - Mung Bean (Green Gram)

Mung bean, an ancient crop native to India, is used as both a green vegetable and a dry bean. In many parts of the world, mung bean seeds are sprouted and sold as bean sprouts. The small, self-pollinating flowers do not open before falling off the developing pods. Any chance of cross-pollination is very unlikely. Mung bean, which is also known as green gram or golden gram, is widely available through commercial seed catalogs.

Vigna umbellata - Rice Bean

Rice bean is commonly grown in Southeast Asia, where the dry seeds are eaten as a rice substitute or in combination with rice. Rice bean plants are very similar to cowpeas in growth habit. The immature bean pods and shelled green beans are eaten like cowpeas. The mature pods are slender, slightly curved and grow to about 3-5" in length. The seeds are white with a tiny black or dark brown eye around the hilum. Rice bean does not cross with any other Vigna species.

Vigna unguiculata var. sesquipedalis - Yard Long Bean (Asparagus Bean)

Yard long might be overstating the length of this Vigna species a bit, but the pods really do grow from 12-30" in length. The plants are fairly day-neutral and can be grown throughout the United States. Yard long beans are usually grown for the immature pods which are favored in Asian cuisines. The pods, when lightly cooked, can be twisted into pretzel shapes to make an impressive garnish. Children who will not eat green beans might be coaxed into eating yard long beans.

The flowers of yard long beans are not attractive to bees. Their pollen is shed before the blossoms open. Crossing rarely occurs even if varieties are grown in close proximity.

Yard long bean is sometimes referred to as asparagus bean. Varieties are available commercially that have white seeds in light green pods, black seeds in dark green pods, and black seeds in purple pods. The purple-podded variety, which has a very heavy layer of anthazion over the chlorophyll, remains purple if cooked for a short period of time in a small amount of water.

THE SOLANACEAE FAMILY

Throughout European history the Solanaceae family has been synonymous with nightshade, and nightshade with poison. Only witches and fairies dealt with tomatoes and sunberries. One bite of their deadly fruits was known to strike children dead. The Europeans didn't know that in other parts of the world, sunberry leaves were being sauteed as green vegetables and tomatoes were being made into salsa.

FAMILY TAXONOMY

Solanaceae family includes about 90 genera and 2,000 species that are mostly native to Central America and South America. Potatoes, tomatoes, peppers and eggplants are the most important culinary members of the family. Tobacco is the most significant inedible member.

Solanacea comes from the Latin word solamen which means quieting. The name refers to the sedative properties of some of the species. Many of the species produce significant amounts of alkaloids. While small amounts of alkaloids can be quieting, larger doses can cause death.

All members of the Solanaceae family have a flower shape that is easy to identify. Sizes and colors vary, but each flower has five united or partially united petals. The petals form a symmetrical, wheel-shaped corolla. The five stamens are attached near the base of the corolla.

Facing Page: Not all eggplants (*Solanum melongena*) are dark purple. Fruit colors include pure white, lime green, bright orange, and violet and white striped.

POLLINATION CHARACTERISTICS AND TECHNIQUES

The cultivated species of the Solanaceae family are self-pollinating. Honeybees are not especially fond of Solanaceae flowers, but many other

Solanaceae in the Garden		
Genus	**Species**	**Common Name**
Capsicum	*annuum*	sweet and chili peppers
	baccatum	kellu-uchu
	frutescens	tabasco, squash pepper
	pubescens	manzano
Cyphomandra	*betacea*	tree tomato (tamarillo)
Lycopersicon	*lycopersicon*	tomato
	pimpinellifolium	currant tomato
Physalis	*alkekingi*	Chinese lantern
	ixocarpa	tomatillo (Mexican husk tomato)
	peruviana	cape gooseberry (poha)
	philadelphica	wild tomatillo
	pruinosa	strawberry tomato (dwarf cape gooseberry)
	pubescens	downy ground cherry (yellow husk tomato)
	subglabrata	purple ground cherry
Solanum	*burbankii*	sunberry (wonderberry)
	integrifolium	tomato-fruited eggplant
	melanocerasum	garden huckleberry
	melongena	eggplant
	muricatum	pepino (melon pear)
	nigrum	common nightshade
	quitoense	naranjilla
	tuberosum	potato

insects are, and a good deal of crossing can result.

Isolation or caging will prevent crossing of different varieties within a Solanaceae species. Seeds should be saved from as many different plants as possible to ensure the greatest genetic diversity within the population.

GENERAL PRODUCTION AND PROCESSING TECHNIQUES

Seeds from the various Solanaceae species are always harvested from fully ripe fruits. Plastic buckets are often used, because the acid in some of the fruits will pit or discolor metal surfaces. The fruits are sliced, chopped, crushed or squeezed to expose the seeds. The chopped fruits are placed in a bowl or bucket, water is added, and the mixture is stirred vigorously. The good seeds will sink, while the fruit particles and immature seeds float and are poured off. More water is added and the process is repeated as many times as is necessary, until all that remains are good clean seeds at the bottom of a bowl of clear water.

The seeds are then poured into a strainer, but always be sure that the seeds are not small enough to pass through the strainer holes. Wipe the bottom of the strainer on a towel to remove as much moisture as possible, and then dump the seeds out onto a glass or ceramic dish to dry. Do not attempt to dry the seeds on paper or other absorptive surfaces as it is extremely difficult to remove the seeds from these surfaces.

Stir the seeds twice daily as they are drying to prevent the seeds from bunching together and to ensure even drying. Never dry seeds in direct sunlight or in the oven.

The dry seeds should be placed in an airtight container and kept in a cool, dry, dark location or frozen for long-term storage.

Capsicum spp. - Peppers

Capsicum annum - Sweet and Chili Peppers
C. baccatum - Kellu-uchu
C. frutescens - Tabasco and Squash Pepper
C. pubescens - Manzano

Peppers were cultivated in Central America and South America centuries before the arrival of Columbus. Most wild peppers have high concentrations of capsaicin, the hot compound found in some types of peppers. The highest concentrations of capsaicin are found in the pepper's interior walls (placental walls). The outer wall and even the immature seeds are rather mild until the capsaicin matures and is shed internally.

Peppers are perennial in warm climates, but are quickly killed by frost. Gardeners in cold areas can dig pepper plants from the garden in the fall and transfer them to a greenhouse for the winter. When the soil warms in the spring, the plants can be set back out in the garden for summer fruiting. In general the hotter the variety, the more tolerant it is to cool, wet weather.

Most pepper fruits are green during their immature stage and undergo color changes while ripening. In their ripe or mature state, peppers turn yellow, orange, red, purple or black. In most parts of the world, green peppers are considered unripe and are not commonly eaten. The widespread use of green peppers is unique to American cuisine.

BOTANICAL CLASSIFICATION

The genus _Capsicum_ contains five

cultivated species and 18 documented wild species. *Capsicum annuum* and *C. frutescens* are the only species of peppers that are grown in the United States. All of the bell peppers and hot peppers found in grocery stores are *C. annuum*.

Tabasco peppers, *C. frutescens*, are grown in tropical areas of the southeastern United States and are the key ingredient in Louisiana Tabasco Sauce. *C. frutescens* also includes several peppers native to the Amazon River Basin. The best known of these is the squash pepper, which is also known as rocotillo. Until recently squash peppers were considered to be members of *C. chinense*. Researchers were unable to find any morphological differences between *C. frutescens* and *C. chinense*, however, and are now recommending that the two species be combined into *C. frutescens*.

C. baccatum varieties are available from members of the Seed Savers Exchange and include escabeche, kellu-uchu and puca-uchu. The plants have very large leaves and large, white flowers. Growers in the United States report that varieties of *C. baccatum* appear to be daylength sensitive.

Plants of *C. pubescens* are covered with a light fuzz, hence their name, and have purple flowers and dark brown or black seeds. The plants are native to Mexico, Central America and high elevations in the Andes Mountains. *C. pubescens* can grow 6' tall with 8" diameter trunks. The plants need support in windy areas, but will tolerate excessive rains and cool climates. Both flowering and fruit set are triggered by short days. Manzano, rocoto, locoto and caballo are available on a limited basis from members of the Seed Savers Exchange.

Squash pepper (*Capsicum frutescens*) was formerly classified as *C. chinense*.

POLLINATION, CROSSING AND ISOLATION

The flowers of all peppers are perfect and self-pollinating. Insect cross-pollination is common, especially by honeybees and tiny sweat bees. A fairly recent study at New Mexico State University showed up to 80% crossing in some populations. Some studies report fruit set in certain varieties is greatly improved if insects visit the flowers, while other studies show little increase in fruit set due to insect visitation.

The pungent or hot gene is dominant in peppers. Sweet peppers that were grown next to hot peppers and then allowed to self-sow, probably account for garden tales of bell pepper volunteers turning hot.

Isolation of 500' is considered sufficient to ensure seed purity. When varieties are grown in closer proximity, caging is required. Only one variety of pepper should be grown in each cage, because ground-dwelling bees are capable of crossing all of the plants within a cage. In hot climates a cage covered with spun polyester acts as a shade cloth and helps reduce blossom drop, which is common in peppers when temperatures exceed 100° F.

Some varieties may need flower agitation or hand-pollination to induce fruit set. Remove the cage between 7-11 a.m. and gently rub or thump each flower. The rubbing simulates an insect visit and "trips" the flower, inducing pollination.

Pepper flowers can also be bagged to prevent crossing. In the evening identify ready-to-open flowers and place a tiny spun polyester bag over unopened blossoms. At the same time place a marker on the flower stem. If a fruit forms, the marker will identify it for seed saving. The marker and bag will fall off with the aborted flower if the fruit fails to form. Always bag blossoms on as many different plants of that variety as possible and then mix the seeds from those fruits at harvest time, which will help retain some variation within the population.

SEED PRODUCTION, HARVEST AND PROCESSING

Peppers seeds are ready for harvest when the fruit is fully mature. Select peppers that are ripe, fully colored and show no signs of disease. When cleaning large-fruited bell peppers, break or cut the flesh off without damaging the internal core. The stem should be left attached to the core and will act as a handle. The blade of a small knife can be used to carefully scrape the seeds off of the core and into a bowl.

Peppers can also be cleaned in a blender or food processor, if the flesh is not going to be eaten. Cut the stems off of the fleshless seed cores, adding enough water to cover the cores. Blend until the cores disintegrate and the seeds are free. Gently stir the mixture and the good seeds will sink to the bottom. The immature seeds and flesh fragments will float and can be poured off with part of the water. Add more water, blend the mixture, pour off more debris, and repeat until clean.

Small hot peppers can also be cleaned using a blender or food processor. Cut off their stems and a little bit of their shoulders, before putting the pods and water into the blender. Always wear thick rubber gloves when working with hot chilies. Chili oil is very pungent and will remain on unprotected fingers even after washing. Touching any area of the face with hands that contain chili oil residue can cause extreme discomfort. Also, be sure to clean chili peppers in a well-ventilated room, because the fumes can cause severe respiratory distress.

After all of the debris has been poured off, dump the remaining water and clean seeds into a strainer. Wipe the bottom of the strainer on a towel and dump the seeds out onto a dish or cookie sheet to dry.

Pepper seeds should be dried away

from direct sunlight, until the seeds break when folded. If the seeds bend instead of breaking, additional drying is necessary.

SEED VIABILITY

Pepper seeds will retain 50% germination for three years when stored in a cool, dry, dark area.

_____ *Lycopersicon spp.* - Tomatoes

Lycopersicon lycopersicon - Tomato
L. pimpinellifolium - Currant Tomato

Tomatoes were domesticated from wild perennial species in Mexico, Central America and South America. When Columbus took tomatoes back to Spain, the plants quickly spread throughout Europe and were considered a poisonous garden oddity. On their way from poisonous to popular, the attitudes of gardeners concerning tomato consumption went through a gradual transformation. The following advice from Harriott Horry's *Receipt Book* in 1602 is typical: "It is alright, but not advisable, to eat the tomato, if it is thoroughly cooked. Tomatoes should never be eaten raw as death

Diversity abounds in the shapes, sizes and colors of tomatoes (*Lycopersicon spp.*).

will be instantaneous."

Although a rich red color is standard for today's tomatoes, many other colors exist. Heirloom varieties include fruit colors of white, lime green, lemon yellow, yellow with red stripes, gold, persimmon, orange, pink, and purple.

BOTANICAL CLASSIFICATION

Garden tomatoes belong to the genus *Lycopersicon* and the species *lycopersicon* (formerly *L. esculentum*). Currant tomatoes, *L. pimpinellifolium*, have red fruits that are only 1/4" in diameter and grow in clusters. Crossing between different varieties of *L. pimpinellifolium* is common.

POLLINATION, CROSSING AND ISOLATION

The extent of cross-pollination in tomatoes has been a controversy among seed savers for a long time. Some say that crossing is rampant, while others have never seen crossing after years of growing different varieties next to one another. Charlie Rick, whose tomato breeding accomplishments are legendary, describes the evolution of the tomato in *Potential Genetic Resources in Tomato Species* (1952). "The ancestral tomato species could not reproduce by self-pollination.... It had a long style, extending far beyond the anther tube, to facilitate cross-pollination by insects.... As this ancestral species evolved into the wild predecessor of the cultivated tomato it developed the ability to self-pollinate.... With this development, the style became shorter but still protruded beyond the anther tube.... As the tomato migrated northward, the style continued to shorten and in some species totally retracted inside the anther tube,

precluding any possibility of insect crossing...."

Most modern tomato varieties have totally retracted styles. Such flower structure severely limits (and may totally preclude) any crossing between these varieties. Three groups of tomato varieties have been found to have protruding styles however: currant tomatoes, *L. pimpinellifolium;* all of the potato-leaved varieties of *L. lycopersicon;* and any fruit formed from double blossoms on beefsteak types of *L. lycopersicon.* Potato-leaved tomatoes have rampant vines and smooth-edged leaves that resemble the leaves of a potato plant.

Although not all tomato varieties have been examined, most modern varieties available commercially will not cross with one another due to their retracted styles. Seed savers should therefore have no problem with cross-pollination when growing one currant tomato, or one potato-leaved variety and any number of modern varieties with styles that are covered by their anther tubes. Caging can be used to prevent crossing when more than one variety of *L. pimpinellifolium* or more than one potato-leaved variety of *L. lycopersicon* are grown in close proximity. Double blossoms, commonly seen in amongst the early flowers of beefsteak tomatoes, often have exposed stigmas, making them more prone to insect cross-pollination. Seeds should not be saved from double fruits for this reason.

To determine the style position for any given tomato variety, choose 10-20 new blossoms from several different plants. Examine each blossom with a magnifying glass to see if the style is recessed or protruding. The anther tube will open as the fruit forms, so it is important to choose newly opened blossoms.

Most tomato varieties will set more fruit if the flowers are agitated or tripped. This increases the amount of pollen traveling down the anther tube. The wind usually provides sufficient agitation, but fans are often used to simulate the wind in greenhouse situations. Daily shaking can be used to increase flower set in caged plants.

SEED PRODUCTION, HARVEST AND PROCESSING

Paste and slicing tomatoes are particularly easy for seed saving. The seeds can be saved and the fruit can be eaten or processed without any waste. Pick and wash fully ripe tomatoes, and then cut the fruits across the middle, not through the stem and blossom ends. This exposes the large seed cavities and makes the seeds accessible without mashing the fruit. Now squeeze the seeds and surrounding gel into a bowl or bucket.

The same process can be used for cherry and currant tomatoes, however grinding the fruits is far easier. Place the clean, fully ripe fruits in a blender or a food processor fitted with a metal blade. Process until all of the fruits are mashed and the mixture is very thick. The small, hard seeds will not be

Left: Seeds and gel are squeezed into a labeled deli tub. Right: After about three days a thick layer of fungus will have grown across the surface of the mixture.

damaged. To aid in seed separation, add one cup of water to each cup of mashed fruit and stir.

Each tomato seed is encased in a gelatinous sack. The gel in these sacks contains chemicals that inhibit seed germination, which prevents the seeds from sprouting inside the wet flesh of the tomato. In nature the ripe tomatoes fall from the plant and slowly rot. The rotting away of the fruits is a natural fermentation process during which the gel sacks are destroyed. Eventually the fruits totally rot away leaving the seeds on the surface of the soil, ready to germinate when conditions are right.

Artificially duplicating the tomato fruit's fermentation process is not difficult. In addition to removing the gel sack, fermentation also kills many seed-borne tomato diseases. The container of tomato seeds and gel should be set aside to ferment for about three days. The mixture needs to be stirred twice daily. Fermentation will proceed more quickly as the daytime temperatures increase.

During this period the container of seeds will begin to stink and will become covered with a layer of white or gray mold. Because of the horrible smell, do not keep the bowl in the house or where it might be tipped over

Left: Seeds, liquid and fungus are poured into a strainer. Right: The seeds are washed until clean by rubbing the mixture against the strainer under running water.

by animals or children. The fermentation process should be stopped when bubbles can be seen rising in the mixture or when the layer of mold completely covers its surface. If allowed to continue too long, the seeds will begin to germinate in the mixture.

Add enough water to double the mixture and then stir it vigorously. The good seeds will settle to the bottom of the container, allowing the mold and debris and hollow seeds to be poured off. Add more water and repeat the process until only clean seeds remain.

Pour the seeds into a strainer. Wipe the bottom of the strainer on a towel to remove as much moisture as possible and dump the seeds out on a glass or ceramic dish to dry. Do not attempt to dry the seeds on paper or cloth or non-rigid plastic, as it is extremely difficult to remove the seeds from these surfaces.

To ensure even drying and to prevent the seeds from bunching together, stir at least twice a day. Never dry seeds in direct sunlight or in an oven. Tomato seeds will begin to germinate if not dried quickly. In hot humid weather, a fan will help speed the drying process.

SEED VIABILITY

Tomato seeds will remain viable for 4-10 years depending on the variety. Completely dried seeds should be sealed in an airtight container and stored in a cool, dry area or frozen for long-term storage.

_____ *Physalis spp.* - Husk Tomatoes, Tomatillos, etc. _____

Physalis alkekingi - Chinese Lantern
P. ixocarpa - Tomatillo (Mexican Husk Tomato)
P. peruviana - Cape Gooseberry (Poha)
P. philadelphica - Wild Tomatillo
P. pruinosa - Strawberry Tomato (Dwarf Cape Gooseberry)
P. pubescens - Downy Ground Cherry (Yellow Husk Tomato)
P. subglabrata - Purple Ground Cherry

The genus *Physalis* includes several species that are little appreciated in the United States, but are widely grown in other parts of the world. Tomatillos, *P. ixocarpa* and *P. philadelphica*, are staples in Mexican cuisine. Translations of Mexican recipes often refer to tomatillos as green tomatoes, which can be confusing for the cook. Tomatillos have a distinctive flavor and texture. They resemble green tomatoes in color only. Tomatillos have small, hard, green fruits that are enclosed in tan, papery husks. As the fruit grows, the husk becomes increasingly filled until, at full maturity, the fruits actually split the husks open.

Chinese lantern, *P. alkekingi*, has very small, edible fruits that are encased in bright red husks. Their small, lantern-like husks are often used in dry arrangements. *P. alkekingi* is sometimes called strawberry tomato.

The other species of Physalis are commonly known as ground cherry, husk tomato, poha, golden berry and cape gooseberry. All of their fruits are formed inside a tan husk and range from 1/4"-1" in diameter. The fruits do

Zuni tomatillo (*Physalis philadelphica*), left, and Large Green tomatillo (*Physalis ixocarpa*), right.

not split the husks open when mature, but simply fall off the plant. Gathering these fallen fruits is the easiest way to harvest. Ground cherries can be eaten out of hand, made into pies, jams, sauces, or dried for use in fruit cakes.

BOTANICAL CLASSIFICATION

Tomatillos belong to the genus *Physalis* and the species *ixocarpa*. *P. ixocarpa* are multibranched and usually sprawl on the ground. The plants can be grown in tomato cages to conserve garden space.

There is a good deal of confusion over the species characteristics, botanical classifications and common names for *P. peruviana*, *P. pruinosa* and *P. pubescens*. While *P. peruviana* is a perennial and will tolerate some frost, *P. pruinosa* and *P. pubescens* are said to be annual plants. Another species, *P. subglabrata*, has sweet purple fruits which make identification a bit easier. Perennial species can grow 4-5' tall and take up a square yard of garden space, but pruning and staking reduces their sprawling nature.

Seed companies often incorrectly refer to tomatillo as ground cherry and rarely list the correct botanical names for various Physalis species. Confusion over the botanical classifications is unlikely to clear up until a definitive study of the genus is completed.

POLLINATION, CROSSING AND ISOLATION

All of the species of Physalis have flowers that are perfect and self-pollinating. Tomatillo, *P. ixocarpa*, will not cross with any other Physalis species. There is widespread confusion about the classification of other Physalis species, so isolation or caging is recommended for seed purity.

SEED PRODUCTION, HARVEST AND PROCESSING

Fully ripe tomatillos and ground cherries are easy to save for seed. Select fruits from as many different plants as possible. The paper husks are removed and the berries are placed in a blender or food processor with enough water to cover them. The seeds, which are small and slippery, will not be harmed by the metal blades. When the fruits are totally blended, empty the contents into a large bowl. Add enough water to double the mixture, stir vigorously and allow the good seeds to settle to the bottom. Gently pour off the debris and hollow seeds. Add more water and repeat the process until only clean seeds and water remain.

The clean seeds are poured through a strainer, but always be very sure that the seeds are not small enough to pass through the strainer's holes. Wipe the bottom of the strainer on a towel to remove as much moisture as possible and dump the seeds out on a glass or ceramic dish to dry.

SEED VIABILITY

Physalis seeds will remain viable for three years when stored in cool, dry, dark conditions.

Solanum spp. - Eggplant

Solanum melongena - Eggplant
S. integrifolium - Tomato-Fruited Eggplant

Eggplants originated in India from bitter-fruited, spiny plants. Centuries of selection and cultivation have produced fruits whose bitterness has been almost eliminated. Records in China show that a non-bitter variety appeared in the 5th century B.C. Eggplants then traveled to Spain, Africa and Italy, where further development resulted in the varieties known today.

The first eggplants grown in Europe were probably small, white, egg-shaped types. Such varieties may have been responsible for eggplant receiving its English name.

Eggplants are perennial, but do not tolerate frost. Cuttings can be rooted, overwintered in a greenhouse, and then set out when the weather warms up the following spring.

BOTANICAL CLASSIFICATION

Eggplants belong to the genus *Solanum* and the species *melongena*. The plants of various varieties of *S. melongena* range from 1-8' in height. The fruits vary from the size of pearls to huge sword-shaped fruits over 18" long. Fruit color is just as variable and includes varieties that are light green, white (maturing to yellow), pink, purple, and white with purple stripes.

Red-fruited and orange-fruited eggplants belong to the genus *Solanum* and the species *integrifolium*. Both bitter and non-bitter types of *S.*

Bright orange, tomato-fruited eggplant (*Solanum integrifolium*).

integrifolium are cultivated in Asia and Africa. Their fruits lack a solid interior and are sometimes referred to as tomato-fruited eggplants or gilos. The plants grow 2-3' tall with fruits that rarely exceed 2" in diameter. Some of the wild types have tiny, bitter, orange fruits that are the size of peas.

POLLINATION, CROSSING AND ISOLATION

Eggplant flowers are perfect and are primarily self-pollinated. Some studies indicate that eggplant pollination is enhanced by insects, while other studies have demonstrated that just as many fruits form on caged plants as form on uncaged plants. Eggplant flowers are not particularly attractive to honeybees, but bumblebees and some solitary bees will work the flowers.

Cross-pollination can be prevented by isolation of 50' or by caging. Bagging the individual flowers is possible, but tedious. Cages covered with spun polyester or screen wire should be in place very early in the season before the flea beetles appear. Any flea beetles that are trapped inside the cage will continue to seriously damage the plants.

SEED PRODUCTION, HARVEST AND PROCESSING

Always grow as many eggplants of each variety as possible to maintain the greatest amount of variation within a population. Six plants should be considered an absolute minimum. Depending on the variety and the length of the growing season, several eggplants can be harvested for eating before the fruits that will be saved for seed are allowed to mature.

To save seeds from eggplants, let the fruits grow far past the edible stage. All eggplants change color when fully ripe: purple varieties become a dull purplish brown; green fruits turn yellowish green; and white fruits turn golden. At their ripe, inedible stage, the fruits are dull, off-color and hard. Seeds saved from immature or ready-to-eat eggplants will not be viable.

Several references have described saving seeds from eggplant fruits that are fully ripe but not rotten. This would seem to contradict nature, as the fruits must rot in order for the seeds to reach the soil and germinate. In most varieties, seeds from partially rotten fruits have germinated well. Harvested fruits can be held at room temperature for several weeks before cleaning. The firm, brown seeds are usually located in the bottom portion of the fruit.

Anyone who has ever picked seeds one by one out of eggplant flesh will appreciate the following method. Grate or blend the bottom portion of the eggplant, which contains the greatest seed density, using a hand grater or food processor. The small brown seeds are firm and slippery, so there is very little damage. The grating exposes the maximum number of seeds to the surface of the flesh. Put all of the gratings in a bowl or bucket which can hold at least twice that capacity. Some of the seeds will have popped free of the flesh and should also be put into the bowl. Add water to within 2" of the rim, roll up your sleeves and begin squeezing the gratings vigorously. The good seeds will come free and will sink to the bottom, and the grated flesh will float. Continue squeezing until very few seeds are left in the flesh. The grated flesh is then lifted out of the bucket and can be fed to the chickens or composted.

Another seed cleaning method requires a food processor with a blunt plastic blade or a blender. Cut the bottom portion of an eggplant into 1/2" squares. Turn on the food processor or blender and gradually add the eggplant cubes. Pour in a bit of water and continue adding the cubes. When the receptacle is full, dump the eggplant mash into a bowl. Repeat if more cubes remain. Add fresh water to the bowl, stir the mixture, let the good seeds settle, and pour off the debris. Repeat until only clean seeds remain in the bottom of the bowl. Add more water and pour through a strainer. Dry the bottom of the strainer on a towel and dump the seeds out onto a glass or ceramic plate. Spread the seeds evenly over the surface of the plate and stir twice daily to ensure even drying, which prevents the seeds from bunching together.

SEED VIABILITY

Eggplant seeds will maintain 50% germination for seven years. Seeds should be stored in a tightly sealed container in a cool, dry, dark location. Thoroughly dry seeds sealed in an airtight container can also be frozen for long-term storage.

Solanum spp. - Sunberry, Huckleberry and Nightshade

Solanum burbankii - Sunberry (Wonderberry)
S. melanocerasum - Garden Huckleberry
S. nigrum - Common Nightshade (Poisonberry)

Sunberry was introduced by Luther Burbank and classified as _Solanum burbankii_. Great controversy immediately arose about its origins, because many people claimed that Burbank had simply reintroduced _S. nigrum_, the common garden huckleberry, as a new plant. In 1957 Charles Heiser set out to put the matter to rest and reexamined the sunberry. Although sunberry does resemble _S. nigrum_ somewhat, its berries are blue and slightly sweet in flavor while common nightshade has dullish black, acrid fruits.

The berries of _S. burbankii_, _S. melanocerasum_ and _S. nigrum_ have long suffered under the same misapprehensions once associated with tomatoes. Talk of poison invariably enters any discussion of huckleberries and usually scares off even the most adventurous. All three species, however, are eaten by various cultures around the world. Even the leaves are cooked for greens in Africa.

Although some varieties may have slightly toxic leaves, the toxicity is destroyed by cooking. Also, studies indicate that the fruits of these three species are not poisonous. This is not to suggest that all small black Solanum fruits picked in the wild are edible. It is best to obtain seeds of known varieties and to grow the plants intentionally. The berries from all three can be used in jams, pies and preserves.

BOTANICAL CLASSIFICATION

Sunberry, which is sometimes called wonderberry, belongs to the genus _Solanum_ and the species _burbankii_. _S. burbankii_ has 1/4" deep blue fruits that are covered with a white bloom.

Garden huckleberries, which belong to _S. melanocerasum_, are commonly grown in the tropics of western Africa. The 3-5' branched plants produce 1/2" shiny black berries.

Common nightshade, which is sometimes called poisonberry or schwartzbeeren, belongs to _S. nigrum_. The multibranched plants grow 18" tall and produce 1/4" dull black fruits that have a strong acrid taste.

POLLINATION, CROSSING AND ISOLATION

Sunberry, garden huckleberry and common nightshade all have flowers that are perfect and self-pollinating. The three species do not cross with one another. If unique varieties were to become available, however, different varieties within each species could be insect-crossed and would require isolation of 50' or caging to maintain seed purity.

Volunteer seedlings usually provide more than enough plants for growing and trading. Seeds need only be collected for preservation and exchange purposes.

SEED PRODUCTION, HARVEST AND PROCESSING

Select fully ripe berries from as many different plants as possible. Grind the berries in a food processor or blender, or squeeze each berry by hand. The berries do not need to be washed or have their stems removed, and a small amount of water can be added during grinding. The blended mixture is poured into a bowl, more water is added, and the mixture is stirred to encourage separation. The good seeds sink to the bottom of the bowl, while the skins, stems and immature seeds will float. The floating debris should be poured off very slowly and carefully. Add more water, stir, pour off the floating matter, repeat this process until only clean seeds remain at the bottom of the bowl. Pour the seeds into a strainer, wipe the bottom of the strainer on a towel to remove moisture, and dump the seeds onto a glass or ceramic dish to dry.

SEED STORAGE

There is no known germination study for sunberries, garden huckleberries, or common nightshade, but experience would suggest that at least 50% germination would be maintained for four years.

Solanum tuberosum - Potato

Potatoes originated in the mountainous regions of Peru where Indian farmers once grew more than 3,000 varieties. The introduction of the potato into Europe is rather obscure. Various references describe the potato as first being grown in the Netherlands, France, Russia and Switzerland. Today the vast majority of the world's potatoes are produced in Europe. The Soviet Union leads all other nations in consuming the most potatoes per person.

Gardeners throughout the United States have recently been introduced to yellow, blue, purple, and striped potatoes. Purple-fleshed potatoes are just as savory as their white counterparts and are a real conversation piece at the dinner table. Yellow-fleshed potatoes appear to have already been buttered.

SEED PRODUCTION, HARVEST AND PROCESSING

Potatoes grown for food are usually planted from tuber cuttings, so those plants are clones of the parent plant. Potatoes are also sometimes raised from true seeds, by either potato breeders or by amateur experimenters.

Potato blossoms will occasionally produce a small, hard, green fruit. The seeds contained in these seed balls do not come true-to-type; nearly every seed will produce a different variety.

Potato seed balls should be picked about two months after they form, when they are completely mature and a bit soft. At this stage they often fall off the plant. Squeeze the seeds from the fruits into a bowl and add enough water to cover. The good seeds will sink to the bottom of the bowl. Add more water, pour off the debris, drain and dry the seeds. Some research suggests that a fermentation period of two to three days may aid germination. Potato seeds germinate best at 60° F. and are treated like tomato seedlings.

Potatoes are almost always propagated vegetatively by planting whole or cut tubers. Unfortunately, viral diseases and root knot nematodes are often carried in the tubers, and several states, including California and Florida, prohibit the importation of non-certified seed potatoes for this reason.

Tuber-transmitted diseases and pests can usually be eliminated by

A few of the 600 potato varieties (*Solanum tuberosum*) being maintained by the Seed Savers Exchange.

utilizing the following method. Plant the tubers in a large pot, using a sterile potting mix. Let the shoots grow 6-8" tall and then cut them off at least 2" above the soil mix. Do not allow the growing shoots to bend over and touch the potting mix, and never let the cut shoots come in contact with it. The shoots are then planted in a flat filled with previously unused sterile soil. The original tuber and the potting medium should be burned to prevent contamination or disease transmission. The sprouts will root in the flat in about 10 days and can be planted into the garden as soon as a good root system has formed.

Cuttings from potato plants can also be taken and rooted whenever weather or insects threaten the crop. Rooted plants can be maintained in a cool greenhouse for up to a year.

Late potato varieties are the best candidates for winter storage. After curing, pack the tubers in baskets or boxes. Avoid storing potatoes near apples. Potatoes will keep for 4-6 months when stored between 32-40° F. and 80-90% humidity.

_____ Lesser Grown Solanaceae _____

Cyphomandra betacea - Tree Tomato (Tamarillo)

Tree tomato, sometimes called tamarillo, is native to Mexico and grown commercially in Australia. The shrub-like plants can grow 10' tall, but are extremely frost tender and will not overwinter in most areas. Tree tomato plants take about 18 months to produce fruit when grown from seeds. The plants reach full production in 3-4 years. In mild winter areas, the fruits mature from October to December. Red and yellow fruited varieties are available from several seed companies in the United States.

Tree tomato flowers are perfect, but must be tripped or agitated for pollination to occur. Different varieties can be insect-crossed, so the flowers must be bagged or taped to maintain seed purity if more than one variety is being grown in close proximity.

Harvest fully ripe fruits and squeeze or pick the seeds out of the fruit. Using a strainer, wash the seeds thoroughly and then dry and store as with other Solanum species.

Solanum muricatum - Pepino

Pepino is native to Peru and is grown commercially in Australia. The plants are easily started from seeds. The flowers are perfect, but require tripping for self-pollination to occur. Different varieties can be insect-crossed. The plants are perennial, multibranched, 2' shrublets.

Pepino fruits are often light greenish yellow, and some also have purple streaks or stripes. Pepino tastes like a cross between a cucumber and a sweet melon, and is usually eaten fresh or in fruit salads. Pepino plants are available from nurseries specializing in tropicals.

Solanum quitoense - Naranjilla

Naranjilla is widely grown in Ecuador for fresh juice. The yellow 2" fruits are filled with a green, gelatinous pulp which is sieved to prepare drinks and sauces. The plants grow for about seven months before flowering and take six more months to produce mature fruits.

Naranjilla plants quickly die in cold, wet soil. The plants are also very susceptible to damage from several different nematodes and do not tolerate any frost.

The stems and leaves of naranjillas are covered with soft, purple hairs. Plants can grow to 5' during their commercial production period, which usually lasts four years. In Ecuador the plants are grown in frost-free valleys at 3,500-7,500'. Seeds and plants are both available commercially in the United States.

THE UMBELLIFERAE FAMILY

The Umbelliferae family includes those groups of plants that have umbrella-shaped flowers. The "pedicels" (individual stems of each flower) radiate from a common point on the stalk. The family is very large with over 200 species. Many are oily and aromatic, and some are poisonous. Carrots, celery, fennel and parsnips are among the most commonly grown vegetables. Dill, parsley and coriander, which are commonly grown as annuals in the vegetable garden, have also been included.

FAMILY TAXONOMY

All members of the Umbelliferae family have flowers which are referred to as umbels. The main seed stalk initially forms the primary umbel, which contains the highest quality seeds. Additional branches form lower on the seed stalk and produce secondary umbels, usually smaller than the primary umbels. Smaller still are the tertiary umbels that form on small branches along the stalks of the secondary umbels.

The umbels develop and mature over a period of 30-40 days. The primary umbels mature first, then the secondary umbels, and finally the tertiary umbels. The maturation process may not be complete until the hottest part of the summer, and the seeds can be damaged when temperatures exceed 100° F. Some growers harvest the seed crop when the primary and secondary umbels are mature, rather than risk damaging their high quality seeds while waiting for the tertiary umbels.

Umbelliferae family members are often divided into those that produce roots and those grown for their foliage. The root crops are biennial, and must be overwintered before producing seeds during their second season.

Several Umbelliferae family members are poisonous. Never presume that all wild plants with umbels are edible.

Umbelliferae in the Garden		
Genus	**Species**	**Common Name**
Apium	*graveolens*	celery, celeriac
Anethum	*graveolens*	dill
Anthriscus	*cerefolium*	chervil
Arracacia	*xanthorrhiza*	Peruvian carrot
Chaerophyllum	*bulbosum*	turnip-rooted chervil
Coriandrum	*sativium*	coriander
Daucus	*carota*	carrot
Foeniculum	*vulgare*	fennel
Pastinaca	*sativa*	parsnip
Petroselinum	*crispum*	parsley, parsley root
Sium	*sisarum*	skirret

POLLINATION CHARACTERISTICS AND TECHNIQUES

Umbelliferae flowers are perfect, but cannot self-pollinate. The anthers shed pollen before the stigma is receptive. The individual flowers on each flower head open over a long period and the stigmas are receptive for 5-7 days depending on the genus. Thus, some of the flowers on any umbel will be shedding pollen and some will be receptive at the same time.

Honeybees and other hairy insects move pollen from one flower to another. In experiments where all insects

---

Facing Page: Harvesting dill (*Anethum graveolens*) seed.

were prevented from visiting the plants, only about 10% of the flowers produced seeds. The pollination that did occur was attributed to the flower bags rubbing back and forth across the flower heads on windy days.

Three methods can be used to save pure seeds of Umbelliferae. The easiest method is isolation. Depending on the size of the crop and the local geography, three miles is usually considered sufficient. In some areas weeds will also have to be controlled. Queen Anne's lace (wild carrot) and wild fennel are examples of weeds that will contaminate a seed crop.

Hand-pollination is also possible with Umbelliferae crops. For good seed production, the flowers must be hand-pollinated every day for at least two weeks and preferably for 30 days. The immature umbels are bagged before any of their flowers open. At least 10 umbels of each variety should be covered using Reemay bags, corn tassel bags, paper sacks or cloth bags. Secure each bag with a removable string or plastic twist tie. Each morning between 7:00-11:00, debag as many flower heads as can be kept free of insects. Rub a camel hair brush over the open flowers, moving from head to head and back again. Cover each flower head twice in rotation. This will help ensure that some of the flowers receive pollen from another plant. Rebag the flowers and repeat the process daily. The bags can be removed when all of the seeds have set, but be sure to tag the hand-pollinated umbels.

Bagged umbels may also be pollinated using the palm of the hand. Although not as effective as using a brush, this technique may be useful with carrots or when using similar techniques for seed-producing onions.

After unbagging the umbels (or onion seed heads), gently rub the palm of the hand over the umbel in a circular motion. This helps insure that pollen will come in contact with receptive florets. Always be careful to just barely touch the umbel, so that the tiny styles will not be damaged. Check your palm for tiny streaks of yellow pollen before moving to the next umbel. Keep as much pollen on the palm as possible while moving from one flower head to the next, so that each umbel will receive pollen from several other plants. All of the umbels must be kept free of insects while you work. Rebag each of the umbels and thoroughly wash your hands, arms, and under your fingernails before working with the next variety.

Two caging methods can be used with umbels. Alternate day caging is the easier method and requires that a cage be constructed for each of the varieties. Each morning one cage is removed; each evening that cage is replaced and an alternate cage is removed the next morning. This method allows insects to pollinate each variety for one day and excludes insects the next. Of course, this method requires isolation from any plants of the same species and any wild relatives. Once all of the seeds have set and flowering has stopped, the cages are no longer needed. Remember to tag the plants that were caged.

Caging with introduced pollinators, a rather complicated and expensive method for the home seed saver, is discussed in Section I.

GENERAL PRODUCTION AND PROCESSING TECHNIQUES

Two different methods are used for growing biennial Umbelliferae. The most common is the seed-to-root-to-seed method. Seeds are planted in the spring and the crop grows to maturity. The roots are carefully dug in the fall, examined and sorted. Healthy roots that are true-to-type are stored through the winter months. In mild winter areas the roots can be replanted almost immediately. In colder climates the roots are replanted in the spring, and the plant that results eventually produces a seed stalk.

In mild winter areas it is also possible to grow biennial Umbelliferae using the seed-to-seed method. The crop is planted in the summer or early fall, grows throughout the winter and bolts to seed during the next spring. Although this method is much less time-consuming, the roots cannot be examined and sorted, so any off-type roots are not removed before cross-pollination occurs. If there is any question about the purity of seeds involved, always use the seed-to-root-to-seed method.

The umbels are cut from the plant when the seeds are fully formed. If further drying is necessary, the umbels can be dried in the sun when temperatures are below 90° F. and then covered at night to protect from the dew.

It is easiest to rub the umbels over a screen to remove the seeds and break up the seed heads. Cleaner seed can be harvested from fully mature, dry umbels attached to slightly green stems. Gently rub the umbels between the hands. Most of the chaff can be removed by screening. Winnowing is sometimes difficult because the seeds are very light.

Apium graveolens - Celery and Celeriac

Celery is 94% water, which makes it a great diet food. Some dieters claim that chewing celery uses more calories than the stalks contain. Despite its low food value, celery is the third most common salad ingredient in the United States.

Wild celery, sometimes called smallage, can be found growing in damp and marshy areas from Sweden to Algeria and also throughout Asia. The wild varieties are rather bitter and were first used by the Greeks as a medicine. Not until the 16th century does the literature indicate that celery was being used as food. At that time the plants were probably very bitter and strong tasting. The stalks were covered with earth and blanched to make them more palatable. Through consistent selection, the stalks became larger and more commonly used as a vegetable rather than as a medicine or seasoning.

Celeriac, also known as celery root or knob celery, was selected specifically for its roots rather than for its foliage. Celeriac roots are usually harvested when about baseball size after a full season of growth, taste somewhat like celery, and are used both cooked and raw. Celeriac is much less particular about growing conditions than celery, and is easily grown throughout the United States.

BOTANICAL CLASSIFICATION

Celery and celeriac are biennials and belong to the genus _Apium_ and the species _graveolens_. Self-blanching celery varieties are usually grown and sold through grocery stores in the United States. In Europe the stalks are still earthed up or wrapped with paper to produce blanched or white celery. Yellow, golden and pink celery varieties have garnered popularity at various times, but are rarely grown commercially.

POLLINATION, CROSSING AND ISOLATION

Celery flowers, like the flowers of other members of the Umbelliferae family, shed pollen before the stigma is receptive. Therefore, the crop relies on insects for pollination. All celery varieties will cross with one another as well as with smallage and celeriac. Celery does not cross with lovage. Isolation, bagging or caging are necessary to prevent cross-pollination between varieties. Pollination techniques are described in the introductory pages of the Umbelliferae family.

SEED PRODUCTION, HARVEST AND PROCESSING

Some gardeners harvest a few outer stalks of celery without pulling the plant out of the ground. This practice can increase the chances of plant injury and disease. If only a few stalks are carefully removed and the plant is not damaged, however, seed production should not be harmed. Celeriac leaves can also be lightly harvested during the growing season without diminishing the seed crop.

In mild climates, both types of *A. graveolens* can be overwintered in the ground. Where winters are severe, the plants must be dug and stored in a root cellar. Celery plants should be trimmed back rather severely and stored in damp earth or sand with the crowns exposed. Celeriac roots should be carefully dug, all side roots trimmed, and tops trimmed to 2". Celeriac will keep for 3-4 months when stored in slightly damp sawdust, leaves or sand at 32-40° F. and 90% humidity.

After being replanted in the garden the following spring, the plants will develop flower stalks that must be prevented from crossing, as was already discussed. Celery's primary umbels mature first and often shatter before the secondary umbels are dry. It is best to hand harvest the umbels as they mature. The seeds can be separated easily as the umbels are harvested and will be fairly clean. Any remaining dust and debris can be removed by screening or winnowing.

SEED VIABILITY

Celery seeds will maintain 50% germination for at least eight years when stored under cool, dry, dark conditions.

_____ *Daucus carota* - Carrot _____

Carrots are the most important commercial member of the Umbelliferae family. Wild carrots are found throughout Asia, Africa, Europe and the Americas. Carrot roots were first used as medicine, but gradually gained importance as a food crop. Records indicate that carrots were first cultivated in Europe about the 10th century. By the 1600s carrots had become such an important crop that early American settlers are known to have brought several varieties from Europe.

BOTANICAL CLASSIFICATION

Carrots are biennial and belong to the genus *Daucus* and the species *carota*. Orange-colored carrot varieties

Carrot plants (*Daucus carota*) in full bloom.

are by far the most common, but white, yellow, red, purple, and black varieties are also available. Yellow and orange carrot varieties are high in provitamin A, while white carrots contain very little. The anthocyanin pigment in red, purple and black varieties does not contribute to their vitamin content.

Carrots range from 2-36" in length. The shorter varieties have been developed for heavy clay soils. Varieties are usually referred to as round, stubby, triangular or tapered.

POLLINATION, CROSSING AND ISOLATION

Carrots are insect-pollinated and attract a wide variety of insects. All carrot varieties will cross with one an-

other as well as with Queen Anne's lace, which is a wild carrot. Carrot varieties being grown for seed must be isolated by 1/2 mile. Techniques for hand-pollination and caging are described in the introductory pages of the Umbelliferae family.

Wild carrots can be a significant source of seed contamination. In areas where Queen Anne's lace is a common weed, isolation is nearly impossible. Even the carrot umbels inside cages made of window screen must be staked, because bees will cross any flowers that touch the sides of the cage. White root color is dominant in carrots, so crossing with the white-rooted Queen Anne's lace will eventually become visible. Such crossing in carrots often becomes apparent in a

Left and Center: Carrot (*Daucus carota*).
Right: Queen Anne's lace or wild carrot (also *D. carota*).

change in root color during the follow-ing generations. Extra care must be taken when growing white carrot vari-eties in areas where Queen Anne's lace is growing, because a change in root color will not be obvious.

SEED PRODUCTION, CROSSING AND ISOLATION

Carrots are best grown using the seed-to-root-to-seed method described in the general production techniques in the introductory pages of the Um-belliferae family. If this is impractical for gardeners in mild winter areas, at least dig down around each root to

make sure it is the right color and right shape before letting the crop go to seed. Gardeners in northern areas should dig carrot roots before a hard freeze. Clip the tops to 1" above the ground, trim the roots to 3", and store in sawdust, sand or leaves. Carrots will store for 6-8 months at 32-40° F. and 90% humidity.

The carrot umbels produced during the second season can be left to dry in the garden, or can be cut when fully mature and air dried for an additional two to three weeks. Many growers harvest the entire crop when the pri-mary and secondary umbels are be-ginning to dry, since those umbels produce the best seeds. Home gar-deners can gather the seeds as each of the umbels dries to a brown color. Some seed savers harvest, clean and save all seeds from the primary umbels separately.

All carrot seeds have a beard or hairs on the seed coat. That may come as a surprise, if you have never seen home-saved carrot seeds. When com-mercial carrot seeds are cleaned, the beard is removed to make the seeds easier to package. Debearding is not necessary and does not affect germi-nation.

Carrot seeds can be easily cleaned by rubbing the umbels over a 22 mesh (1/22") screen. The seeds will fall through such a screen and be partially debearded in the process. A second screening using a much smaller screen will remove any remaining dust and loose hairs. Carrot seeds are very light and should be winnowed with care.

SEED VIABILITY

Carrot seeds will maintain a high rate of germination for three years, af-ter which the rate falls off very quickly.

Petroselinum crispum - Parsley and Parsley Root

Curly leaf varieties of parsley are the most commonly used garnish in the world. Flat leaf varieties are usually processed into dried parsley flakes which are widely used for flavoring. Hamburg parsley, also known as parsley root or turnip rooted parsley, is savored in Europe but not often grown in the United States. Its leaves are flat and can be used as either a garnish or an herb. The roots are harvested after a full season of growth and have a mild parsley flavor when used like parsnips in soups and stews.

BOTANICAL CLASSIFICATION

All types and varieties of parsley belong to the genus _Petroselinum_ and the species _crispum_. Parsley is a biennial and does not cross with any other vegetable species.

POLLINATION, CROSSING AND ISOLATION

Parsley plants produce umbels which rely on insects for pollination. Like other Umbelliferae family members, a large variety of insects visits parsley flowers. A wild parsley exists that is native to Europe where it crosses with cultivated parsley, but the plant is not common in the United States. Isolation of one mile is commonly recommended for commercial crops. When more than one variety of parsley is grown in close proximity, use the hand-pollination or caging techniques described in the introductory pages of the Umbelliferae family.

SEED PRODUCTION, HARVEST AND PROCESSING

Parsley varieties can be lightly picked during the first year without harming the quantity or quality of the seed harvest. All varieties can be overwintered in the ground where winters are mild. Leaf parsley varieties store best when cut back and actually planted in earth or sand with their crowns exposed in a storage area where a temperature of 32-40° F. can be maintained all winter. Although somewhat cold-tender, parsley will tolerate below zero temperatures in the ground when covered with 2-3' of straw or leaves. Parsley root should be carefully dug, and then tops are trimmed to 2" and all side roots are removed. The roots will keep 3-4 months when stored in sawdust, leaves or sand at 32-40° F. and 90% humidity.

Parsley seed heads, produced after replanting the next spring, will shatter easily and are usually harvested individually as each one becomes dry. The primary and secondary umbels will produce the highest quality seeds. The seeds that are dry can be rubbed off of the umbel during harvest. If the seeds are fully formed but not completely dry, the umbel can be cut and dried further. Small stems and other debris can be removed by winnowing or reverse screening. A very fine mesh screen will remove dust and small debris, while leaving the seeds on top of the screen.

SEED VIABILITY

Parsley seeds will retain 50% germination for three years when stored under optimum conditions.

_____ Lesser Grown Umbelliferae _____

Anethum graveolens - Dill

A seed head of dill is an essential ingredient in most cucumber pickle recipes. Dry dill seeds are also used to flavor breads, pickles and stews. Several shorter varieties of dill have recently been developed.

Dill will not cross with any other vegetables or herbs. Different varieties of dill can be crossed by insects. Dill is

an annual and goes quickly to seed. Time isolation is often used, when attempting to save seeds from two varieties of dill. Plant the first variety early, and then sow the second variety when the first variety is beginning to flower. The first variety should set seeds before the second begins to flower.

Each dill plant produces several umbels which are usually allowed to dry in the garden. The seeds shatter from the heads very easily during cleaning. To avoid losing seed, select fully mature, dry umbels whose stems are slightly green. Rub the umbels gently to free the seed. Any small stem pieces or other debris can be winnowed or screened. Dill seeds do not need any further treatment and will maintain 50% germination for five years when stored in a dry, cool, dark location.

Anthriscus cerefolium - Chervil

Chervil has feathery leaves which impart a delicate anise flavor to foods. The leaves are usually chopped like parsley and included in salads and vegetable dishes. Chervil is also an important ingredient in French fines herbes mixtures.

In mild winter climates where the plants can be mulched or protected with frames, chervil seeds are often sown in the fall for winter harvest. Chervil does not do well in the heat of the summer and often bolts before producing much useful foliage. Abundant water and a shaded location may be useful in delaying seed production.

Chervil is an annual and produces an umbel with small, white flowers. Seed catalogs rarely list different varieties of chervil, but various insects, including

Heads of dill (*Anethum graveolens*) ripen unevenly and shatter easily. Individual umbels are harvested as they mature.

bees, are attracted to the flowers and could easliy cross-pollinate any separate varieties grown near one another. Chervil will not cross with turnip-rooted chervil, *Chaerophyllum bulbosum*. Isolation distances are unavailable.

Chervil plants produce small, oval seeds which shatter easily. Consequently the plants are noted for re-seeding themselves, and daily harvest is necessary for maximum seed yield. Chervil seeds are easily separated from the umbels, and winnowing will remove any debris.

Chervil seeds will retain 50% germination for three years.

Arracacia xanthorrhiza - Peruvian Carrot

Peruvian carrot is native to the highlands of the Andes Mountains, where it is a very important crop for several Indian populations. The roots taste like a cross between carrot and celeriac. Documented varieties include roots that are white, cream, yellow, orange, and purple.

Peruvian carrots are usually grown from crown cuttings and grow well during cool temperatures. Each plant produces about 10 carrot-sized roots during the 10-month growing season. The plants do not tolerate any frost and require short days for root production. There are no known commercial sources of Peruvian carrot seeds in the United States.

Chaerophyllum bulbosum - Turnip-rooted Chervil

Turnip-rooted chervil, native to southern Europe, is a biennial plant with divided leaves and violet-colored leaf stalks. The 3" roots look like stubby carrots with gray or black skin and yellow or cream-colored flesh. Seeds are produced on umbels from roots left to overwinter in the ground. The seeds shatter easily and care must be taken to harvest mature seeds on a daily basis. If different varieties of turnip-rooted chervil still exist, they would be cross-pollinated by insects if grown in close proximity. Isolation distances are unavailable. Turnip-rooted chervil does not cross with salad chervil, *Anthriscus cerefolium*.

The seeds of turnip-rooted chervil have very difficult germination requirements and only remain viable for six months to one year. Seeds can be sown in a prepared bed in the fall, barely covered with sand. A straw mulch should be applied before snow cover. Germination will occur in the early spring. Alternatively, seeds can be harvested and immediately stored in a cool place folded in a cloth between layers of sand in a box or jar. The seeds can then be sown the following spring.

Coriandrum sativium - Coriander

Grown nearly worldwide, this plant is known as coriander to Americans, cilantro to Mexicans, har dhania to Indians and uen sai to the Cantonese. The plant's green leaves are either hated or craved depending on personal tastes. Coriander's flavor is considered to be an absolute necessity in Southeast Asian cuisine, where it is used extensively. In ancient times coriander was used as a medicine in European countries, but has gradually found its way into the kitchen as a seasoning.

Coriander is easily grown, bolts quickly to seed and will not cross with any other vegetable or herb. Most seed companies that sell coriander do not identify any distinct varieties. Different varieties would be insect crossed, if grown within 1/2 mile of each other. The time isolation technique described for dill would also be well suited for coriander.

Foeniculum vulgare - Fennel

Fennel holds an interesting and important place in vegetable history. The ancient Greeks grew it for use as a medicine, food and insect repellent. Fennel tea was also served just before important battles to instill courage in Greek warriors.

Fennel is available in three different forms. In many parts of the United States, fennel grows wild as a leafy herb. Fennel leaves and seeds are used in baked goods, teas and as a flavoring in candy. Sicilian fennel, which grows in southern Italy, has tender stems that are eaten like celery. Florence fennel, also called finocchio, is grown for its thick leaf stalks which form a bulb at the base of the plant. Sicilian fennel and Florence fennel are both biennials.

All types and varieties of fennel can be crossed by insects. Different varieties should be isolated by 1/2 mile. When more than one variety is grown in close proximity, hand-pollination or caging can be used to ensure seed purity. Fennel seeds are easily harvested from the dry umbels and will retain 50% germination for four years.

Pastinaca sativa - Parsnip

Parsnip is a favorite vegetable in northern Europe. The plant is a biennial and its seeds are very difficult to germinate. In mild winter areas parsnip seeds can be sown in the fall, but will not form large roots before bolting to seed during the next spring. Parsnip grows best, however, when sown in the early spring in cold winter climates. Parsnip roots keep very well in the ground in nearly all parts of the country and develop a sweet, delicate flavor after exposure to freezing temperatures. In areas that have extremely cold winters, the roots should be carefully dug and the tops trimmed back to 2-3". Parsnips will keep 4-6 months when stored in sawdust, leaves or sand between 32-40° F. at 90% humidity.

Some books claim that parsnips left in the ground during the winter become poisonous. Such statements are not true. USDA has investigated many such claims and found that in all cases the poisonings can be traced to cicuta,

Left: Cultivated parsnip (*Pastinaca sativa*).
Right: Wild parsnip (also *P. sativa*).

the water hemlock that closely resembles parsnip in appearance.

Parsnip is insect cross-pollinated. Different varieties should be separated by at least one mile depending on the number of plants and the geography of the region. Parsnip can be grown either seed-to-seed or seed-to-root-to-seed. In many regions of the United States, parsnips have escaped from cultivation and become weeds. These weedy types will cross with cultivated varieties.

Juice exuded from the stem and leaves of parsnips can cause serious skin rashes. Gardeners should never touch their faces if there might be any parsnip juice on their hands. Workers in commercial fields wear special overalls, long-sleeved shirts, hats, goggles and gloves.

Parsnips are very similar to carrots in seed development, pollination, crossing and harvest. Unlike carrots, however, parsnips are totally hardy and will overwinter in the ground without protection in all but the coldest climates. Parsnip seeds remain viable for only one year.

Sium sisarum - Skirret

Skirret is a hardy perennial that produces several wrinkled, grayish brown roots from the center of its crown. Like many other root vegetables, skirret's flavor is better after frost. The roots can be braised, stewed, baked or creamed and are often mixed with potatoes or salsify. Skirret often has a central core that cannot be chewed, which should be removed after the root is boiled.

In mild winter areas, skirret can be grown as a perennial. The plant's new roots can be removed for eating as desired. Skirret plants will produce seeds each summer after the second year. In climates where the ground freezes, skirret can be left in the ground if mulched with straw or leaves. Skirret seeds are difficult to find in the United States, but are available from a few members of the Seed Savers Exchange.

If different skirret varieties exist and were grown near one another, they would be crossed by insects. The plant's seeds are formed and harvested much like carrots. Skirret seeds will germinate well for 10 years.

III

OTHER FAMILIES
WITH VEGETABLE MEMBERS

THE AMARANTHACEAE FAMILY

Much of the Amaranthaceae family, particularly the genus *Amaranthus,* is in botanical disarray. In other words, the family's botanical classifications are a mess. Some researchers believe that all grain amaranth originated from a single species in Mexico and Guatemala, and then spread to Africa, India and North America perhaps 400-500 years ago through established trade routes. These scientists think that the various grain amaranths known today evolved as this single species adapted to its new environments and was subjected to human selection. Other researchers believe that several distinct species of grain amaranth originated in different parts of the world.

The definitive study of amaranths, resulting in a reclassification of *Amaranthus* genus, has yet to be made. As a result, it is extremely difficult to make conclusive seed saving recommendations. After consulting with amaranth researchers all over the country, however, a few general guidelines are available. Research is continuing and more classification changes will undoubtedly be made. For the moment, the following seed saving guidelines should result in the maintenance of pure varieties.

One other genus in the Amaranthaceae family is edible. *Celosia cristata* or cock's comb has edible leaves and flowers, and *C. argentea* or quail grass has edible leaves. All varieties of *C. cristata* and *C. argentea* have tiny, perfect flowers which are generally self-pollinated. Celosia leaves are served raw in salads or cooked like spinach. Very young celosia flowers can be included in salads or vegetable dishes, but become rather coarse and hard to chew as they mature.

Amaranthus spp. - Amaranth

Amaranth was a sacred food of the Aztecs. During sacrificial ceremonies, amaranth seed was mixed with human blood and offered to the gods. Red seed heads were often associated with blood in Aztec legends that explain the origins of the plants. When the Spanish Christians invaded Central America and Mexico, they forbade the growing of amaranth because of its association with pagan rituals. As a result the crop nearly became extinct in Mexico.

In Asia, varieties of *Amaranthus tricolor* have been grown as a green vegetable since the beginning of recorded history. The leaves of all amaranth species are high in calcium and iron, but have a high oxalic acid content which diminishes nutritionally available calcium. Amaranth seeds are high in lysine, an important amino acid that is missing in most grain crops. This means that amaranth, when combined with another grain, provides a complete protein.

BOTANICAL CLASSIFICATION

All amaranths belong to the genus *Amaranthus* and one of several different species. Various studies have docu-

Facing Page: Grain amaranth (*Amaranthus spp*.) seed head.

mented crossing between *Amaranthus retroflexus* (also called pigweed or redroot), *A. hybridus* (grain amaranth from India which has become a North American weed), *A. hypochondriacus* (grain amaranth), *A. cruentus* (grain amaranth) and *A. caudatus* (Love-Lies-Bleeding). Some of the crosses are extremely rare and result in sterile offspring. Crosses between *A. retroflexus* and some grain species do produce viable seed, but it is very weak. The research on crossing between the various amaranth species has not been completed. Eventually the five species mentioned above may possibly be combined into a single species known as *A. hybridus*.

Many of the names used for amaranth species in seed catalogs are botanically incorrect, or are outdated and no longer in use. *A. gangeticus* has been replaced with *A. tricolor*, *A. silicifolius* is now referred to as *A. retroflexus*, and *A. paniculatus* has become *A. cruentus*.

Several other amaranth species names also appear. *A. blitum*, a North American Indian species, is not known to cross with other species. Also two weedy species, *A. powelli* and *A. viridis*, are not known to cross with each other or with any other species.

A. caudatus, commonly called Love-Lies-Bleeding, was once thought to be incapable of crossing with other grain species. Recent studies have demonstrated, however, that *A. caudatus* will cross with *A. hypochondriacus*. Other crosses may possibly occur, but are not known at this time.

A. tricolor includes the vegetable amaranths, which are sometimes called tampala. All members of *A. tricolor* have black seeds, but not all black-seeded amaranths are *A. tricolor*. Varieties of *A. tricolor* also bear flowers in clusters along the stems of the plant. Varieties within the species will cross with each other, but not with any other amaranth species.

Grain amaranth plants can grow 9' tall and 3' wide. The golden or burgundy colored seed heads are very attractive in the flower garden as background plants. Leaf amaranth varieties usually grow about 3' tall, but frequent pickings can result in even smaller plants.

POLLINATION, CROSSING AND ISOLATION

Grain amaranths and leaf amaranths are both wind-pollinated and produce male and female flowers on the same plant. Insects are also capable of cross-pollinating different varieties within the same species, but amaranth flowers are so small that such crossing is rare. Honeybees will visit amaranth if other pollen is not available.

Amaranth pollen is very small and light. Some research suggests that amaranth pollen has limited viability and is not carried great distances. The minimum isolation distance between two leaf amaranth varieties is 500' with a tall crop in between to help prevent pollen drift. The isolation distance between two varieties within a grain amaranth species may need to be as great as two miles, if absolute seed purity is to be ensured.

Amaranth flower heads can also be covered with corn tassel bags to prevent crossing. Inbreeding depression, which often results from self-pollination, can be avoided by growing five plants closely together in a hill, possibly surrounded by a round, funnel-shaped wire tomato cage. The crowded plants will grow a bit smaller than usual. When the flower heads have formed but before any individual flowers open, make a bag that will protect all five heads. Spun polyester is the easiest material to use. Insects can be excluded from the bag by stuffing cotton batting around the five stalks where the bottom of the bag is taped or tied. The wind should do an adequate job of moving the flower heads within the bag. A vigorous shake each morning will also help move pollen from the male to the female flowers.

The bag should be left in place until the seeds are harvested, since each flower head will continue to produce flowers at its tip even after the seeds at the bottom of the head are mature. Larger groups of plants can be grown in greenhouse-sized cages and with wind produced by fans.

SEED PRODUCTION, HARVEST AND PROCESSING

Amaranth leaves can be lightly harvested from both grain and leaf varieties without damaging the seed crops. Plants that are weak or not true-to-type should not be used for seed production.

Amaranth seeds mature unevenly along the seed stalks from bottom to top. To produce the maximum amount of seed, the heads can be harvested as the seeds mature by shaking into a bag each day. It is much more convenient, however, to harvest the entire crop of seed heads when most of the seeds are ripe. The seed heads should be placed on a covered surface to finish drying, but the heads should not be dried in the direct sun, especially in hot summer areas.

Always wear gloves when handling dry amaranth seed heads, because their flowers can be very stiff and sharp. Leaf amaranths and small amounts of the grain types can be rubbed by hand to free the seeds. Wearing gloves, rub the seed heads and allow the seeds to fall into a bowl. Amaranth seeds are very small, so baskets are not recommended.

For larger amounts of seeds, place the seed heads on a tarp, cover with a second tarp and jog in place on top of both. Turn the seed heads several times and continue to jog until most of the seeds are free. Beating the seed heads together is also an effective threshing method. Holding the stalk of a seed head in each hand, beat the heads together while standing over a tarp.

Some people cut the mature seed heads while still moist and remove the seeds by rubbing before the heads have dried. This method is much easier on the hands, but the moist chaff and seeds should be dried quickly or mold may possibly develop.

Dry seeds that have been threshed can be placed in a bowl and swirled around several times. Large pieces of flowers will rise to the top and are easy to remove. Most of the cleaning can be completed by just tipping the bowl and raking out the chaff. Small particles of dirt and other material can then be removed with a fine mesh screen. Regular window screen is the perfect-sized mesh, once the seeds have dried. Winnowing in a light breeze will remove the remaining papery seed caps, but the seeds are very light so be careful.

SEED VIABILITY

Germination rates for the various species are not available, but amaranth is a long-lived seed.

THE BASELLACEAE FAMILY

The Basellaceae family includes two rarely grown vegetables, basella and ulluco. *Basella alba* and *B. rubra*, commonly called Malabar spinach, are discussed below. Ulluco is a native of the central Andes Mountains of South America and thrives in cool, moist conditions with bright sunlight. The plants are very frost resistant and produce tubers which are eaten fresh like potatoes. The crop is also dehydrated by placing the tubers out to freeze at night. In the morning the tubers are stomped on to release their moisture and then left in the sun to dry. This process is repeated for several days until the tubers are totally dry. Prepared in this way, ulluco is called chuno and has been known to store for five years. Ulluco rarely sets seed and is usually propagated from stem cuttings or tubers. There is no known commercial source for ulluco tubers in the United States.

Basella alba - Malabar Spinach

Malabar spinach is a beautiful, frost sensitive, perennial vine. The plant is native to Africa and Southeast Asia, and prefers hot, humid weather which produces fast, luxuriant growth. Each seed is encased in a berry-like seed coat. The dark red juice from the seed coat is a potent dye and has been used as an ink substitute in India.

The thick leaves of Malabar spinach are not bitter and are used in salads in place of spinach. The leaves are somewhat "mucilaginous" (slimy), but that quality is easily overcome with salad dressings that include vinegar.

BOTANICAL CLASSIFICATION

Malabar spinach belongs to the genus *Basella* and the species *alba*. *Hortus Third* lists *B. rubra* as a variety of *B. alba*, while some references consider *B. rubra* to be a separate species. *B. alba* has a light green vine with dark green leaves. *B. rubra* has a red vine with greenish red leaves. Both species are available from several seed companies in the United States.

POLLINATION, CROSSING AND ISOLATION

Malabar spinach flowers are perfect and self-pollinating. The flowers are covered by perianth segments and never open to expose the stamens. Malabar spinach varieties, including *B. alba* and *B. rubra*, do not cross with each other or with any other garden vegetables.

SEED PRODUCTION, HARVEST AND PROCESSING

A continuous light harvest of Malabar spinach leaves does not appear to reduce the quality or quantity of the seeds. Malabar spinach is easy to grow and nearly pest-free, but is one of the messiest plants for seed savers. Each fully ripe seed is encased in a black fruit that is firmly attached to the branch of the plant. When subjected to frost, Malabar spinach plants literally melt into a black slime, depositing their seeds on the ground. In its native climate, birds and small animals eat the berries and excrete the seeds.

Malabar spinach: *Basella rubra,* left, and *B. alba,* right.

In long season climates, some of the fruits will dry around the seeds. These can be harvested without any further cleaning. It is very important that the seeds be thoroughly dry, however, or mold can form on the moist seed coats.

In most areas of the United States, the purplish black fruits must be picked individually. Always be sure to collect fruits from as many different plants as possible. The fruits are then placed in a metal strainer that is partially submerged in a bowl of soapy water. When rubbed against the sides of the strainer, the fruits disintegrate exposing the seeds.

A food processor can also be used instead of a strainer. Insert the blunt plastic dough blade and process the fruits with an equal amount of water for 30 seconds. This method will crack some of the seeds, however, and the plastic bowl of the processor will have to be bleached to remove the purple stains.

Rinse the seeds in clear water and dry the bottom of the strainer on a towel to remove as much water as possible. The seeds are then placed on a glass or ceramic plate to dry. Seeds should never be dried in direct sun or in an oven. Stir the seeds twice daily to ensure even drying. The seeds will turn light tan when completely dry.

SEED VIABILITY

Malabar spinach seeds will remain viable for five years if stored in an airtight container in a cool, dry, dark location.

THE CONVOLVULACEAE FAMILY

The Convolvulaceae family includes sweet potatoes, one of the world's most important food crops. Another member of the family, water spinach or swamp cabbage, is a significant vegetable in Asia.

Ipomoea aquatica - Water Spinach (Water Convolvus)

Water spinach has a long history in China, where reference was made to its use about 300 A.D. The plant is grown in shallow water or muddy areas. Water spinach can become a serious perennial weed in frost-free regions, if allowed to escape into waterways. For this reason, the seeds and plants cannot be sent to Florida, Louisiana or California. The plants can be started from either seeds or cuttings.

BOTANICAL CLASSIFICATION

Water spinach belongs to the genus *Ipomoea* and the species *aquatica*. The plants have hollow stems which allow the vines to float on top of the water. Two distinct types of water spinach exist. Ching quat is best adapted to mud culture and pak quat prefers aquatic culture.

POLLINATION, CROSSING AND ISOLATION

Water spinach flowers are perfect and self-pollinating. Different varieties grown in close proximity would probably be cross-pollinated by insects. Isolation distances are not available.

Mature seeds drop into the mud or water and are difficult to find. Daily collection of the mature seeds will result in the greatest harvest. In Asia the shoots are harvested until the plants begin to flower. The fields are drained when the seeds begin to mature, so that the pods can be harvested and dried. Workers walk or run over the seedpods to free the seeds.

SEED PRODUCTION, HARVEST AND PROCESSING

Water spinach leaves and shoots can be harvested prior to the blooming period with little decrease in seed quantity or quality.

Place the harvested pods in a warm place to finish drying. The dry pods are put into a pillowcase or feed sack with the open end taped or tied shut. Roll a rolling pin over the sack until the majority of the pods are broken open and the seeds are free. The seeds should then be dried for several additional days away from direct sunlight.

SEED VIABILITY

Water spinach seeds should remain viable for three years when stored in cool, dry, dark conditions.

Ipomoea batatas - Sweet Potato

Sweet potatoes have been cultivated since prehistoric times and are thought to have originated in tropical America. The tubers come in an assortment of colors which include white, yellow, orange, red, and purple. Sweet potato vines are used as a cooked vegetable in Asia.

Sweet potato (*Ipomea batatas*) vines and flowers.

BOTANICAL CLASSIFICATION

Sweet potatoes are members of the genus *Ipomoea* and the species *batatas*. Some of the orange and red varieties of *I. batatas* are incorrectly referred to as yams. True yams belong to a different botanical family, Dioscoreaceae, and are not related to sweet potatoes.

SEED PRODUCTION, HARVEST AND PROCESSING

Sweet potatoes are propagated vegetatively. Placed in a warm, moist medium, shoots form along the sides of each tuber and take root. The shoots can also be broken off and rooted in a seed flat. Unfortunately serious diseases and pests, including root knot nematodes, reside in sweet potatoes and can be transmitted from garden to garden when the tubers or shoots are planted. Several states, including California and Florida, prohibit importation of sweet potatoes.

The following method may eliminate some of these problems. Place each tuber in a pot filled with sterile potting mix, covering half of the tuber with mix. Allow new shoots to grow 6-8" long without touching the potting mix. Cut the shoots off several inches above the tuber and re-root them in a new flat. The original tuber and the potting soil should be burned to prevent contamination or disease transmission.

Sweet potato tubers store well in a root cellar. After several days of curing to harden their skins, unblemished roots are wrapped in newspapers or packed in baskets of sawdust, making sure that the roots do not touch. Sweet potatoes will keep 3-5 months when stored at 50-60 degrees F. and 60-70% humidity.

THE GRAMINEAE FAMILY

Gramineae is an extremely large botanical family which contains nearly all of the grains and grasses. Only two genera and species, *Zea mays* and *Sorghum bicolor*, are commonly grown in the vegetable garden.

_____ *Sorghum bicolor* - Sorghum and Broom Corn_____

Sorghum is an important source of sugar syrup in areas where sugar cane is not grown and maple syrup is not produced. In the fall, sorghum stalks are stripped of their leaves and cut into workable lengths. Then the stalks are ground up and pressed, and the sweet, green juice is cooked down like maple syrup. Different sorghum varieties produce subtle flavor variations in the syrup, which is used like honey.

Broom corn is grown specifically for the plant's stiff tassels, which are made into brooms and brushes. Broom making can be a unique and enjoyable craft experience. Without good instructions or a helpful neighbor with old-time knowledge, however, the process can also be very frustrating. The *Foxfire* series and other craft books offer excellent broom-making guides.

BOTANICAL CLASSIFICATION

All sorghums and broom corns belong to the genus *Sorghum* and the species *bicolor*. Three types of sorghums have been developed and refined over several hundred years: sweet sorghums, broom corns and grain sorghums. Broom corn is usually considered to be a variety of sweet sorghum. Grain sorghum, which is also referred to as milo and kafir corn, is primarily used as a rather low-quality livestock feed in the United States.

POLLINATION, CROSSING AND ISOLATION

Sorghums have perfect florets that are self-fertile and are generally self-pollinated. The wind is probably sufficient to trip the flowers and increase their pollination. A small amount of crossing may occur between all types and varieties of *S. bicolor,* but is easily prevented by bagging the plant's tassel as soon as it begins to emerge. Weather resistant corn tassel bags work well, but paper or spun polyester bags can be used in dry climates. The bags should remain in place until all of the seeds have formed. Seed should be saved from as many plants as possible.

SEED PRODUCTION, HARVEST AND PROCESSING

The seed tassels can be cut when the stalks begin to dry. Sorghum seeds are easily rubbed off by hand and can then be winnowed in a moderate wind or with a fan. Continue drying the seeds for several days, but not in direct sun. Several of the seeds can be hit with a hammer to test for dryness. If the seeds shatter, the crop is ready for storage. If the seeds are mashed instead of shattering, continue drying.

SEED VIABILITY

Sorghum seeds remain viable for at least four years under ideal conditions.

Facing Page: Mature seed head of broom corn (*Sorghum bicolor*).

Zea mays - Corn

Corn is one of the three most important cereal crops in the world. The corn plant first evolved in tropical America and has grown there since pre-Columbian times. Trading between Indian tribes gradually spread corn from the South American Andes to southern Canada. Many tribes hold a special reverence for corn as a gift from the gods. The first white settlers on this continent received corn as a gift from the Indians, a gift that allowed their new settlements to survive. Today more acreage is planted to corn than any other crop in North America.

Hybrid sweet corns have nearly taken over the home garden market. Many gardeners find these hybrids, especially the new super-sweets, hard to resist. Other gardeners think the super-sweets are too sugary and prefer open-pollinated varieties for their old-fashioned flavor. Even many of the older dent and flint varieties can be eaten like sweet corn in a very immature state.

Popcorn is a must for every child's vegetable garden. Many of the tiny, multi-colored popping ears that are beginning to show up in trendy supermarkets aren't really new. Some are as old as the Indian tribes that have selected and isolated their characteristics over several centuries.

The tiny immature ears of corn being served by many fancy restaurants are also not really a new vegetable item. Originally these tiny ears were harvested in the Orient from suckers and the small secondary ears which formed after the main harvest. Their use was simply an attempt to harvest as much food as possible from each planting, not as a delicacy. When the royal families of China developed a taste for the tiny ears, Chinese farmers began planting corn very close together and harvesting the tiny immature ears. Then, over time, varieties that produced an abundance of smaller ears were bred especially for that purpose.

BOTANICAL CLASSIFICATION

All corn varieties belong to the genus *Zea* and the species *mays*. Teosinte, a wild ancestor of corn, has historically been referred to as *Z. mexicana*. In the 1970s a perennial teosinte was discovered in Mexico. It has subsequently been named *Z. diploperennis*. Since that discovery, *Z. mexicana* has been increasingly referred to as *Z. mays subsp. mexicana*. Teosintes will cross with *Z. mays* varieties, however the tetraploid teosintes do so with difficulty.

POLLINATION, CROSSING AND ISOLATION

All corn varieties are wind-pollinated and cross readily with each other. Pollen is produced by the tassel that forms at the top of each stalk of corn, which is the plant's male flower. As the tassel ripens, tiny structures called anthers emerge along the branches of the tassel and start to shed pollen. Healthy corn plants produce one or more ears along their stalk. The ears and the silks that emerge from them are the female parts of the plant. The wind blows grains of pollen from the tassel onto the silks. Each silk that is pollinated results in a kernel of corn developing on that ear. Corn pollen is light and can be carried for long distances by the wind. Isolating a variety

The incredible diversity displayed by traditional Native American corns (*Zea mays*).

of corn by two miles will ensure purity.

To provide maximum pollination in isolated patches, corns should always be grown in blocks rather than in long, single rows. If you choose to grow just one corn variety in isolation, grow 200 plants and break off the tassels of any off-type plants. Time isolation is also possible, which sometimes allows a gardener to save seeds from two varieties without having to hand-pollinate. Seed can be saved from both an early and a late variety that are planted near each other, if the tassels of the early variety finish shedding pollen before the silks of the late variety begin to emerge, and if the silks of the early va-

riety dry up before the late variety starts to shed pollen. Time isolation sounds logical but variations in weather and maturity dates can be quite tricky, so the technique should probably not to be counted on when working with rare varieties.

POPULATION SIZE

Most corn varieties are quite susceptible to inbreeding depression. If seeds are saved from too few plants for even one year, the loss of genetic diversity within the population is immediately noticeable and irreversible. Undesirable traits will begin to appear, such as the plants getting progressively shorter, yielding fewer ears and developing later in the season.

Inbreeding depression can usually be avoided by growing 200 plants of each variety (100 plants at the *very* least), which should maintain adequate genetic variability and diversity within a population. Out of those 200, work with about 100 of the best plants that are the most true-to-type.

Inbreeding depression can also be minimized by never working with both the tassels and the ears on the same plants and being sure to make a mixture of seed from 25-50 ears taken from different plants. Always try to bag the tassels of 50 plants and the ears of 50 *other* plants (25 of each is an absolute minimum).

HAND-POLLINATION OF CORN

Hand-pollination, which is time-consuming but not difficult, is the only alternative for persons wanting to maintain the purity of two or more varieties of corn that are tasseling nearby at the same time. Uncontaminated pollen must be collected from the tassels and sprinkled onto the silks of their ears. Bags must be placed around the ears before the silks appear and also around the tassels when the first anthers are beginning to emerge and shed pollen, in order to successfully control the pollination of the corn plant and produce pure seed. This process was refined in Midwestern states where the air is saturated with corn pollen each summer when pollination is occurring, so the process does succeed in an atmosphere that is highly contaminated with foreign pollen.

Tools and materials needed to hand-pollinate corn include a pocketknife and stapler, as well as shoot bags and tassel bags purchased from the Lawson Bag Company (PO Box 8577, Northfield, IL 60093, phone 708/446-8812). Lawson's bags are made from tough materials that will not decompose in the rain. Their #217 shoot bags are good for a wide range of ear sizes, and the #402 tassel bags are a good all-around size. Lawson Bag Company has agreed to sell these two styles of bags to home gardeners in lots of 1,000. (See "Supplies for Seed Savers" at the end of Section I.)

The process for hand-pollination of corn usually lasts two or three days, and possibly even longer if drought is slowing the rate of growth. (Sometimes an extremely diverse population can take more than a week, because the plants are not all at the same stage of development.) The two-day process would involve bagging ears on the first day, bagging tassels on the morning of the second day, and making the pollinations around noon on the second day. The three-day process would involve two days of bagging ears at the beginning.

The hand-pollination process begins just before the silks start to emerge from the tiny ears. The first indication of that happening will be the appearance of husk leaves along the nodes of the stalk. Sometimes, however, the silks emerge almost before the tips of the ears become apparent. Many popcorns are difficult to work with for that reason. Any silks that emerge before the ear is bagged will be contaminated with foreign pollen, which ruins that ear for seed saving purposes. If silks are already visible, the process should have been started sooner.

When it becomes apparent that the silks will soon emerge on a lot of the plants, bag as many ears as are ready that first day. Always bag the top ear, because the plant feeds that ear first and also aborts it last during drought. Find an ear with husk leaves that are protruding, but from which no silks have yet emerged. Grab the leaf that is covering the ear and, in one smooth downward motion, tear that leaf completely off the plant.

Cut the tip off of the husk leaves with a pocketknife, cutting off enough of the husk to expose the silks, which will look like a pea-sized circle in the center of the cut. Be careful not to cut too far down or the tip of the developing cob may be damaged, which can encourage smut. More of the tip of the husks can be cut off than first imagined, but be careful with ears of popcorn which often have cobs that grow high inside the ear. How far to cut can be estimated by tearing open and examining a couple of ears on off-type plants that would not be used anyway.

The ear is then covered with a small white "shoot bag" that covers the whole ear and is wedged next to the stalk. If the shoot bag cannot be wedged behind the ear, make a small vertical cut with the knife downward behind the stalk. The cut is often tricky to make. Try to just barely slit the base of the leaf that wraps around the stem. Be careful, because the ear can easily be cut off completely. It is always hard to wedge the bag into place if the leaf that covers the emerging ear is not torn off. The number of ears that can be bagged the first day will depend on how many have silks that are about ready to emerge. More ears can also be bagged on the second day (and possibly the third, and the fourth, etc., depending upon the synchrony of the variety), especially if the tassels are still not shedding pollen.

The next objective is to staple a brown "tassel bag" around each tassel just as it begins to shed pollen. Close observation of the developing plants will reveal a green tassel emerging from the whorl of leaves at the top of each plant. As each tassel ripens, its lateral branches gradually droop away from the main vertical stalk of the tassel and eventually become horizontal. Tassels that are bagged when still too green will stop developing and not shed pollen at all, and green tassels can actually cook inside the bag in the hot sun. The perfect time to bag the tassel is when the "anthers" (tiny pollen-bearing structures) start to emerge along the tips of both the lateral branches and main vertical branch of the tassel.

Grab the stalk just below the tassel and give the tassel a vigorous shake. That will usually get rid of any foreign pollen that may have floated in and contaminated the tassel. Then pull all of the lateral branches upward and place the "tassel bag" over the tassel. The stalk of the plant should be placed in the corner of the tassel bag. Fold the opening of the bag back toward the stalk and then away again, before stapling the bag shut right beside the stalk. There are several folding techniques, but their common objective is to fasten the bag tightly enough around the stalk to keep the powdery pollen from falling down and out of the bag.

Avoid the large amount of pollen that collects in the whorl of leaves just below the tassel, which is usually old and contaminated. Staple the tassel bag well above that point, or tear off those leaves to clear that area.

Most pollen is shed from mid-morning until noon, as the dew dries

 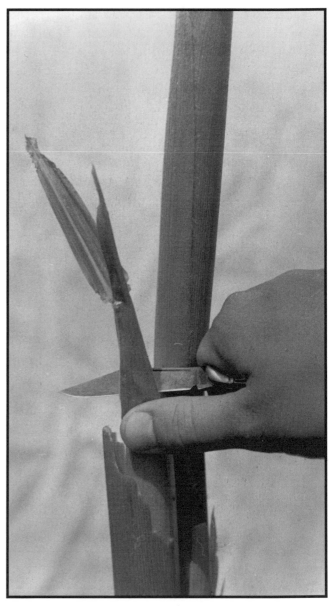

Left: In one smooth, downward motion, the leaf covering the ear is torn completely from the plant.
Right: The tips of the husk leaves are cut off to expose the silks.

off and the tassel bags begin to heat up. The intense heat of the afternoon sun can kill the pollen inside the bags. If the tassel bags are left in place throughout an afternoon, the pollen collected will only be of fair quality and much larger amounts will be needed to get a decent set of seeds. A much better method is to put on tassel bags in the evening or the next morning after

the dew dries, and then make the pollinations late that same morning or in the early afternoon.

In the late morning or early afternoon, pollen is collected from all of the tassels that were bagged. Bend each brown tassel bag over at a slight downward angle, but not enough to break the tassel or the plant. Give the tassel bag a couple of sharp whacks or

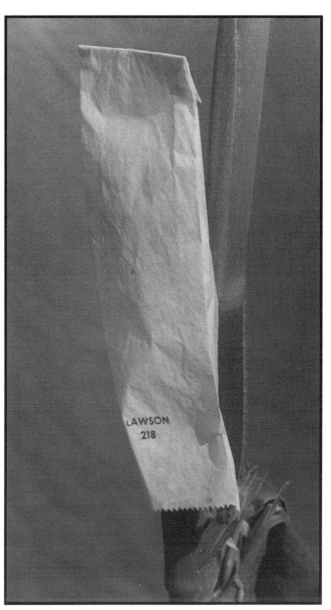

Left: Be careful not to damage the tip of the developing ear by cutting too deeply; remove just enough to expose a pea-size circle of silks. Right: A white shoot bag is wedged tightly between ear and stalk.

vigorous shakes to dislodge as much pollen as possible. Unfasten the staple and, with the bag still held at a slightly downward angle, gently shake the tassel while pulling it out of the bag to dislodge even more pollen.

To help maintain as much genetic variability as possible, make a pollen mix by pouring the contents of all the tassel bags together into one of the bags and then shake the bag vigorously. The mix will contain pollen, a lot of dead anthers and quite a few live bugs. Pour the contents from the large brown tassel bag into the small white shoot bag taken from the first ear that will be pollinated. Gently shake the mixture along a seam of the brown tassel bag. The anthers will reach the lip of the bag first and can be carefully

Left: Tassels should be bagged when the anthers emerge and begin to shed pollen. Right: A brown tassel bag is stapled tightly around the stalk to prevent the pollen from falling out of the bag.

poured off and discarded. Then pour the pollen, which is the bright yellow, very fine powder, into the shoot bag. It is much easier to make the pollinations by shaking the pollen from the smaller shoot bag than from the large, clumsy, brown tassel bag.

Although the shoot bags are made out of white paper, the emerging silks can actually be seen through the sides of the bags. Each white shoot bag should be left in place until just before time to sprinkle the pollen onto that ear's silks. Too much pollen may be floating in the air to risk exposing the silks for any longer than necessary. Pollinations are easiest to make on a short 1" brush of silks which form a fairly even surface. If the silks are a lot longer than that or are ragged and dif-

 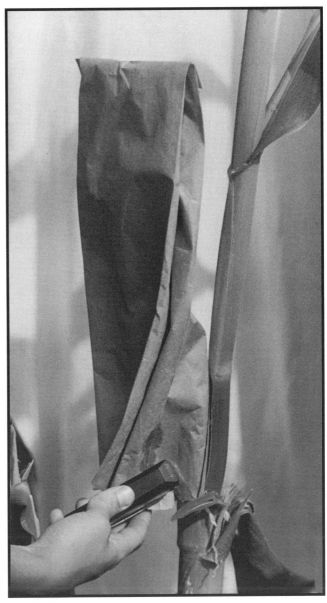

Left: A portion of the pollen mix is shaken evenly onto the silks. Right: A used tassel bag is stapled loosely around the ear to prevent contamination and allow for further growth.

ferent lengths, just cut back the silks to a 1" brush. That won't cause any damage or problems, because the pollen doesn't enter on the tips of the silks. Each strand of silk is receptive along its entire length, so the pollen can enter anywhere.

Try to estimate the amount of available pollen to be divided among the bagged ears that need pollinating. At

first, it is difficult to guess how far the pollen will go, so be conservative. With a little gentle shaking, the pollen will settle to the bottom of the white shoot bag and any remaining anthers will float to the top. Make a small cut in one of the bottom corners of the shoot bag and shake pollen from that hole onto the silks. Shake on just enough so that the pollen is visible on the silks, probably about half a level teaspoon if there is that much for each ear. Sprinkle the pollen around uniformly, trying not to dump all of it in just one spot on the silks.

Now cover the pollinated ear with one of the brown tassel bags that was used to collect the pollen. Wedge the back of the bag between the ear and the stalk, into the old cut, and then pull the bag's bottom corners around *behind* the stalk and staple them a couple of times. The bag should be fastened rather loosely around the stalk to give the ear room to develop, but tight enough so the wind cannot blow it off. The bags can be left on until harvest to mark the ears that have been hand-pollinated. Also an indelible pen can be used to write the pollination date and other varietal data right on the bag, which will stay with the ear.

There are several potential sources of contamination which must be avoided. Always make sure that the tassel bags used to re-cover the ears are ones that were used on that same variety, or use new ones. Bags that were used in an adjacent block of corn will contain traces of other pollen. An easy way to make sure that tassel bags stay in the right block is to do only one population at a time, and throw away any extra tassel bags when you finish that population. The white shoot bags can be reused once or twice, but always wait at least a week to make sure that any remaining traces of pollen are dead. There is also a good possibility that pollen can be carried on a person's body or hands from one variety to the next. Avoid touching the insides of tassel bags, and always brush off clothing and wash hands thoroughly between varieties, concentrating on the fingernails.

HARVEST AND PROCESSING

Ears of corn are usually left on the stalks until completely dry. If insect or animal damage or weather conditions make that impossible, mature cobs can be removed, husked and dried under shelter. The drying should be done at a moderate temperature (less than 95° F.). To prevent damage, corn kernels should not be removed until both the cob and the kernels are dry. Electric and hand-cranked corn shellers work well when processing large quantities. For smaller amounts, simply rub two cobs together to remove the seeds from both. Any silk or cob debris mixed in with the seeds should be winnowed out. Kernels that are not completely formed should also be discarded. In a final attempt to minimize inbreeding depression, always make a mixture of seeds from 25-50 ears taken from different plants, taking more or less equal numbers of seeds from each ear.

SEED VIABILITY

Corn kernels should be completely dry before being stored. Sweet corn varieties will maintain 50% germination for three years when stored in cool, dry, dark conditions. Flint corns, dent corns and popcorns will retain high germination rates for 5-10 years and sometimes much longer, depending on the variety and storage conditions.

THE LABIATAE FAMILY

The Labiatae family includes about 180 genera and 3,500 species of herbs and small shrubs. Basil, the most renowned member of the family, has been included here because it is so commonly grown in vegetable gardens. Perilla and Chinese artichokes are both commonly grown vegetables in Asia, but are little known in the United States.

Ocimum basilicum - Basil

Numerous varieties of basil are native to India and have become important culinary additions to many cuisines around the world. Italian dishes are just not the same without basil. Holy basil grown near the doorstep keeps bad spirits from entering Pakistani homes. Anise and cinnamon basil fill a kitchen with lovely aromas that are said to stimulate the appetite. Lemon basil adds an unmistakable tang to salad dressings. Bush basil and purple basil make lovely additions to any edible flower garden.

Basil is an Old-World plant with an interesting but sometimes marred history. Chrysippus, who lived 200 years before Christ, condemned its use as "an enemy to sight and a robber of wits." The ancient Greeks, however, extolled its virtues and recommended basil for its medicinal properties as well as general culinary use. Roman gardeners believed that the tiny seed would not germinate unless they cursed the crop as it was being planted. Italian gardeners found that basil combined with olive oil and Parmesan cheese made the perfect pasta sauce and dubbed the concoction pesto.

BOTANICAL CLASSIFICATION

Basil belongs to the genus *Ocimum* and the species *basilicum*. The plants form small, multiple-branched bushes which, depending on the variety, can grow anywhere from 8-48" tall.

POLLINATION, CROSSING AND ISOLATION

Basil flowers require insects for pollination and are frequently visited by thrips and small bees. Different varieties can be cross-pollinated by insects, but isolation of 150' will maintain seed purity. Alternate day caging can also be used, which would allow two or possibly more varieties to be grown simultaneously.

SEED PRODUCTION, HARVEST AND PROCESSING

Flower racemes mature progressively from the bottom of the stem to the top. When the bottom seed capsules start to turn brown, the stem can be cut and allowed to dry away from the direct sun in a well-ventilated area. Basil plants will continue to produce leaves and flowers even after the flower raceme is cut.

Each flower contains four seeds, which are difficult to extract from the dried seedpod. When processing small quantities, rub each raceme over a fine wire mesh and winnow off the chaff. A seed thresher is recommended for larger quantities. Place the chaff and seeds in a bowl and very carefully swirl the contents around in the bottom of

Left to right: Lemon, bush and sweet basil (*Ocimum basilicum*) in seed.

the bowl. The seeds will gather in the bottom of the bowl and the chaff will be on top. Tip the bowl until the chaff can be raked off and discarded. Then blow the rest of the chaff out of the bowl very carefully, because the light seeds can be blown away quite easily.

SEED VIABILITY

Basil seeds will remain viable for five years when stored in a cool, dry, dark location.

Perilla frutescens - Perilla

Perilla, a native of the Himalayas, is widely grown and much appreciated in Asia. Although closely related to basil, perilla leaves are not as fragrant. The leaves are widely used in pickling and as a condiment, and are highly valued for the beautiful red color that they impart to other vegetables. Turnips or white daikon radishes cooked with perilla turn a bright pink.

A leaf of perilla is often included in pickle jars in Asia. Like grape leaves in the United States, the pickles are thought to be crisper when the leaf is included.   Ume boshi, a salt-cured plum, is wrapped in perilla leaves in Japan. Historically, the leaves have also been used as a seaweed replacement by Japanese Americans when seaweed was difficult to obtain in the United States.

BOTANICAL CLASSIFICATION

Perilla is a member of the genus *Perilla* and the species *frutescens*. The plants, which resemble an ornamental coleus, sometimes grow 6' tall but can be kept smaller by frequent picking. Both a green and a purple leafed variety are available in the United States.

POLLINATION, CROSSING AND ISOLATION

Perilla flowers require insects for pollination and are frequently visited by thrips and small bees. Different varieties can be cross-pollinated by insects, but isolation of 150' will ensure seed purity. Alternate day caging can also be used. Perilla seeds are harvested and cleaned like basil.

SEED VIABILITY

Perilla seeds will remain viable for five years when stored in cool, dry, dark conditions.

Stachys affinis - Chinese Artichoke

Chinese artichoke produces 2" pearly white tubers that are slightly pointed toward one end and are segmented like beads, like the rattles on a rattlesnake. *Stachys affinis* grows 10" tall and has square mint-like stems. The plants produce pegs like peanuts, with each peg producing a tuber. Any tubers left in the ground will resprout and can become a nuisance.

Stachys affinis is little known in the United States but is grown throughout Asia and has been cultivated in China since the 14th century.   Chinese artichoke is known as choro-gi in Japan, where it is an esteemed vegetable crop. French gardeners refer to the vegetable as crosnes du Japon, while English gardeners call the plant knotroot.

BOTANICAL CLASSIFICATION

Chinese artichokes belong to the genus *Stachys* and the species *affinis*.

Both a white-flowered and a red-flowered variety are cultivated in Asia. A full season of growth and ample amounts of water will produce numerous tubers 3-6" below the surface of the soil. In most areas, the tubers can be left in the ground to overwinter.

SEED PRODUCTION, HARVEST AND STORAGE

Chinese artichokes are cultivated by tuber division. If the plants are grown without interruption for several seasons, white or red flowers will occasionally be produced and also possibly seed.

Chinese artichoke tubers are dug in the fall or as needed throughout the winter in mild climates. Unwashed tubers also store well in plastic food containers in the refrigerator.

THE LILIACEAE FAMILY

The Liliaceae family includes asparagus and day lilies, two common garden edibles. Liliaceae does not include onions, which are now classified as members of the Amaryllidaceae family. Day lilies make a nice addition to any vegetable garden. Their blossoms are edible at all stages and make a beautiful garnish on plates and buffet trays. In China dried day lily blossoms are used in soups and vegetable dishes.

Asparagus officinalis - Asparagus

There are 240 genera within the Liliaceae family, but only asparagus is cultivated primarily as a food crop. Asparagus plants produce tender, edible spears early each spring. When asparagus plants are started from seeds, there is a three to five year wait for edible stalks. Step-by-step growing instructions are available in most garden books.

BOTANICAL CLASSIFICATION

Asparagus belongs to the genus *Asparagus* and the species *officinalis*. About 15 varieties are still commercially available in the United States.

POLLINATION, CROSSING AND ISOLATION

Each asparagus flower develops with two sets of sexual organs. One set of organs aborts as the flowers mature, leaving all male or all female flowers on the plant. The flowers rely on insects, usually honeybees, for pollination. Wind is not considered a factor in asparagus pollination.

Asparagus varieties being grown for seed are easily crossed and should be separated by two miles. Alternate day caging has not been tried on a garden scale, but should work well.

SEED PRODUCTION, HARVEST AND PROCESSING

Asparagus can be eaten and also saved for seed, however seed quality and quantity will decline with each harvested stalk. Female asparagus flowers produce round, reddish, 3/8" berries containing six seeds. Birds find the berries tasty and often damage crops that are not caged or covered in some way. The ripe berries should be harvested before they drop from the plants. The fruits can be rubbed over a screen to free the seeds, which are then washed in several changes of water. Dry the seeds away from direct sunlight for several days before storing.

SEED VIABILITY

Asparagus seeds will maintain 50% germination for five years when stored under ideal conditions.

THE MALVACEAE FAMILY

Many members of the Malvaceae family are cultivated for their beautiful flowers. A number of species are edible, but only roselle and okra are grown as food crops.

Roselle, *Hibiscus sabdariffa*, is grown for its slightly acid-tasting red flowers which are steeped in sugar water and used for a refreshing beverage or as a base for jelly. The beautiful plants, which are also known as Jamaica sorrel and jelly plant, are often grown in flower gardens.

Roselle's flowers are perfect and do not cross with okra, cotton or hibiscus. If more than one variety of roselle is grown, isolate the crops by 1/2 mile or bag individual blossoms to prevent cross-pollination by insects.

Abelmoschus esculentus - Okra

Okra's origins are obscure at best. Some European references cite Central and South America, but the species probably originated in Ethiopia and the Upper Nile where numerous wild varieties have been found. Several perennial varieties have also been found in West Africa. The presence of okra in the Americas can probably be traced to African slaves who most likely brought along seeds of the cherished plants.

BOTANICAL CLASSIFICATION

Okra belongs to the genus *Abelmoschus* and the species *esculentus*. Prior to the release of *Hortus Third, A. esculentus* was sometimes referred to as *Hibiscus esculentus*.

POLLINATION, CROSSING AND ISOLATION

Okra flowers are perfect and self-pollinating, but are also large, showy, full of pollen and very attractive to bees. Different varieties are easily cross-pollinated by insects and must be isolated by one mile. Okra does not cross with roselle, cotton or hibiscus. To prevent crossing, entire plants can be caged or individual blossoms can be bagged. Muslin 4" x 6" drawstring bags make ideal individual blossom bags. Pieces of nylon hosiery or spun polyester are also easily adaptable.

Healthy, true-to-type plants should be selected for seed saving. In the late afternoon or evening put a bag over each okra blossom that is ready to open the next morning. The flowers will be fat, will have a light green striped appearance, and may also be starting to show some color. Each bag must be secured using a drawstring, rubber band or masking tape, making sure that insects are unable to wiggle in and pollinate the blossom. Self-pollination takes place shortly after the blossoms open, and the flowers are completely unreceptive to pollen by noon. Leave the bags on during the next full day after the blossom opens, and then remove the bags the following day. At the same time that the bags are being removed, tag those blossoms with poultry bands, yarn, string or plastic ribbon. Okra pollen can remain viable for up to 24 hours, especially on cool days, so the bags should not be reused on other blossoms for at least 48 hours.

Unripe, ready-to-eat okra pods (*Abelmoschus esculentus*).

SEED PRODUCTION, HARVEST AND PROCESSING

Okra plants that are harvested consistently will continue to produce pods over a long period of time. A light harvest early in the season will have a very minimal effect on the number of pods available for seed production.

Green okra plants often cause skin irritations, but the dry pods are downright nasty. *Always* wear gloves when harvesting and cleaning okra pods. Still green but fully mature pods can be picked and left to finish drying away from direct sun until they split open.

Wearing gloves, break each pod open and let the seeds fall into a bowl or tightly woven basket. Dry pods can also be secured inside a feed sack or pillowcase. Place the sack on a hard surface and jog in place on it, which will break the pods open and free the seeds. Remove any crushed pieces of pods and dirt by using a hair dryer or fan to winnow the seeds.

SEED VIABILITY

Okra seeds will maintain 50% germination for five years when stored under ideal conditions.

THE MARTYNIACEAE FAMILY

All three genera of the Martyniaceae family have sticky, hairy leaves, orchid-like flowers and woody, beak-shaped pods. The seeds of the yellow-flowered *Ibicella lutea*, which is native to South America, are not commercially available in the United States, although the species occurs as an occasional weed in California's Central Valley. Introduced members of the *Martynia* and *Proboscidea* genera are often found growing as weeds in the southwestern United States.

_____ *Martynia* and *Proboscidea spp.* - Devil's Claw (Unicorn Plant) ___

Martynia annua - Devil's Claw
Proboscidea fragrans - Devil's Claw
P. louisianica - Devil's Claw

Devil's claw is a rather attractive plant with fragrant, orchid-like flowers. The green pods are edible when immature and can be cooked like okra with tomatoes and onions. Many farmers spray the wild plants with herbicides, so never eat pods from plants found growing near cultivated fields. Martynia pickles are a favorite in some parts of Mexico. The seeds can be opened and eaten like sunflower seeds or pressed to produce oil. American Indian tribes in the desert Southwest soaked the black pods in water and used the fibers in basket weaving. Seeds are difficult to find commercially, but are available from Native Seeds/ SEARCH and from members of the Seed Savers Exchange.

BOTANICAL CLASSIFICATION

There is very little difference between the *Martynia* and *Proboscidea* genera. Martynia flowers have a calyx with five separate sepals and two fertile stamens. Proboscidea flowers have four fertile stamens.

Proboscidea fragrans, a dark purple-flowered species native to Brazil, is often found growing wild in the southwestern United States. *P. louisianica*, which has white flowers with violet and red spots, is most often seen in Gulf Coast states. *Martynia annua*, which has creamy violet flowers, is found throughout the United States and is classified as a noxious weed in some states.

POLLINATION, CROSSING AND ISOLATION

The three devil's claw species do not cross with one another, however different varieties within each of the species can be cross-pollinated by insects. When two or more varieties of a species are grown in close proximity, seed purity can be ensured with isolation of 1/2 mile or by using alternate day caging.

SEED PRODUCTION, HARVEST AND PROCESSING

When devil's claw pods begin to dry, the green outer husk falls away exposing the black, woody, beak-like pods. Completely dry pods split open exposing the seeds. The curved tips of the

Foliage, flowers, immature pods and dry pods of South American devil's claw (*Martynia spp.*).

pods are very sharp and can cause serious injury if lodged in the legs or feet of pets or farm animals. Care must be taken during seed cleaning to avoid puncturing or lacerating fingers and arms.

SEED VIABILITY

Various reports state that devil's claw seeds germinate well for only two years, but personal experience indicates that the seeds will maintain 75% germination for five years or longer.

THE POLYGONACEAE FAMILY

Two members of the Polygonaceae family commonly appear in the vegetable garden. Both rhubarb and sorrel have been used as vegetables and medicines since before the time of Christ. Dioscorides, a Roman doctor, used rhubarb to treat Anthony and Cleopatra for weakness of the stomach. Dioscorides also used preparations made from rhubarb to treat ringworm and diseases of the liver.

Rheum rhubarbarum - Rhubarb

Rhubarb plants produce both flowers and seed stalks, however rhubarb seeds do not produce plants that are true-to-type. When rhubarb seeds are planted, a wide variety of plant types will result which may or may not look anything like the parent plants. If it is impossible to transport cuttings of a favorite rhubarb plant to a new garden, seeds can be used. Start 20 or more plants from seeds and select those which most resemble the desired variety.

Rumex spp. - Sorrel

Rumex acetosa - Garden Sorrel
R. alpinus - Mountain Sorrel
R. scutatus - French Sorrel

Sorrel is the common name for three different species with acid-tasting green leaves. Common garden sorrel or sour dock belongs to *Rumex acetosa*. *Rumex alpinus* is often called maiden sorrel, monk's sorrel or mountain sorrel. *Rumex scutatus* is referred to as French sorrel, white sorrel, lettuce sorrel or blonde sorrel. All three species have been collected in the wild and cultivated in gardens for centuries. The plants are easily divided, so vegetative propagation is common. The plants produce both male and female flowers, requiring insects for pollination. If more than one variety of the same species is grown in close proximity, alternate day caging will prevent crossing.

THE PORTULACACEAE FAMILY

Edible members of the Portulacaceae family are considered by various persons to be either noxious weeds or succulent salad greens. Miner's lettuce grows in the winter and early spring, while purslane grows during the summer months. Other Portulacaceae family members are grown as ornamental flowers in the warmer regions of the world.

Claytonia parvifolia - Miner's Lettuce

Miner's lettuce is commonly referred to as winter purslane in Europe. The delicate leaves appear in moist, shady, wooded areas in the early spring. The self-sowing plants are rarely planted and are most often foraged for like fiddlehead ferns.

Plants of miner's lettuce develop two types of leaves during their short life. The first leaves appear on 4-6" stems, are kidney-shaped and very succulent. Pretty round leaves appear later, encircling the flower stalks. The leaves are much sought after by restaurants and deserve a place in more gardens. Miner's lettuce produces early, rarely interferes with other crops and is easily intercropped between later vegetables.

BOTANICAL CLASSIFICATION

Miner's lettuce belongs to the genus *Claytonia* and the species *parvifolia*. Different varieties of miner's lettuce have been mentioned in literature, but may only be variations in growth caused by differences in altitude, climate, shade, etc.

POLLINATION, CROSSING AND ISOLATION

Miner's lettuce flowers are perfect and self-pollinating. The flowers do not seem to be attractive to insects, but that may be due to their early spring emergence. There is no information available on different varieties or crossing between varieties. If true varieties do exist and were grown in close proximity, caging would prevent any possible cross-pollination by insects. Miner's lettuce does not cross with purslane.

SEED PRODUCTION, HARVEST AND PROCESSING

Miner's lettuce can be lightly picked for eating and still grown for seed. Tiny white blossoms emerge from the center of the round leaves and quickly form small seedpods. The top portion of the seedpods falls off and tiny, shiny black seeds fall out before the plant has started to dry. The seeds shatter easily and are hard to collect.

Entire plants are sometimes collected and put in pillowcases to dry, however that can be risky. The plants are very succulent and with damp early spring weather a moldy mess is likely to result, rather than a tablespoon of black seeds. It is easier to dig miner's lettuce plants and set them out to mature and drop seeds where the plants are to grow. Collected seeds can be air-dried away from direct sun for several days before being stored.

SEED VIABILITY

Under ideal conditions, miner's lettuce seeds remain viable for five years.

Portulaca oleracea - Purslane

Purslane may be indigenous to the Himalayas, southern Russia and Greece. The plant was originally thought to have been brought to America from Europe, but current research suggests it may be indigenous to the Americas as well. Improved varieties of purslane are cultivated for market in Egypt and also in some parts of Central and South America.

Purslane, which is usually considered a weed, appears in the early summer when warm nights and moist conditions coincide. Recent nutritional studies have discovered that purslane contains omega-3 fatty acids, compounds found in certain seafoods which are thought to lower blood pressure and reduce the incidence of heart disease. Thus, an annoying garden weed has been added to the growing arsenal of foods that may combat disease.

Purslane does have some negative nutritional qualities. Like spinach, the plant's leaves can accumulate nitrates and contain oxalic acid which prevents calcium absorption. Too much of a good thing may actually be harmful. Eating excessive amounts of purslane to lower blood pressure could lead to calcium deprivation and weak bones.

BOTANICAL CLASSIFICATION

Purslane belongs to the genus _Portulaca_ and the species _oleracea_. Wild varieties form a mat on the surface of the ground with individual plants reaching 12" in diameter. Improved garden varieties with large leaves can grow 10" in height. Both the golden and large leaf varieties produce upright, slow to bolt plants with large, tender leaves. Seeds for selected garden varieties are available from seed companies specializing in herbs.

POLLINATION, CROSSING AND ISOLATION

Purslane flowers are perfect and self-pollinating, but they are also visited by many bees, small flies and butterflies. Studies have not yet determined when pollination occurs. If the flowers self-pollinate before opening, cross-pollination by insects is probably not possible. If, however, the flowers open before the pollen is ripe, various improved varieties and the wild type probably can be crossed. Since improved varieties of purslane are not grown commercially in the United States, no information on crossing is available. If more than one variety is being grown, isolation or caging would ensure purity. Purslane will not cross with any other vegetable or flower.

SEED PRODUCTION, HARVEST AND PROCESSING

Purslane can be lightly picked for eating with almost no decrease in the amount of seeds produced by each plant. Yellow blossoms appear on the tips of each branch of the plant and quickly develop into capped seedpods. The top portion or lid of each cap falls off as the seeds mature. The seedpods mature and release their seeds while the plants are green and continuing to grow. The pods shatter very easily, so seeds must be collected on a regular basis.

SEED VIABILITY

Purslane seeds will remain viable for seven years.

THE **TETRAGONIACEAE** FAMILY

The Tetragoniaceae family includes only one vegetable species, New Zealand spinach. Sir Joseph Banks discovered the plant in New Zealand in 1770 and sent specimens to the Kew Gardens in England. From Kew, New Zealand spinach found its way into seed catalogs around the world. G. Don discovered three distinct varieties in Chile in 1834, which included a variety with smooth leaves, one with leaves that are smooth on top and hairy beneath, and a third with very small, glabrous leaves.

Tetragonia tetragonioides - New Zealand Spinach

New Zealand spinach is grown in many of the hot summer regions of the world. While not a true spinach, the plant's leaves are often used as a substitute for spinach in cooked vegetable dishes. The leaves are high in oxalic acid which some people find disagreeable.

The plants form vines with attractive spear-shaped leaves and inconspicuous greenish yellow flowers. New Zealand spinach will not tolerate any frost and does not begin growing until the soil is very warm and air temperatures are well into the 80s.

BOTANICAL CLASSIFICATION

New Zealand spinach belongs to the genus *Tetragonia* and the species *tetragonioides*. Although three varieties of *T. tetragonioides* are known to exist, American seed companies offer only generic New Zealand spinach. Until recently the species was included in the Aizoaceae family and was formerly classified as *Tetragoniaceae expansa*.

POLLINATION, CROSSING AND ISOLATION

The flowers of New Zealand spinach are small and not showy. Two flowers usually grow tightly together in each leaf apex and may be mistaken for a single unit. The flowers are perfect and self-pollinating. Insect crossing might be possible if two varieties were grown near one another. In such cases, isolation or caging would ensure seed purity.

SEED PRODUCTION, HARVEST AND PROCESSING

New Zealand spinach seeds ripen progressively along the length of the vine. Its hard fruits each contain several seed capsules and change from green to brown at full maturity. The mature fruits often fall off the plant and are difficult to see on the ground. Full-sized green fruits can also be picked and allowed to dry until brown. Although picking the individual seedpods off of the vine is time-consuming, no further treatment of the seeds is necessary.

SEED VIABILITY

New Zealand spinach seeds will maintain 50% germination for five years when stored in cool, dry, dark conditions.

THE VALERIANACEAE FAMILY

The Valerianaceae family includes about 10 genera and 400 species of herbs and small shrubs. Valerianella is the only genus that is grown as a vegetable.

Valerianella spp. - Corn Salad

Valerianella eriocarpa - Italian Corn Salad
V. locusta - Common Corn Salad

Like Portulaca, corn salad is a common weed in many parts of North America, Europe, North Africa and Asia. For centuries the delicate rosettes of leaves have been collected in early spring for sale in European markets, especially in France where the corn salad plant is called mache. Until recently corn salad was considered a weed in the United States, where the plant is sometimes called lamb's lettuce. With the current surge of interest in both gardening and cuisine, however, corn salad is becoming a fashionable food sought after by restaurants and greengrocers.

BOTANICAL CLASSIFICATION

Corn salad belongs to the genus *Valerianella* and to two distinct species. Italian corn salad, *V. eriocarpa*, grows 16" tall with 5" leaves that are somewhat hairy. Common corn salad, *V. locusta*, forms rosettes that are 3-6" high with either smooth or crinkled leaves.

POLLINATION, CROSSING AND ISOLATION

Italian corn salad, *V. eriocarpa*, will not cross with common corn salad, *V. locusta*. Different varieties within each of the species, however, will cross with one another. Corn salad growing in the wild can also cross with the cultivated varieties.

Corn salad plants rely on insects for pollination. No information on isolation distances is available. Alternate day caging would ensure purity if more than one variety of a species is grown for seeds.

SEED PRODUCTION, HARVEST AND PROCESSING

Corn salad plants form bluish white flowers with the onset of warm weather. The flowers quickly form seeds which drop when mature and self-sow. The plants are so small and go to seed so early that warm season crops can be planted among the maturing corn salad plants without difficulty.

When the plants are beginning to dry, carefully collect the entire plant in a pillowcase. Shake the plants to free as many seeds as possible and then remove the seeds from the bag. The plants can be left in the bag to dry a bit further and the process can be repeated. Dry the seeds out of direct sunlight for several days and winnow to remove small pieces of debris.

SEED VIABILITY

Corn salad seeds will maintain 50% germination for five years when stored under ideal conditions.

SEED SAVING ORGANIZATIONS

Seed Savers Exchange

Several thousand backyard gardeners are searching the countryside for endangered vegetables, fruits and grains. They are members of the Seed Savers Exchange (SSE), a nonprofit tax-exempt organization that is saving old-time food crops from extinction. Kent and Diane Whealy founded SSE in 1975 after an elderly, terminally ill relative bestowed three kinds of garden seeds brought from Bavaria four generations earlier. The Whealys began searching for other "heirloom varieties" (seeds passed down from generation to generation) and soon discovered a vast, little-known genetic treasure.

Since the Mayflower first landed, gardeners from every corner of the world have brought along favorite seeds when their families immigrated. Many of these heirloom varieties are still being maintained by gardeners and farmers in isolated rural areas and ethnic enclaves. Today, due to constantly shrinking rural populations, elderly gardeners often cannot find anyone who will continue growing their living heirlooms. When elderly seed savers pass away, unless their seeds are replanted by other gardeners, their outstanding strains become extinct. Future generations will never enjoy them and invaluable genetic characteristics are lost forever to gardeners, orchardists and plant breeders.

SSE's members are maintaining thousands of heirloom varieties, traditional Indian crops, garden varieties of the Mennonite and Amish, vegetables dropped from all seed catalogs and outstanding foreign varieties. Each year 900 members use SSE's publica-

tions to distribute such seeds to ensure their survival. Perhaps you are growing beans your grandmother raised, or tomatoes a friend's family brought from the old country, or some unique vegetables discovered on a trip abroad. SSE has no monetary interest whatsoever in any of these varieties and wants only to save them for future generations to enjoy.

You don't have to be keeping heirloom seeds to join SSE; your desire to try some of these beautiful, highly flavored varieties is enough. If you've never grown vegetables for their seeds, SSE will teach you easy seed saving techniques. Nongardening members also enjoy SSE's publications immensely and their annual memberships provide vitally needed financial support. SSE's three annual membership publications include more than 500 pages of exciting horticultural information and provide access to thousands of heirloom varieties that are not available elsewhere. Your garden and the enjoyment derived from it will never be the same. In addition, your support and involvement will help save what remains of our vanishing vegetable heritage.

Each winter SSE publishes a 304-page *Seed Savers Yearbook* which contains names and addresses of 900 members and 6,000 listings of rare vegetable and fruit varieties that they are offering to other gardeners. Seeds are obtained by writing directly to the members who are listing those varieties. Since SSE was founded in 1975, its members have distributed 400,000 samples of seeds that were not available through catalogs and often on the verge of extinction.

SSE also publishes a 100-160 page *Summer Edition* in July/August which contains: Plant Finder Service used by members and historic gardens to locate lost varieties; Plant Profiles of SSE's finest heirlooms; informative articles; transcripts of speeches; and fascinating interviews. SSE's *Harvest Edition*, published in October/November and also 100-160 pages, has articles about: SSE's Campout Convention; activities at Heritage Farm; and genetic preservation projects working with flowers, herbs, fruits and endangered breeds of livestock and poultry.

An annual membership to SSE, which includes the three issues described above, is $25 (with optional reduced rates of $20 or $15 for low income families). If you would like to learn more about SSE before joining, send $1 for a four-page color brochure that describes the organization's projects and publications to: Seed Savers Exchange, Rt. 3 Box 239, Decorah, IA 52101.

Native Seeds/SEARCH

Native Seeds/SEARCH (NS/S) is a nonprofit seed conservation organization working to preserve the traditional native crops of the U.S. Southwest and Northwest Mexico. For centuries Native American farmers have grown corn, squash, beans and other crops under a variety of growing conditions. NS/S encourages the continued use of these plants in their native habitats, and also distributes them widely to home gardeners, researchers and free of charge to Native American farmers. Wild relatives of crops - such as wild beans, chiles, gourds and cotton - are included in Native Seeds/SEARCH's conservation efforts.

Native Seeds/SEARCH is a membership organization that publishes a fact-filled quarterly newsletter called *The Seedhead News*. Each issue contains recipes, previews of workshops and other special events, gardening tips, book reviews and feature articles on Native American farmers and crops. Members also receive a 10% discount on all items for sale. Membership starts at $10 per year.

NS/S's informative annual seed catalog lists more than 200 varieties for sale. Each crop listing includes seed saving information as well as culture and folklore. You can obtain NS/S's current seed catalog by sending $1.00 to: Native Seeds/SEARCH, 2509 N. Campbell #325, Tucson, AZ 85719.

The Flower and Herb Exchange

The Flower and Herb Exchange (FHE) is a new organization patterned after the Seed Savers Exchange (SSE). Founded in 1989, FHE has been set up as a project of SSE in order to utilize SSE's office staff and computer system, but is financially independent and has its own Board of Directors.

Flowers and herbs are an important part of most gardens. For several years SSE has not had room in its publications to list anything but food plants. Many seed savers are also keeping heirloom flowers and herbs that hold special memories. We are very grateful for the families who have had the respect and foresight to keep these living heirlooms from being lost. FHE provides a system so that gardeners can share and preserve this precious legacy.

FHE is trying to locate varieties of flowers and herbs that are heirlooms or unusual, and are not commercially available. If you are keeping such plants and are willing to share their seeds with other gardeners, or if you are interested in growing rare flowers and herbs, FHE would be pleased to have you join our efforts.

Last year *The Flower and Herb Exchange* contained 180 members who were offering nearly 700 listings. The 48-page booklet was filled with old-time flowers whose simple beauty is seldom found in modern catalogs. Many of the herbs and wildflowers being offered were not even available commercially. FHE is making this heritage available to other gardeners who will treasure these plants and continue to exchange their seeds.

FHE is a separate organization from SSE and has its own publication and membership fee. To receive a copy of *The Flower and Herb Exchange*, send your name and address along with your $5 membership fee to: The Flower and Herb Exchange, Rt. 3 Box 239, Decorah, IA 52101.

The Heritage Seed Program

The Heritage Seed Program (HSP) is a project of the Canadian Organic Growers, a charitable organization. The purpose of this project is to search out and preserve heirloom and endangered varieties of vegetables, fruits, grains, herbs and flowers. HSP's members are backyard gardeners, farmers, historical sites, museums, horticultural historians, botanical gardens, scientists and plant breeders.

The heart of HSP consists of its network of growers who multiply endangered varieties in their gardens, practice the proper seed saving techniques to keep the varieties pure, save seeds, and make these seeds available to other members free of charge. In this way, someone somewhere is always

growing these endangered varieties so that they will not become extinct. HSP is a living gene bank.

Three times each year, HSP publishes a periodical which has articles on heritage gardens, heirloom varieties, seed companies which sell heirloom and regionally adapted nonhybrid varieties, and projects in Canada and around the world which work to preserve our horticultural and agricultural heritage. Information is available through the organization on how to save your own seeds.

In December of every year, HSP publishes a *Seed Listing* of all the varieties which its members have to share. This listing is different from a seed catalog in that those who take seeds from it are asked to grow the seeds, practice the proper seed saving techniques and save seed to share with other members.

Anyone is welcome to join HSP, even if they do not wish to become a grower, and your membership fee will help support HSP's preservation projects. As a member you will receive the three annual periodicals including the yearly *Seed Listing* from which you can choose seeds which you might wish to adopt. Membership fees are: Regular $10, Fixed Income $7, Supporting $20, U.S. and Foreign $15.

Our ancestors have bequeathed us a rich agricultural and horticultural heritage of vegetables, fruits, grains and herbs which are delicious, nutritious, beautiful and resistant to insects and diseases. With a little effort we can preserve these wonderful varieties and ensure that they will survive for our children to enjoy. Please consider becoming involved in this exciting project.

SELECTED REFERENCES

Allard, R. W. *Principles of Plant Breeding*. New York: John Wiley and Sons, 1960.

Andrews, J. *Peppers: The Domesticated Capsicums*. Austin: University of Texas Press, 1977.

Antunes, I. F., J. G. C. da Costa and E. H. Oliveira. *Natural Hybridization in Phaseolus vulgaris*. The 1973 Report of the Bean Improvement Cooperative, 1973.

Bailey, L. H. *Hortus Third, A Concise Dictionary of Plants Cultivated in the United States and Canada*. New York: Macmillan Publishing, 1976.

Bird, R. *Growing From Seed*. Jackson, New Jersey: Thompson & Morgan, 1988.

Correll, D. S. *The Potato and Its Wild Relatives*. Renner, Texas: Texas Research Foundation, 1962.

Creech, J. L., and L. P. Reitz. "Plant Germplasm Now and for Tomorrow." *Advanced Agronomy* 23:1-43 (1971).

Culp, T. W., W. K. Bailey and R. O. Hammons. "Natural Hybridization of Peanuts, Arachis Hypogaea, in Virginia." *Crop Science* 8:108-111.

Dahlen, M., and K. Phillipps. *A Popular Guide to Chinese Vegetables*. New York: Crown Publishers, Inc., 1983.

Doty, W. L. *All About Vegetables*. San Francisco: Chevron Chemical Company, 1973.

Dremann, C. C. *Ground Cherries, Husk Tomatoes, and Tomatillos*. Redwood City, California: The Redwood City Seed Company, 1985.

Elving, P. *Fresh Produce: A to Z; How to Select, Store & Prepare*. Menlo Park, California: Lane Publishing Company, 1987.

Erwin, A. T., and E. S. Haber. *Species and Varietal Crosses in Cucurbits*. Ames, Iowa: Agricultural Experiment Station, Iowa State College, 1929.

Fehr, W., and H. Hadley. *Hybridization of Crop Plants*. Madison, Wisconsin: American Society of Agronomy, 1980.

Fisher, H. *The Flower Family Album*. Minneapolis: The University of Minnesota Press, 1942.

Freeman, O. L. *Seeds: The Yearbook of Agriculture*. Washington, D.C.: The United States Government Printing Office, 1961.

George, R. A. T. *Vegetable Seed Production*. New York: Longman Inc., 1985.

Haplin, A. M. *Gourmet Gardening: 48 Special Vegetables You Can Grow for Deliciously Distinctive Meals*. Emmaus, Pennsylvania: Rodale Press, Inc., 1981.

Harrington, J. F. "Drying, Storing and Packaging Seed to Maintain Germination and Vigor." *Seedsmen's Digest* 11:16-56 (1960).

Hedrick, U. P. *Sturtevant's Edible Plants of the World*. New York: Dover Publications, Inc., 1972.

Heiser, C. B. Jr. *The Fascinating World of the Nightshades: Tobacco, Mandrake, Potato, Tomato, Pepper, Eggplant, etc.* New York: Dover Publications, Inc., 1987.

Heiser, C. B. Jr. *The Gourd*. Norman: University of Oklahoma Press, 1985.

Heiser, C. B. Jr. *Of Plants and People*. Norman: University of Oklahoma Press, 1985.

Heiser, C. B. Jr. *The Sunflower*. Norman: University of Oklahoma Press, 1985.

Herklots, G. A. C. *Vegetables In South-East Asia*. London: George Allen & Unwin Ltd., 1972.

Hills, L. D. *Save Your Own Seed*. Essex, England: The Henry Doubleday Research Association, 1978.

Jabs, C. *The Heirloom Gardener*. San Francisco: Sierra Club Books, 1984.

Jardin, C. *Kulu, Kuru, Uru: Lexicon of names of food plants in the South Pacific*. Noumea, New Caledonia, 1974.

Johnson, C. *The Seed Grower*. Marietta, Pennsylvania: Redwood Seed Company, 1906.

Johnston, R. Jr. *Growing Garden Seeds*. Albion, Maine: Johnny's Selected Seeds, 1983.

Justice, O. L., and L. N. Bass. *Principles and Practices of Seed Storage*. Washington, D.C.: Agricultural Research Service, United States Department of Agriculture, 1978.

Knott, J. E. *Handbook for Vegetable Growers*. New York: Wiley and Sons, Inc., 1957.

Larkcom, J. *The Salad Garden*. New York: The Viking Press, 1984.

McGregor, S. E. *Insect Pollination of Cultivated Crop Plants*. Washington, D.C.: Agricultural Research Service, United States Department of Agriculture, 1976.

McLean, J. G., and F. J. Stevenson. "Methods of Obtaining Seed on Russet, Burbank and Similar Flowering Varieties of Potatoes." *American Potato Journal* 29:206-211 (1952).

Miller, D. C. *Vegetable and Herb Seed Growing for the Gardener and Small Farmer*. Boise, Idaho: Seeds Blum, 1984.

Nieuwhof, M. *Cole Crops: Botany, Cultivation and Utilization*. London: Leonard Hill, 1969.

Owen, E. B. *The Storage of Seeds for Maintenance of Viability*. Bucks, England: Commonwealth Agriculture Bureau, 1956.

Proctor, M., and P. Yeo. *The Pollination of Flowers*. New York: Taplinger Publishing Company, 1972.

Rick, C. M. "The Role of Natural Hybridization in the Derivation of Cultivated Tomatoes of Western South America." *Economic Botany* 12:346-347 (1958).

Rick, C. M., M. Holle and R. W. Thorp. "Rates of Cross-Pollination in Lycopersicon pimpinellifolium." *Plant Evolution* 129:31-44 (1978).

Riley, J. M. "Solanaceae." *Solanaceae Quarterly*. Santa Clara, California, 1988.

Roberts, E. H. *Viability of Seeds*. London: Chapman and Hall Ltd., 1972.

Rogers, B., and B. Powers-Rogers. *Culinary Botany: The Essential Handbook*. Kent, Washington: Brant Rogers and Bev Powers-Rogers, 1988.

Rogers, M. *Growing and Saving Vegetable Seeds*. Pownal, Vermont: Garden Way Publishing (Storey Communications), 1978.

Ryder, E. J., Ph.D. *Leafy Salad Vegetables*. Westport, Connecticut: AVI Publishing Company, Inc., 1979.

Schneider, E. *Uncommon Fruits & Vegetables: A Commonsense Guide.* New York: Harper & Row, Publishers, Inc., 1986.

Shinohara, S. *Vegetable Seed Production Technology of Japan Elucidated with Respective Variety Development Histories, Particulars: Volume I.* Tokyo, Japan: Authorized Agricultural Consulting Engineer Office, 1984.

Taylor, R. L. *Plants of Colonial Days.* Williamsburg, Virginia: Colonial Williamsburg, Inc., 1952.

Thompson, H. C., Ph.D., and W. C. Kelly, Ph.D. *Vegetable Crops.* New York: McGraw-Hill Company, Inc., 1957.

Vietmeyer, Noel, et al. *Lost Crops of the Incas.* Washington, D.C.: National Academy Press, 1989.

Vilmorin-Andrieux, MM. *The Vegetable Garden.* Berkeley: Ten Speed Press, 1885.

Whealy, K. *Harvest Editions* and *Winter Yearbooks* of the Seed Savers Exchange. Decorah, Iowa: Seed Savers Exchange, 1981-1988.

Whealy, K. *Garden Seed Inventory: Second Edition.* Decorah, Iowa: Seed Saver Publications, 1988.

Whealy, K. *Seed Savers Exchange: The First Ten Years.* Decorah, Iowa: Seed Saver Publications, 1986.

Whitaker, T. W., and G. H. Davis. *Cucurbits.* New York: Interscience Publications, 1962.

Yamaguchi, M. *World Vegetables: Principles, Production, and Nutritive Values.* Westport, Connecticut: The AVI Publishing Company, Inc., 1983.

Yanovsky, E. *Food Plants of the North American Indians.* Misc. Publication 237. Washington, D.C.: U.S. Department of Agriculture.

GLOSSARY

Accession: A sample of seeds from a particular plant (or group of plants) entered into a collection or seed bank.

Aerial: Growing in the air instead of in soil or water.

Annual: Plants that are started from seed and produce seed themselves within one growing season.

Anther: Pollen-bearing structure supported by a filament, which together form the stamen of a flower.

Anthesis: The moment when a flower first opens, when the anthers and stigmas become functional.

Asexual Reproduction: Non-sexual reproduction, such as plants which are cloned from vegetative growth, cuttings, tubers, etc.

Biennial: Plants that require two growing seasons to complete a life cycle, usually exhibiting vegetative growth during the first year and producing seed during the second year.

Bolt: The development of a seed stalk, as in "hot weather caused the lettuce plants to bolt."

Bulbil: A small aerial bulb that forms on a flower stalk and is capable of forming a new plant, commonly seen in some types of onions.

Chaff: Pieces of stem, leaf and other debris that may be mixed with seed before the winnowing process.

Clone: A plant or group of plants produced from the same genetic parent using vegetative propagation (asexually) instead of from seed (sexually).

Cross-Pollination: Transfer of pollen from an anther on one plant to the stigma of a flower on another plant, and also often used to refer to situations that result in crossing between varieties.

Cultivar: An abbreviation for "cultivated variety," usually a named variety.

Day-Neutral: Plants which flower and produce fruit or seed regardless of the number of hours of sun.

Dioecious: A species that produces male flowers and female flowers on separate plants.

Dormancy: A state during which buds or seeds will not sprout even though conditions are favorable.

Edible: A portion of a plant that may be eaten, but is not necessarily palatable.

Family: A category of taxonomic classification ranking above a genus, forming a group of plants that includes one or more similar genera.

Fermentation: The natural microbial decomposition of fruit-bearing vegetables, sometimes induced deliberately to help clean the seeds and destroy seed-borne diseases.

Fertilization: The union of pollen with the ovule, which eventually produces seed.

Filament: The stalk of a stamen which bears the anther.

Genera: The plural of genus.

Genetic Diversity: The total range of genetic differences displayed by plants of the same species.

Genetic Erosion: The gradual, persistent loss of genetic resources.

Genetic Vulnerability: A condition which occurs when plants within a species become so genetically uniform that the continued evolution of the species is at risk.

Genus: A category of taxonomic classification ranking above a species, which forms a group of closely related species.

Germination: The sprouting of a seed, which marks the beginning of plant growth.

Germplasm: The total of the hereditary materials (inherited characteristics) within a species.

Heirloom Vegetable: A non-hybrid vegetable variety that has been passed down from generation to generation, usually a long-time family favorite.

Hilum: The scar on a seed, marking the spot where it was attached to the seed stalk or seedpod.

Hybrid: The offspring of a cross between parent varieties (usually of the same species) that are genetically different.

Imperfect Flower: A flower that has a stamen (stamens) or a pistil, but not both.

Inbreeding Depression: Loss of vigor and variation due to the crossing of two genetically similar plants.

Isolation: Separating one plant (or group of plants) from another to prevent any crossing.

Long-Day: Plants that flower or mature only when the length of daylight exceeds a certain minimum amount of time.

Monoecious: A species that forms male flowers and female flowers separately on the same plant.

Mutation: An unexpected inheritable genetic change.

Open-Pollinated: Non-hybrid plants produced by crossing two parents from the same variety, which in turn produce offspring just like the parent plants.

Ovary: The enlarged portion of the pistil, which contains the ovules (egg cells).

Ovule: A rudimentary seed that has not yet been fertilized.

Palatable: An edible portion of a plant that is pleasant or acceptable to the taste.

Peduncle: The stalk of a flower (or group of flowers) or, after fruit formation, the fruit-to-plant attachment as with squash.

Perennial: Any plant which lives more than two years, usually producing flowers and seeds from the same root year after year.

Perfect Flower: A flower that contains both a stamen (stamens) and a pistil.

Pistil: The female portion of a flower, which consists of an ovary, style and stigma.

Poison: A naturally occurring constituent in a plant or plant part that is capable of killing a human if eaten.

Pollen: The male spores or dust-like grains of reproductive material produced by the anthers.

Propagation: Increasing the number of plants by vegetative means or by planting seeds.

Raceme: An unbranched flower cluster consisting of a single central stem along which individual flowers grow on small stems at intervals.

Radicle: The embryonic portion of a seed which develops into the primary root.

Rogue: A non-typical, usually inferior plant within a varietal population.

Roguing: The removal of any plants that are not true-to-type in order to purify the variety.

Scape: A leafless flower stalk usually growing from the crown of the plant.

Scarify: To nick, cut into or abrade the hard coat of a seed, allowing water to enter in order to aid germination.

Seed: A fertilized and mature ovule capable of forming a new plant, typically consisting of an embryo with its protective coat and stored food.

Selection: The process, either natural or with human intervention, by which plants displaying desirable characteristics are retained within a population.

Self-Incompatibility: A trait associated with some perfect flowers whose pollen cannot grow in a flower on the same plant, but grows normally when transferred to a flower on another plant of the same variety.

Selfing: The transfer of pollen from one flower to another flower on the same plant.

Self-Pollination: The transfer of pollen from an anther to the stigma in the same flower, or to the stigma in another flower on the same plant.

Short-Day: Plants that flower or mature only when the length of daylight is shorter than a certain maximum amount of time.

Sibing: The transfer of pollen between flowers on different plants of the same variety.

Silque: A seedpod containing two segments or compartments on either side of a thin membrane bearing the seeds, especially characteristic of the Brassicaceae family.

Species: The units of taxonomic classification into which a genus is divided, each of which forms a maximum interbreeding group of plants that is reproductively incapable of crossing with other species.

Stamen: The male portion of a flower which produces the pollen grains, consisting of filaments and anthers.

Standard Variety: A non-hybrid variety, usually the end result of a breeding program cross, selected generation after generation until completely stabilized.

Stigma: The portion of the pistil that receives the pollen grains during fertilization.

Style: The elongated portion of the pistil that connects the stigma and the ovary.

Taxonomy: A system of arranging plants into related groups based on common characteristics, in descending order from most inclusive: kingdom, division, class, order, family, genus and species.

Threshing: Breaking the seeds free from the seedpods and other dry plant material.

Toxin: A natural constituent of a plant or part of a plant which, if eaten, will make humans sick, but not fatally.

True-to-Type: A plant (or group of plants) that conforms exactly to the known characteristics of that particular variety, the basis or standard for comparison.

Umbel: An umbrella-like cluster of flowers with stalks of nearly equal length radiating from the same point.

Variety: Closely related plants with nearly identical characteristics which form a subdivision of a species.

Vegetative Propagation: Reproduction by asexual methods, not from seed.

Vernalization: A period of cold temperatures that is necessary before some plants are able to form flowers for seed production.

COMMON NAME INDEX